D1430431

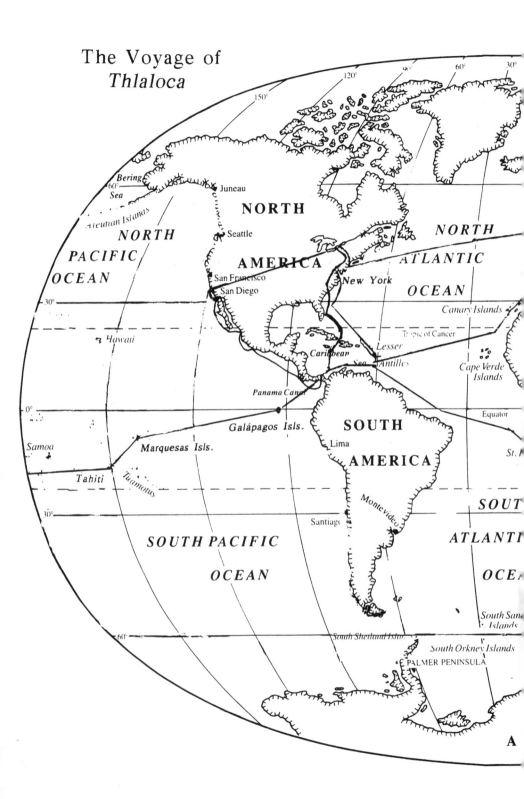

The Voyage of
Thlaloca

Thlaloca under sail

WEST! SAIL WEST, MAN!

Around The World In Twenty Feet

by

Hein Zenker

Illustrated

Windjammer Books

Printed By Hignell Printing Company, Winnipeg, Canada

Library of Congress Catalog Number 97-90189

ISBN 0-9658773-0-2

West! Sail West, Man!

Hein Zenker
89 Forest Haven
White Stone, Va. 22578
USA.

To

Siggi, my wife, who became my competent and loyal First Mate; my hero "the wind beneath my wings."

And to

Margitta, my precious and patient daughter, who waited much too long.

ACKNOWLEDGEMENTS:

Encouragements to write this book came from many quarters, but none was stronger than that of Siggi and our good friends John Frye and Jim Rankin. Their suggestions and help are much appreciated.

CONTENTS

FOREWORD

Our hats off to Siggi and Hein, followed by a deep bow. We felt that way as soon we came to know them and little *Thlaloca*. Their big accomplishment in sailing around the world must call up the admiration of every sailor. We felt richer by being their friends.

Though the sizes of *Thlaloca* to our 96-foot brigantine, the *Yankee,* made our experience at sea very different, Irving and I had seen enough of the oceans of the world in our seven circumnavigations to find much in common with Siggi and Hein. "Anything can happen at sea," someone told me as I set off on my first sailing ship, in which I met Irving. But, as I read Hein's account I also marveled at how unfailingly he could appreciate the beauty of the world he was seeing so bravely.

Irving would have followed minutely all the troubles with rudder, skeg, and bolts that gave way. On our canal cruise with *Thlaloca*, the tales I remember most vividly still, are the near wreck on the Mexican coast; Hein's desperate underwater work at sea (with no such a thing as scuba gear of course) when all the bolts that held the fin-keel to the boat had loosened. And there was Siggi's extensive scalding on their way to New Zealand, when the whole stove with boiling water fell on her. It seemed they could overcome any disaster. I notice they give credit to Lady Luck, and so must every sailor. Also, Hein says, "For a couple in love a 30ft. boat well equipped would be perfect. If 'love' is on the shaky side, chances are that even the largest vessel would not suffice."

Hein, on every page gives Siggi full credit for her great contribution to their voyage. That makes pleasant reading. She put up with great discomfort, much uncertainty, real danger at times. But along with mutual love they both wanted the same thing, as Irving and I did: the success of their venture with a ship and the sea.

I well remember going below on *Thlaloca* and seeing how the galley was the space between Siggi's knees, seated practically on the floor, with the stove at arm's reach. It was indeed doghouse space, but I disagree that theirs was a "dog's life". It was life for two remarkable, farseeing humans. It is encouraging to read how much good they found in the world and its people when one gets discouraged by daily accounts of crime, hatred and violence.

World cruisers always say, the big bonus is the wonderful people you meet. And so it was for Siggi and Hein. They were never freeloaders; they paid or worked their way. I remember how touched we were with their parting gift of the picture, the expensive chocolate bar and the ten dollars.

When they talked about building *Thlaloca Dos*, I said, "You should name the boat *'Spirit.'*" Hope Atkinson countered, "They should name this one 'Guts!'"

Mrs. Irving Johnson
Hadley, MA

PROLOGUE

WEST! SAIL WEST, MAN! is the story of our little ship *Thlaloca* (Goddess of water in Aztec mythology). She was conceived out of pure desire to break away from the drudgery of everyday life in a mining town of Northern Ontario, Canada.

Thlaloca was perhaps the minimum size boat in which a couple could venture far offshore and cross oceans. She is twenty and one-half feet long and six feet and as many inches in beam. She is also a direct sister to a boat called *Trekka* in which John Guzzwell circumnavigated the globe single-handed.

She was well designed by Laurent Giles & Partners of Lymington, England. In strength and ocean performance, she took second to none. She had that one ingredient so desirable in an ocean going boat, our feeling of complete safety and confidence in her. Another ingredient equally desirable she did not have and could not have, that was room and comfort.

We owned this handsome vessel for twelve years and had lived on her for six. She had carried us safely over a distance of 55,000 nautical miles.

We built her in the Georgian Bay area of Canada. When nearly finished, we hauled her overland to California, to be launched in the greatest of all oceans, the Pacific. That was in 1962, a long time ago. From there she sailed us on the normal "milk-run" route around the world. Almost four years later we were back where she was built.

In July of 1968, she was game to take us across the North Atlantic, from New York to Falmouth, England, on the great circle route. It took her forty-one days to make harbor. That it took that long wasn't her fault. In fact she is a very speedy vessel. But the weather was foul and she had to cope with an incredible amount of head winds.

In due course she sailed as far as Germany where she took on the swift Rhine River to gain the peace and quiet of the French canals, and on to the Mediterranean Sea.

On this inland excursion she wasn't able to proceed under her own steam; the 2 hp Seagull outboard motor was no match for the swift currents en route. So we had to rely on the barges of the Rhine River to get us as far as Koblenz. Later it was the *Yankee* with Irving and Exy Johnson who offered their services. We had met them in one of the locks of the *Canal d'Este*. Irving handed us the end of a nylon line, saying, "Here, hang on." And hang on we did for the next three weeks.

Once in the Mediterranean Sea, we sailed along the Spanish coast to Gibraltar, to Morocco, the Canaries, across to the West Indies, the Bahamas, and to the United States. As we sailed into the Chesapeake Bay and up the beautiful Rappahannock River towards Carters Creek, where we wanted to visit Canadian friends, we reflected on how lovely it would be to call this gorgeous area our home. Never again would we have to lower the mast, motor several hundred miles up and down rivers and canals, negotiate three dozen locks, and never again freeze our bones during Canadian winters.

There was another argument that cried out for a change of locale, namerly, that there are no people in the world that say "welcome" so sincerely as do the people of the United States. And no people say it more convincingly as those of the Northern Neck of Virginia. It is our home since.

Here we sold our gallant *Thlaloca* and built our present cutter *Thlaloca Dos*. But that is another story.

☆

The origin of my independent lifestyle goes back to 1951, the year I emigrated to Canada; my first job there as a lumberjack. Isolated amongst forests, lakes and hundreds of miles distant from civilization gave me the first taste of absolute freedom. Absent was television and newspaper, present only hard work, the companionship of coworkers, the snow, the cold and always the magnificent spectacle of nature. My God, did I love it!

Language, of course, was a problem we immigrants tried to improve by reading books drawn from the camp's library (of which were ninety-nine percent western novels).

By nine o'clock at night, the power generating plant shut down, which at the same time was the signal for everyone to keep their blooming mouth shut, a demand we young fellows found almost unbearable. The older folks, mostly farmers in their forties, (with field work in limbo for the winter) old hands but also very camp-wise, had occupied the best places in the bunkhouse, the leeward side. We, as new hands, inexperienced but enthusiastic, had our bunks on the windward side where the missing caulking between the logs caused a drafty exposure. Frequently, when the icy north-wind was howling outside, the draft through the cracks drove us out of our bunks, and we huddled around the barrel stove all night to keep warm. And then not talk?

Anyway, the two hours or so we had available after work for reading wasn't much, but whatever newly found words we had acquired we exercised on the native employees during the day, (who must have had some hilarious laughs within the "inner circle"). However, all were wonderful and they helped us untiringly.

As I recall, there was only a single copy of a hard cover book, lying flat on the top shelf. It caught my curiosity - a biography of George Washington. Enquiring who this man even was I thought, hell, since I was unable to read in any coherent manner it made little difference in what I was reading, as long I found words to bug my friends with. With the help of German comrades whose English was much more advanced, I "battled" through the pages of that voluminous book rather enthusiastically, and to make a long story short I came across a passage that became my "star to steer by" to this very day:

"Far better it is to dare mighty things, to win glorious triumphs, even though checked by failure, than to rank with those poor spirits who neither enjoy much nor suffer much, because they live in the gray twilight that knows not victory nor defeat".

I wrote it down neatly, careful not to make a mistake, and hid it away among my most precious belonging, the wallet, which outside of a few pictures of my girlfriend back in Germany, at once harbored a most significant document - the guiding beacon of my future course. These words, although rewritten many times over the past decades are in my wallet even today.

If overly fastidious, one may find these words a bit pompous applied to an ordinary fellow whose only desire was to break free of traditional values - so be it. To me it was a clear message, to do everything possible to avoid the drudgery of an "eight to five" ritual. We are all free to reach for the stars - call it glory if you will - if we fail, well, so be it! We can always try again, or lick our wounds and forget it, as long we strive to avoid ". . . live in the gray twilight that knows not victory nor defeat."

This then is the inspiration, the pursuance of which eventually found its fulfillment in sailing a tiny boat around the world; an adventure, its magnitude that affects us (Siggi and me) in a spiritual sense, why? Because we experienced the grandeur of nature, and the basic goodness of all people on our wonderful planet earth.

I

A NEW LAND

The sea and a sailor's life weren't entirely foreign to me; I was part of it at fourteen years of age when I was admitted to the Nautical School at Elsfleth in Northern Germany. Months of hard training and learning followed. I then was transferred aboard a cargo ship.

My initial purpose of joining the Merchant Marine Service was certainly a desire to help my country in her struggle fighting a war. A duty of a citizen of any country!

After several supply runs to Kurland, where a German army was cut off, and being pounded by Russian shore batteries, I thought about my decision very seriously. That was live ammunition they were shooting, and they meant to kill. I realized I had opted very unwisely. My young enthusiasm, of course, was far distant from what actually happened - I didn't want to be killed! I had imagined ships plowing blue ocean waves and visiting foreign places, and mingle with people in a world soon at peace. A representative of that peaceful world entered my vision in one of the Baltic seaports - the training barkentine *Horst Wessel* (now the United States Coast Guard's *Eagle)*.

☆

This was the first sailing ship I had seen, and the grand sight had me staring in disbelief. Although a magnificent sight, her hull badly needed paint and her spars with their tightly woven rigging looked neglected. Several coats of varnish would have made the teak and mahogany sparkle. But the country was at war and sailing ships did not contribute; not entitled to even a decent coat of paint. I saw the ship as I wanted her to look, what she was when she was loved and cared for in better days.

1

WEST! SAIL WEST, MAN!

I walked her decks and thought, what a ship, what a beautiful creation of men! I saw her powerful lines and could see her sweeping bow with the long bowsprit, cutting ocean waves and sending spray flying. Aloft the sails were nicely furled. A splendid sight it must be to see her under the full spread of canvas, driven by trade winds on the courses of a past era. On subsequent visits, a small number of men from ships lying in the harbor were delegated to conduct fire drills under navy supervision. A wonderful opportunity to satisfy my curiosity.

In the lines of a sailing ship I saw my future. Right there I heard the wind in the rigging, the scent of south sea islands creeping into my nostrils. I saw my own little ship - *Thlaloca*. I was fourteen and a romantic.

Aboard the cargo ship I was assistant to the "chippy" (the ship's carpenter) to repair the never ending damage caused, particularly when loading ore. One should think an iron ship is wholly of iron. Not so! Judging by the workload, I thought there was more wood than iron. My boss was also a dedicated ship model builder in his spare time; my spare time I spent watching him. In time he trusted me enough to allowed me to use his tools, and I started to carve my own ship models. I discovered that working with wood was my calling. It became my trade which I pursue to this day.

That Germany was in trouble I first noticed on May 8, 1945, the day of her surrender.

The end of the war was also the end of my career as a merchant seaman. The ships that survived were taken away by the victors, and that was the temporary end of the German Merchant Marine Service.

Like millions of others I was locked up in one of the prison-of-war compounds because the Merchant Marine Service was declared by the Allies "The followers of the armed forces," therefore, every former member was treated like a soldier, to be encamped, registered and discharged.

Later the call went out for volunteers to sweep mines in the English Channel. "Instead of being locked up indefinitely, we guarantee that you will be discharged in six months," was the way it was presented.

My grandfather, a veteran of World War I, had one standard saying:

"Never, ever volunteer," I did!

The job was lousy, but the food excellent, At least in

2

quantity! Three square meals a day was the highest reward anybody could expect in those days. Compared to most of my countrymen who were walking about with empty stomachs, we were living like kings.

What made life so exciting was the fact that I was back on a ship. Not very big, a bit over one hundred feet long and a beam of fifteen. They were called R-boats (Räumboote) meaning sweepers. Wooden vessels with two powerful M-A-N Diesels gave them a speed of up to twenty-four knots, power they needed to drag the heavy sweeping paraphernalia.

Not six months as promised, but twenty-seven it took to clear up the shipping lanes sufficiently for vessels to travel again in reasonable safety.

To bring home the magnitude of the operation, here are some figures: Hundreds of thousands of mines were placed in the channel for one reason or another. A field of mines, say twenty thousand strong, was laid in a specific area, exactly charted. With luck we found a dozen or two. The rest had disappeared, either torn loose by storms, or simply corroded and sunk. Better them than us!

The real bonus of the operation was educational. Among the hundreds of men in our flotilla of small ships and the mother ship, were all kinds of highly educated and trained men who for lack of anything else to do to kill time, started training programs in many professions. These lectures were certified, and later on counted as bonus points towards further professional training.

Our teacher was in prewar days associated with the design-staff of the Burmeester yard in Bremen. An expert on wood construction, he was a thorough and persistent teacher. Of course, it was all theoretical; hands-on experience had to be gained in civilian life after discharge.

On December 2, 1947, I was discharged. A clear pass for home. But home was in the Russian-occupied zone of Germany. I was home one day when the authorities ordered me to enter the Russian POW compound in Leipzig. The reason given was for delousing and a clear bill of health. We lived on starvation rations and never saw a doctor. The camp was run by German communists who did everything possible to demonstrate their newly acquired power, at the same time glorifying messiah Stalin and the splendid future of a communistic world. After six weeks of that I was "home free."

WEST! SAIL WEST, MAN!

What followed was a nightmare. Day after day, month after months we lived on starvation ration. I recall that I went to bed unable to sleep because the hunger pangs in my stomach were so painful. Mother would say: "Cover yourself real good so the hunger won't see you." I'm sure it wasn't said lightly.

For much too long I had closed my eyes to the fact that the economic situation in the eastern part of Germany was catastrophic, and could never amount to anything because the leadership was only trained in ideology and the entire lot had no understanding of proper and efficient economics. The result was empty stomachs and disillusionment. Whatever the fruits of our labor, these were siphoned off by the great lover of all working people, the Soviet Union. Not to mention the political hierarchy and army of East Germany that numbered all out of proportions to the labor force. (Thanks to God that this farce has found its inglorious end). So I packed my bags and headed for a place where, so we had heard, the sun was shining a bit brighter - the western zone of Germany. This was before that most gigantic, and most expensive monument to suppression, The Wall, was built.

What was West Germany like in those days? Everybody worked hard and long hours for good money. A huge labor force was engaged in clearing rubble and erecting skyscrapers as a visible sign of everlasting prosperity. Konrad Adenauer, the chancellor, in his inauguration speech promised the German youth that they would never have to carry weapons again. (When my ship left Bremerhaven two years later to carry me to a new land, the *Bundestag* was debating whether the new German Army should press for tactical nuclear weapons).

My mind was set to leave this phony theater and go anywhere that promised a bit more stable rhetoric. When Canada called for lumberjacks, I dropped my tools on the spot and rushed for the employment office.

☆

The ship *Fairsea* left Bremerhaven in the middle of October, 1951, loaded to the gunwales with immigrants. One of them was me!

We had a fair passage, and I felt unbounded joy to be on a ship again, to feel her undulating motions and to see her struggle against the westing wind and sea.

I said to myself, "Someday I will have my own ship - I swear!"

4

There were no individual cabins for us; we were housed community-fashion, where the only division was between the sexes. It was always noisy, either from the constant movement of people, or the occasional scream of a fellow who just got doused by a half-digested meal from the chap in the top bunk.

The ship docked in Quebec Harbor on the eleventh day out. We had arrived in a land that would give each of us either all, little or nothing of what we expected. I loved it from the first moment on.

On debarking we each carried a dog tag around the neck that identified us by name and serial number. Nobody had a rank!

Each waiting train loaded certain numbers into each of the cars, destined all over that giant land. It was all very well organized.

☆

As steadily as the hands on my watch rolled off the time - minutes, hours, days - so did that long train puff us forever deeper into the no-man's-land of Northern Ontario. Only here and there did it stop as if out of breath, in the middle of nowhere, for no apparent reason. Occasionally, the stop lasted for hours, much to our annoyance.

All of us were hungry, very hungry. The last meal we had was aboard ship more than a day past, (no doubt there were logistical problems). When we did receive our first food, it was in shifts in the dining car - two eggs, two pieces of toast and a cup of coffee. It was delicious. Never before had I eaten toast made in a toaster, with butter melting on top a golden crust. We could have eaten loaves of it!

This was the only food for at least half of us on the entire journey, which lasted two days. Considering that there was only one dining car for so many people, someone was out to make a buck, because we were promised regular meals. Also our car was the farthest away from the dining car, a fact that we cursed the entire trip.

Finally the train stopped on high ground overlooking a shallow valley. There we spotted wooden buildings from which smoke rose skyward as straight as a plumb line. It was cold, but we were home!

People were there to greet us in a language we did not understand. Only very few of us spoke a limited English. But we understood their motions that pointed to a bunkhouse we should go to.

Inside were tables that seated a couple of dozen people each. The tables were without table cloths and the seating benches were of plain, beautifully well-worn and polished wood. After having evaluated the goodies that loaded down the tables to capacity, they are still the best looking tables I've ever seen.

Who had ever tasted, much less seen, a steak one inch thick and overlapping the plate by several more? If one wasn't enough, have another one . . . no problem. Who had ever tasted, much less seen, etcetera . . . !

This was *Schlaraffenland* (land of milk and honey), and a lot more.

Many times I have thought about that first day in our new home. What did the management think of that herd of hungry wolves, fifty strong, who devoured almost the entire spread on those tables, perhaps a couple of hundredweight of meat alone? Whoever was in charge of economics surely had doubts in terms of investment versus profit.

Now that I have carried the story this far, it is probably time to direct attention to the fine print in our contract. It committed everyone of us to the spot to hack down trees until every cent of the employer's expense was repaid. Only fair.

Not so fair, however, was the bill. Before we could claim one penny as our own, we had to pay off the transportation fare, which amounted to a stiff two hundred and forty dollars each. The bill stated several meals on the train ride, of over ten dollars each! In 1951 one could book passage on an ocean liner for less, and have a semiprivate cabin to boot.

As far as I was concerned, I gave my honest best, worked harder than ever before, (because I like working hard in any case), enjoying every minute of it, for sixty-four cents an hour, while my Canadian neighbor was earning two dollars an hour for doing exactly the same work. Lack of English precluded any grievances we may have had - the ten-bucks-plus per meal really hit us below the belt line!

I hold no grudge. With my decision to emigrate, I knew I would be starting out at a disadvantage until I learned the ropes and the language.

Many of my colleagues were freeloaders, but only in a sense because they never had to work hard before. Also the general inexperience most of us had in felling trees, and the harsh winter weather none of us ever imagined. For us Europeans it was a wake-up-call what Canada is all about.

This, then, was the beginning of a new life in a new country. Once my contract was fulfilled, I became a drifter. Helped by the sheer phenomenal size of Canada, I always imagined that the grass grew a bit greener on the other side of the fence, and to put my mind at rest, I had to explore it. Consequently, a prospective employer had to be pretty hard up for men before he hired me, considering my job history. Normally, though, I worked my heart out on the job, and I never had much trouble getting the former employer's endorsement for the next job.

My weakness was cars. Expensive cars! The payments were mostly so steep that they committed me to job hunting for the highest pay. Boat-building paid so little that I had to explore other fields.

Another weakness I fell for was the name of a job that had a 'ring' to it. I recall that when I first heard the name lumberjack it brought to mind vividly the Canadian wilderness, trappers and grizzly bears. Then it was "hard-rock-miners," which reminded me of Jack London and his wonderful stories, (sailing followed later). I knew I had to try it, simply because it was paying excellent money, which I needed to prevent repossession of my car.

That was about the time I spotted a very attractive girl, and she fitted my dreams exactly. She liked the car first sight but wasn't at all sure about the driver, even though I did my best to present a good showing. Before she was convinced of it all, we had driven many, many miles. She gave her "yes" to marriage after the first ride in another of my brand new automobiles - apparently a real "convincer!"

Sigrid (Siggi) is her name, my lovely wife now, and you will meet her all along our story.

Siggi had come to Canada from Germany in about the same way I did, the main difference being that she had her own cabin. But she endured very stormy weather, which resulted in a great aversion to anything to do with the open sea (a bad omen for my stock should I ever try to sell her some).

She was born and raised much closer to the sea than I was, in the middle of the Ruhr Valley. Her parents owned a market, and there she worked most of the time once her schooling was completed. Her adventurous spirit (the bonus I needed to sell my stock) led her to visit her relations in Canada with the intention of staying if she liked it.

Well, she did, and in time "found me," and we make a wonderful couple.

The harmony was complete, but hit a rock when I suggested, "We should sell everything we own, buy a sailboat and sail the world."

"How much is that proposed sailboat supposed to cost?" she asked. I mumbled (sensing already the case lost) something about the size, rig, equipment, etcetera . . !

"Oh, about five thousand dollars."

"Hmm ... five thousand you say ... I recall you said sell everything we own. What do we own? Surely you realize that much of what we own still belongs to the finance companies?"

I conceded, resolved not to broach the subject until a more opportune time.

That time came sooner than I expected. It was only a couple of days later when Siggi reopened the subject with a suggestion:

"Listen to what I have to say! (Her normal expression in opening a case, usually a straight finger pointed at me to underline the seriousness.) You get out of that stupid mine and thus spare me the constant worry for your life, I will join forces to find a way where we could have a little sailboat and sail around the bay.

This was wonderful. With Siggi on my side I knew nothing was impossible. Of course, I had to promise! Also I knew, that by building it ourselves the cost of the product would be considerably less.

We were ready to plunge into an adventure of which both of us had no idea where it would end. Would it be my way, where the horizon is the limit? Or Siggi's way, a home and family?

II

BUILDING

In our discussion of a suitable boat, we were never encumbered by consideration that exceeded the minimum. Our sole concern was to find a proven design of sufficient size that could accommodate two people and all the necessary stores for an extended voyage. (Extended voyage was my concern, that I could not possibly discuss with Siggi at that time).

It was then that I remembered a book called *Sopranino*, about a boat by the same name. At the library I found it again, and for a month we studied every morsel of information.

This little boat was only nineteen and one-half feet long, but with a remarkable record for that time (in the middle fifties). With a crew of two it had crossed the Atlantic. The book read so adventurous, the excitement I transformed into measurements on the floor of our mobile home. I asked Siggi for her opinion.

"Pinch the ends to nothing, or almost, we have nothing." A shattering observation, but so true.

But I loved the design and wanted it badly. We agreed to ask for study plans to get a better idea.

Back came, from the good offices of Laurent Giles & Partners, not only one study plan, but two. The enclosed letter explained in detail the history of the other design, named *Columbia Class*. It was an enlarged *Sopranino*, a foot longer and a few inches more in beam and height, really only minor alterations, but those inches amounted to nearly double the living space. It was in fact the *Trekka*, which at that particular time was on its way around the world.

Again I resorted to the measuring tape to lay out the given data on our porch, much more exact than previously to give us a fair perspective. While doing the layout, even indicating the

9

"pinched ends" according to the plan, I searched for a convincing opening statement that would give Siggi very little room for opposing remarks. I tried it with:

"Siggi, this is some huge boat. I'm so pleased we found it," putting emphasis on "huge" and "we."

"If you want the truth, it is an oversized doghouse!"

"A doghouse perhaps in our latitudes but a 'doghouse in paradise': in the tropics . . . blue water . . . sandy beaches . . swaying palm trees . . . " I countered.

"Don't you get any ideas! I suppose it will do for the lakes, so lets get started." Her statement compelled me to remind her, that from the start we opted for the minimum. This happened to be the maximum we could afford!

With that we had resolved the preliminaries. Next to the nitty-gritty.

Once we got the full set of plans, the first concrete step towards building our little ship was the felling of a fair sized rock elm. We carved it up according to the length of scantlings needed to shape the numerous timbers to construct the backbone. This lumber we brought to the nearest sawmill to have it sliced and kiln-dried.

Next we invited Dennis Scott, our friend and owner of the trailer park, to one of the noisy parties that were going on regularly in one or another of the dozen mobile homes in the park.

Dennis Scott preferred Scotch, as any good Scot worth his salt would. He was given a voluminous dosage, followed at a suitable time by our request that some of the trees in the park had to be removed in order to create room for a building site. His wife's possible opposition was muted by her favorite: Bols Mint Liqueur.

A friend had given us a used army tent, large enough to accommodate the boat and just enough space to work around it.

The offsets were properly lofted on the building floor, which gave us a full size blueprint that helped us to cut and shape everything that was required in the major construction of the boat.

Once the skeleton was in place and trued with all necessary care, strip planking was used to plank up the hull. After completion, we called upon our splendid friend Herb Janke, (who, incidentally, had come across the ocean on the same ship as I) to help us applying two layers of fiberglass for added

10

strength and making the hull impervious to any intrusion of water, teredo worms and the like.

The hull was then rolled right-side-up, and steam-bent ribs were placed every four and one-half inches center vertically along the inner hull.

The interior was completed before the deck and cabin went on. With all this finished, we covered it with two layers of fiberglass as well. We then had a boat.

Backing up some, when we had just rolled the hull right-side-up, the open hole really looked gigantic and I had the feeling that Siggi was much impressed. Once, however, when the interior was completed and the deck and cabin in place, that "gigantic" hole had indeed shrunk to the size of a doghouse. That even surprised me. Siggi lost no time expressing her disappointment.

"Well, it will do for the lakes!" She mumbled.

In time the tent was removed, and there for the first time this splendid vessel stood all by herself, freshly painted in blazing sunlight for the world to admire. It was an emotional moment for both of us. It was also a moment, I'm sure of, that Siggi imagined for the first time, what was ingrained in me from the beginning . . . blue water . . . sandy beaches . . . swaying palm trees . . . all the wonderful things that make up dreams.

A hull is not a boat, not by a long shot. Before it would sail, there was still a lot of work to be done, and a lot of money required. As the saying goes: "A boat is a hole in the water to dump money in."

We were then two and one-half years from the day we felled that rock elm. Any attempt to speedier building was stymied by the abominable weather of Northern Ontario. The summers were hot and humid, the mosquitoes and black flies terrible. The winters were appallingly cold. We vividly remember one particular week with temperatures constant at around fifty below zero. Also, there were massive amounts of snow that collapsed the tent twice and tore it to pieces.

With another winter upon us, and no desire to live through it, we decided to finish the boat in California where the climate promised to be more cooperative.

Above: A Rock-Elm for scantlings. Below: Construction

Above: Construction. Below: To California.

III

CALIFORNIA

Surrounded by clouds of mosquitoes and black flies, I built a boat trailer. We shaped and finished the hollow wooden mast. By the end of May, 1962, we shifted the boat to the trailer and lashed her - more securely than ever to a dock - for the start of a safe journey of three thousand miles. Our good friend Scotty hauled the loaded trailer over a steep and bumpy trail to a smooth road with his tractor. Our car took over from there.

We had disposed of our belongings, no doubt the hardest test of our determination. All that we had worked for over the years we gave away for not much more than a song, including the mobile home, Siggi's pride and joy. Only very slowly did she overcome her grief. Understandably, because what she had to look forward to was insecurity and living quarters measuring four by eight feet, with four feet of headroom. A "doghouse," she stated correctly all along. It was up to us to find paradise to make it habitable.

Thinking back over the years brings to mind the many people who, through our example, expressed enthusiastically their desire and determination to do likewise. Some had suitable boats that would have been a delight to live on. None of them (as far as we know) ever sailed away. Why not? Because it takes "guts" to trade jobs and security for something so insecure as a dream. This is no criticism because we all have our priorities, as changeable as time.

WEST! SAIL WEST, MAN!

Within six days we exchanged the timbered hills of the north with the hot and dry wastes of the desert. The heat seemed unbearable at times and we suffered, the car even more. It stalled, often on a steep grade when the engine got so hot that the gasoline vaporized before it reached the carburetor.

Once, when the engine had involuntarily died, I tried to back up in order to clear the highway completely because the traffic was exceedingly heavy. Unfortunately it didn't work. The trailer jackknifed, which put the rig in an almost perfect blocking position. Cars and trucks squeezed through the remaining gap at a snail's pace. Surprisingly, most of the people expressed encouraging words, never any abuse. I told Siggi, "If this would happen in Germany, we would be stoned."

With great effort the car boiled its way up the steep High Sierra grades. Once over the summit we saw below us the green of cotton fields, and only a few miles separated us and the mighty Pacific Ocean.

First there were the palm trees, bent by the prevailing wind, then the blue water glittering under the hot afternoon sun. We pulled off the road to let our eyes gaze over the western horizon, that precise line we wanted to reach out for soon.

☆

I took a job in a boatyard. Unfortunately it paid so little that I feared we would have to delay sailing away indefinitely, for lack of funds to buy necessary equipment. "Siggi," I said, "this will not work." I finally got her to give me leeway in my promise of some years ago, not to work in the mines anymore.

The promise of quick money had us boiling up the High Sierra again, to Bishop, California, a few miles short of the Nevada border, to take a job in a tungsten mine.

Bishop is a small, clean town with breathtaking scenery, favored by the film industry as a setting for many western movies. There was hardly a day we didn't spot one of the stars in the street or in one of the many saloons.

The job was hard but challenging, blasting out and timbering service shafts. That was my specialty for years. Good money was the reward to buy all the fittings for our boat and the half-ton keel to be cast for us in Long Beach.

Very enjoyable were the high temperatures in combination with low humidity. For the boat it was murder. It complained bitterly by showing large patches of fiberglass peeling off the hull, which had shrunk under the blazing sun, as it drew every

14

molecule of moisture out of the wood. We tried to slow the process by covering the boat with watered down foam blankets. It may have helped, but the damage was done. With water being so scarce and expensive, I saw no other way but to quit my job and take *Thlaloca* to a better environment.

☆

In Long Beach we found a boatyard that accommodated the boat and us as live-aboards. We ripped the fiberglass off the hull and bonded the new cloth with epoxy resin, a glue of superior adhesion properties compared to polyester resin.

On November 17, 1962, we bolted the fin-keel to the hull. That readied the boat for the plunge. However, there was one vital item missing to make it successful - the bottle of champagne. We had sent Peter, one of our helpers, off to fetch a bottle. We waited, not knowing that he was helplessly bogged down in traffic.

"What are we going to do? Hold everything, please!" Siggi was begging almost in tears. The crane had the boat already in slings, and the crane operator in a foul mood about the delay.

Thanks to God there was Ruth Billhofer, always a good friend, always practical, who handed Siggi a bottle of soda pop as a substitute. It also improved the mood of the impatient crane operator.

Siggi took several powerful swings. Missing she nearly launched herself before the boat. Then the bottle broke, splattering raspberry fizz all over that graceful bow.

"I name you *Thlaloca*," she said solemnly, giving our beautiful creation the name of an Aztec goddess of water.

Once the slings were slacked, the boat settled beautifully. A very satisfactory moment because it confirmed that up to that point we had done everything as it should be. We were two very happy people.

That night we were much too excited to find sleep, and instead wandered around the boatyard, about as restless as was the boat, tugging on her mooring lines. Our wonderful creation illuminated dimly by the lights of the boatyard.

The following morning the mast went in and we had the rest of the day to complete the rigging. As the sun slowly dipped below the skyline of a great city, we bent on the dacron sails, and then were actually ready for our first sail, to the nearby yacht club and our rented berth.

Neither of us had ever handled a sailboat. I vaguely remembered sail exercises at the German nautical school eighteen years before where we were trained mostly to applaud the cunning maneuvers of our instructors, and all we ever did then was drift with the tide.

Nevertheless, in Siggi's eyes I was a competent sailor. If I had handled sailboats in the boisterous North Sea (so I had told her over the years to win her confidence) there should be no problem taking *Thlaloca* across a crowded harbor in nearly calm winds. It was the crowded harbor that had me frightened as hell.

She wanted to cast off, I didn't. Still too many people around, I wanted no gallery if I was to make an ass of myself. I needed darkness and solitude, and stalled Siggi's impatience with "jobs I still must do."

When all movement in the immediate vicinity seemed to have stopped, I raised the mains'l with a silent prayer, then up went the jib. Quickly I raced back to the cockpit to take control of my first moving sailboat.

The wind had almost died and we barely had steerage way. After my first tack, apparently well executed because Siggi hugged me and praised my skill. I shrugged it off with, "Oh, that's nothing," but I was grateful for the encouragement.

The next maneuver did not go so well. I missed a tack just as we entered the yacht harbor. Before *Thlaloca* regained steerage way for another try, she bumped into a moored motor yacht's stern. It scraped the paint, and the praise I had gained only minutes before. Eventually we sailed into our berth with shouts and fend-offs, but felt competent to cross any ocean.

☆

We sailed local waters to get acquainted with all the good and bad points of our little craft. What a relief that she seemed to have only good points, upon which we called many times. This in turn saved the pride of the two greenhorns sailing her. We had no motor, and the wind was mostly nil. When it did blow, it was so fluky that we bumped into almost everything that got in our way. If it was a manned object, we said ,"Sorry about that." Siggi's terrific smile always elicited a forgiving reply. If the object was unmanned, it reacted to no smile, no matter how sweet. The replies were crunching, and we had to mend them with putty and paint.

☆

On one magnificent day we were drifting about the outer

16

harbor. It was a weekend, and there were dozens of pleasure boats around, on as many courses. Our course was set for a moored American Navy cruiser that was having "open house," as indicated by the long line of people milling about, awaiting their turn for admission. We were sailing toward the stern of that huge man-O-war, where cables stretched aft a long way to a pier.

Our *Thlaloca* must have looked terrific. Her sails stood exactly according to the book. All her bruises were mended, her hull gleaming a brilliant white, with just enough copper paint showing at the waterline for contrast.

Her crew looked as terrific, clad in white shorts and shirts by *Izod Lacoste*. Above it all fluttered the star-spangled Banner, twelve by eighteen inches, on her starboard spreader. Proudly waving astern was the Canadian Ensign, a bit larger. What a pleasing picture she must have made.

"Ready to tack!" I commanded. "Go!"

But go she wouldn't.

"We must have lost the rudder," Siggi exclaimed.

"You are kidding," I said, hoping I was right.

The boat forged ahead, straight for the mooring cables twenty feet up in the air, with us a hundred feet from them.

"It will snap the mast," I yelled as I stripped off my *Izod Lacoste* (it was brand new). The white shorts (of at least equal quality) I had to leave on for obvious reasons. In twenty seconds flat I hoisted my 215 pounds of muscles (some say blubber) up the mast, to be there to cushion the impact of the greasy mooring cable and our forestay.

"Look," Siggi screamed up to me, her finger pointing to a strange roll of vegetation just off our stern. We had not seen anything like that before - tumbleweed! It had lodged between the skeg and rudder, making rudder action useless.

Apparently we gave the people ashore and on the cruiser a good show. They applauded spontaneously. When we spotted several cameras pointed our way, we responded with smiles and waves.

☆

It was obvious that the normal light wind conditions we experienced here would never test *Thlaloca* sufficiently to give us an indication of her capabilities. We had heard there was wind between California and Hawaii, and there I wanted to sail. I felt it was not possible to harness a real sea boat indefinitely.

WEST! SAIL WEST, MAN!

Thlaloca was a thoroughbred, designed by a team of experts and built by us very carefully with the best materials we could find.

My proposal of sailing to Hawaii unleashed in Siggi a more than usual strong reaction, "like hell we will!" Being the much more sensible person of the two of us, she preferred a coastal passage to gain experience. What she feared more than sharks and other creatures of the sea was my ignorance of celestial navigation, a subject I feared more than the IRS. Also, Siggi has the uncanny aptitude, inherent in most members of the lovable female species, turning a man's decision in their favor.

Fear it or not, I had to face it if I ever wanted to venture beyond the horizon. A run down to Globe & Nautical in San Pedro confronted me with a score of nautical instruments, one of them called a sextant. Unfortunately, it has nothing to do with sex, or I would have shown interest in it at an earlier age.

Throughout my seafaring years I had seen these things on the bridges of ships, nicely boxed in mahogany or teak. I had never seen one used. What I had heard about them led me to believe that the computation was past my knowledge in arithmetic. So I had never a desire to even look into those boxes. Now Siggi wanted me to buy one, box and all!

Captain Jorgenson, the store's proprietor, humbled me into silence as he demonstrated the pros and cons of each instrument, using nautical terms I'd never heard before. And I don't know what shook me more, the price of the sextant or his question: "Do you have tables?"

I responded by describing the layout of the boat and the platform we use as table. All along thinking, what the devil has tables to do with a sextant. A broad grin spread across his face. What's so funny? I wondered.

Since his question was in the plural, I asked, "Why more than one table?"

He handed me a book, answering, "These are tables!"

Only minutes before I had told the captain of our proposed voyage to Hawaii. Now that I had given myself away and couldn't sink much lower in his opinion about my navigational skills, I asked him for more advice.

If every syllable he uttered over the next half hour, giving us a lecture on celestial navigation, equaled one mile, the sum of them was how far Hawaii had drifted out of reach.

Besides the sextant, we bought six Hydrographic Office Altitude and Azimuth Tables, a Nautical Almanac, and a couple books on celestial navigation. I believed strongly in the number of books should my brain fail me!

I studied diligently for many hours a subject I found completely alien. Without some expert help, I couldn't seem to master it. Eventually I saw Hawaii only as a rapidly darkening smudge on the screen of my dream. It forced me to concede to Siggi's more realistic plan - a coastal passage.

IV

CHARLIE

It was a hot, sultry day when our Mercury clicked off the miles driving south on highway #1 towards Los Angeles. The huge city lay engulfed in a dense layer of brown-yellowish smog, already noticeable as a painful sting in our eyes. Siggi, sitting beside me, remarked: "This stinking hole we have to go back to. Isn't there something else in this world? "

"Listen," She said, "since we are in the area, why not pay Charlie a visit." Super idea!

We rolled off the highway onto a secondary road that wound its way into the hills, where Charlie owned a modest home surrounded by a sea of flowers - his hobby.

We had met him some time before in one of the bars along Malibu Beach. After we had downed several Mount Gays, with Siggi still nursing her first Bloody Mary, Charlie became talkative. By the time the barman had given the unmistakable sign (refusing to serve) that the bar was closing for the night, Charlie, Siggi and I swore to each other eternal friendship. Siggi, by that time had finished her second drink of the same, and that had put her in the mood to swear to anything.

Charlie was an extraordinary man, a real sailor. He had worked himself up "through the bilges" of sailing ships, tramps and the most modern vessels of his time, and had earned a master's ticket. He knew the oceans from Cape Horn to the China Sea, as well as the harbors from Newcastle to Pernambuco.

WEST! SAIL WEST, MAN!

He was a skinny man, and not much over five and one-half feet tall. Some said he was eighty-three years old, he claimed ten years less (curiously, along our path we should meet later a man with exactly the same credentials). All we knew was that his heart was young, and that is all what matters.

We detected several remarkable things about him. One, his eyes, pale blue and always a bit moist. The cause may well have been his fondness for rum, but most likely it was from gazing to windward during his long years at sea. And there were his enormous hands a size that didn't fit his frail physique. His outstanding trait, however, was his ability to tell a good story. Exactly the reason for Siggi's suggestion of a visit.

At a liquor store we purchased a bottle of Mount Gay, that never failed to help Charlie remember more stories.

It was another super evening, enhanced considerably by a smooth passage home, with no cop in sight!

Something else of significance happened on that trip home. Siggi in her enlightened mood actually spoke of places far, far away. "Shall we sail there? "I asked very cautiously.

"Perhaps we should!" Her reply emphasizes the amazing power of Mount Gay. It made my day!

Some months later, while we were in Mexico, we learned that Charlie had rounded his last cape. Bless his soul!

What he loved more than rum was people - all of them. His love for the human race we took with us on our voyage around the world. We weren't disappointed once. Let this be the last one, Charlie - pass the bottle!

V

DEPARTURE

"Let's sail down the coast and turn a hard right once we have solved the celestial nightmare." So we decided. And so we planned a voyage which may take months, even years.

We got busy preparing for a voyage that differs from an ocean passage insofar that it requires a lot more preliminaries. Especially since the passage would be entirely along a chain of countries considered very poor, and a lot of things unobtainable.

As far as terrestrial navigation was concerned, there was no problem. I was well acquainted with it from the navigational courses I had while in the service.

A trip like that is also infinitely more expensive. Apart from a lot of charts, Sailing Directions, etc., there are visa fees, harbor dues, and simply more occasions that entice one to spend money. An example is Siggi's standard suggestion: "...reason to celebrate." This could mean a juicy steak with beer and ice cream for dessert. Or just a cup of coffee with a dollop of rum or the like.

What worried us a lot was the high percentage of calms and foul winds on our proposed route, as indicated on the Pilot Chart. Our friend Ames Waterbury, a long distance sailor, lectured: "You must be out of your cotton-picking mind to sail that coast without a motor!" Siggi agreed, I bought one. Ames also insisted on a Walker-log (an instrument that shows speed and distance sailed) and an inflatable dinghy.

"That man is right, Hein," And Hein bought both. Ames suggested . . . Siggi agreed. I finally called it quits before our grand voyage ended before it started because the dollar bills were running out faster than the Treasury could print them. The man who could have been of great help, at least more in my line of thinking, was Charlie. Unfortunately, he lived far away and had no transportation to help us (me) in our conflict with ideas and suggestions. There was no doubt about the sincerity of suggestions received from people. All had in mind our well-being. What they failed to grasp were our meager resources, and that we only had a twenty-foot boat with limited stowage. Also, the boat is basically a one-man vessel. Carrying two people was in itself one hundred percent above capacity.

Every day we bought and stored. A constant flow of people came by to chat. Those with experience pointed out harbors and anchorages of interest and beauty. Often when we returned from errands we found notes stuck to the cabin, saying, "Sorry we missed you. Best of luck on the voyage." Twice those notes were on boxes of food; choice food we considered luxuries.

I shaped a pair of downwind poles. Siggi was feverishly engaged in solving the stowage problems. We bought another jib, equal in size to the one we had, for downwind sailing, and to make the boat self-steering. Once the compass was compensated, we thought we were ready.

We were exuberant. Our thoughts were on smooth seas and blustering winds that would make *Thlaloca*'s wake a gleaming white line while self-steering herself to places of exotic beauty our friends had talked about. We thought of us, lying exposed on the foredeck under a glorious sun, our hides tanned to the color of bronze, happy and laughing all the way to any destination we choose. Like hell we did!

☆

We embarked on a voyage we didn't know where it would take us, or end. It didn't matter. Important was that we pursued the dreams that had evolved in a mobile home three years before. Along our path south we would shed that dream world and face reality with the same determination - a reality that is expressed more to the point in the words so eloquently presented by our friend Nancy Griffith:

"He who goes to sea for fun will go to hell for pleasure."

24

The first entry in our first logbook was marked February 20, 1963, the date of our departure, Some people were there to say a last "Good Luck!" Some were friends, some were strangers. One woman handed Siggi a miniature Bible. A fellow asked, "Do you have a shoehorn?" "What would I need a shoehorn for?" I asked. "To get into that nut shell of yours, mate!"

We slipped the moorings, and off we went. Very slowly *Thlaloca* gathered way. We waved back until we lost sight of all the people we left. Are we ever going to see them again? A question no one could answer.

In a light breeze we crept towards the breakwater just as the aircraft carrier *Kearsarge* entered the harbor on her return from Southeast Asia, with white-clad sailors standing parade. As we drew abreast of the giant vessel, Ames and Charlie, who had followed us by car along the shore, snapped a photo, a telling example of the minute size of *Thlaloca*. Yet she was destined to sail the same oceans as any huge ship, and get away with it.

VI

EARLY DISASTER

We tied up to the Coast Guard dock in San Diego two days later. While Siggi showered in the Coast Guard's fabulous facilities, I stripped down the outboard motor again, as I had so many times since Ames outburst: "You must be out of your cotton-picking mind . . . " It gradually dawned on me that there was indeed something wrong with me for having bought a piece of junk called Golden Jet 500. Anyway, I got it running again.

The wind blew fair on leaving the bay but had petered out abreast the Coronado Islands. The Golden Jet had quit again, so we drifted about until midnight when a bit of wind kissed the sails and pushed us past Punta Descano by daybreak. Then the fog rolled in. It was cold. I paddled to work up a sweat and to propel us in the direction of Ensenada, Mexico, while keeping a disgusted eye on that confounded motor, which was getting a free ride. Later, Siggi worked the paddle while I stripped the motor again. Casually Siggi remarked, "There must be a railroad close by, I can hear a train!" I listened and, sure enough, a train must be rolling by close. A little later, Siggi said, "Look, there is something white off our port bow."

I got the binoculars. "Hell," I screamed, "those are breakers!" We paddled furiously until the "white" disappeared back into the fog.

While Siggi continued paddling, I doubled my effort to

make the motor start. Once it did, we marveled at the lovely sound a motor makes when needed most. It prompted Siggi to pump the Primus - "to celebrate" with a cup of coffee laced with a tot of rum.

The fog we didn't like at all. But with a steaming cup of coffee as company and the motor purring a soothing song, the fog didn't look as dense as it really was. What was that?!

"Oh, my God, what is it?" Siggi exclaimed with heartbreak in her voice.

The motor had ground to a halt - no news there. What disturbed us that we were motionless, surrounded by the strangest plants we ever saw - kelp.

"You know," Siggi said, "we never thought of fog, did we?" "Right, Sig, neither did we think of kelp, did we?"

At Ensenada we cleared into Mexico. We only tarried long enough to sample the different brands of *cervezas* and ice cream. We provisioned the boat and loaded up on *agua purificada*. Then we were off. (Little did we know that we would be back soon).

☆

Out on the ocean we were back to drifting and the usual battle with the outboard. In two days we had drifted as far as Colnet Bay. Tired out by all this, we decided to enter the bay and anchor for a well earned rest.

Colnet Bay is large, with high country to the north, low and barren elsewhere, except for the impressive Cabo Colnet where it meets the ocean. Except for any wind from the south through west, the anchorage is well protected, but even though a heavy swell was rolling in on that fateful day. Our chart had no detail of the bay. The only caution we had was from the Sailing Direction - shallow bay.

No problem, we should see the bottom in plenty of time. Unfortunately, the ground was stirred up by the swell therefore we could not judge the depth of water. Depth sounder we did not have; and being still so far offshore, casting the lead seemed premature.

When I dropped the anchor it hit the ground very quickly. I hauled the line plumb, and estimated the depth about seven feet. This wasn't much water. And not knowing the stage of the tide, I thought it prudent to find deeper water farther offshore. With the anchor back on deck, I went aft to start the motor. But what did I see?

Early Disaster

A huge swell curling some four feet high and breaking just off the stern. It sure didn't look right. What I did next led to disaster: trying to start the obstinate Golden Jet. As usual it refused to start. In the meantime, every breaker drove the boat into shallower water until she touched ground. All seemed lost.

There is no use saying that boats should not go aground or that good skippers don't do it. As we know, Columbus stranded *Santa Maria* off Santo Domingo and so did many others. This was our turn. Admittedly it came mighty early in our adventure. We had sailed only 250 miles.

I jumped into the water and floated the anchor on a life vest offshore to the end of the line. For the next four hours we worked our hearts out, struggling to pull the boat back into deeper water. It was a fruitless effort, even after three American scuba divers, who were exploring the bay, came to help.

The breakers constantly threw the boat onto her beam ends. The heavy keel pounded the hard sand, and she trembled from trunk to keel. Obviously, no vessel could stand this abuse for long. She would break up shortly if we failed in our effort.

The tide was falling, that made her pound harder, it became unsafe to be around her. I was determined to try one more trick; climb up the mast and hope that my weight would suffice and keep her on one side, thereby reducing draft, to give Siggi and the helpers a chance to float her free.

It took all my strength to climb half way up the mast that swayed violently with the motions of the boat. The end came fast. The mast broke at deck level with a splintering noise and buried me underneath it. The end of the steel jumper strut hit me below the left shoulder blade and broke several ribs. It was the temporary end of our struggle - and almost of me. It had knocked me out cold, and we were so fortunate that Siggi had the help of the husky American men who dragged me ashore where I regained consciousness. Blood was flowing from the deep gash in my back, Siggi bandaged with some clean cloth provided by the people ashore.

We looked out to our darling little ship and I cursed being unable to help relieve her agony. Everything looked so unreal. Only hours before, we had sailed into this bay with our world and the future bright and promising. And now, this promising world was disintegrating before our eyes. And there was nothing we could do to prevent it. Three years of planning and hard labor were being pounded to pieces by a merciless sea within hours. What a terribly high price to pay for having goofed only slightly.

But in that darkness of doom shone a brightly lit beacon of hope; my lovely Siggi. She was pale and exhausted from being in the chilly water for hours, shivering uncontrollably from exposure, work and heartbreak. We sat on a boulder ashore, tightly embraced to give warmth to each other. Siggi repeatedly uttered the words: "It's you now who is important. All will be all right!" in an effort to console my wounded body and mind.

We looked about the barren land and saw nothing of interest except a couple of adobe huts very close to the beach on a patch of high ground. Living in one of the huts was the Melling family, Señora Melling and her eighteen-year-old son and a daughter two years younger. (Melling is not a Spanish name, but is one of the most common names in the area. It is attributed to a Norwegian sea trader who apparently traded not only in commodities, but also looked after the people's needs in body and soul).

Señora Melling invited Siggi to her home. I boarded the station wagon of our American helpers, who insisted that I see a doctor, some twenty miles away.

The road was only a winding donkey path through the flat countryside. The numerous potholes jolted the car and had me choking. The town was nothing but a cluster of huts, reminiscent of a typical frontier town of the "Old West."

At the doctor's office I was laced up, and on leaving was given a bottle of painkilling tablets. All was free of charge. At the sheriff's office I inquired about a call to San Diego - my American helpers had insisted that I get in touch with the U.S. Coast Guard. But the language barrier soon stalled our fitful conversation, except that we were left with the impression that there was a man with some command of the English language in a town "ten or twenty" kilometer farther along the road.

We found the town and the man as well. He took us to the sheriff's office, over a trail better suited for a Caterpillar tractor. Via the interpreter, I told the sheriff about our calamity on the beach and requested a call to San Diego. *No problema!*

He was a very helpful chap. That he demonstrated by grabbing the phone and calling Ensenada for a relay to San Diego. Also demonstrated was his powerful status, in the shape of an enormous revolver that weighed down heavily his port side. But all his official power did not budge the operator in Ensenada, who requested our presence there so that all charges could be settled at the head office, unless a reliable person would guarantee the charges.

No problema there. What other man was more reliable than a sheriff. With a dollar bill stuck under his nose, he was more than willing. We couldn't follow what the two characters were talking about, but we gathered from the great excitement in the sheriff's voice and the gesticulation that things did not go well. Apparently, the problem was that the previous sheriff was convicted for embezzlement, a felony that reflected badly on the present sheriff. Not only had I lost a dollar, but also all hope of making our plight known to the outside world.

What followed is an example what humanity can do helping each other if there are will and compassion.

It was then that our interpreter vaguely remembered some of his relations in Ensenada. But try as he did, he couldn't recall their names. I gambled another dollar, plus a cold *cerveza*, instructing him to take it easy and come up with a name. Fifteen minutes later I handed him another beer; already doubting the wisdom of my action - payment before results.

When he finally raised his lanky body from the squeaking bench, it wasn't because he remembered the name of any person, but that he definitely recalled the street name his cousin lived on in former days, operating a bakery. This he told the operator and pleaded with her to locate the party.

As time dragged on we sat around in the hot sun. The apathetic Mexicans squabbled among themselves while my dejected thoughts were with Siggi and the boat. Will it still be alive? The pain in my chest bothered me terribly, and the burning heat had me close to fainting many times. I fought with all my will power against it. Yet I was forced to adopt the attitude of my Mexican crowd - wait and take it easy - *mañana*!

It was discouraging. Also it seemed unreasonable to expect that any operator would be allowed to take out time to locate a party, furnished with such scant description. But strange things happen in Mexico. The party was located and without argument agreed to guarantee the charges.

When the phone rang and a voice said, "U.S. Coast Guard, San Diego," it was music in my ear. Having described my plight, I was connected to the proper department - Search and Rescue - which told me that a plane would be over the area the following morning to investigate. Also that I should mark the "wreck" by a light at night so that a cutter, which was presently engaged in assisting a stranded yacht two hundred miles farther south, could find us on its way home within the next forty-eight hours.

Overjoyed by such encouraging news, I returned to Siggi and the boat. If *Thlaloca* would last another day, we had a chance to save her. We had every reason to rely on the efficiency of the U.S . Coast Guard.

Siggi had already made a home for us in one of the adobe huts offered by Señora Melling. Out in the foaming breakers our gallant little ship still fought for her life. We could not lighten her agonizing struggle, and that was enough to drive us mad. We thought about freeing her and let the seas drive her ashore where she would be out of the constant pounding, but that would reduce our chances of ever getting her back into deep water. What finally decided against it was the solid line of large boulders that fringed the beach, and would surely crush the hull.

That night was full of horrible nightmares. The pain in my chest immobilized me and made breathing an ordeal. Siggi stood watch to keep an eye on the kerosene light we had elevated on a stick on the highest point ashore.

With the rising tide came the awful roar of breakers and the distinguishing sound of *Thlaloca*'s pounding. I could not restrain myself, I had to help her. I must have been crazy even to try it in the condition I was in, but I was desperate. Mauled by the breakers I struggled to get through. What finally made me give up was Siggi's frantic hold on me, and her tears.

Early next morning we found the boat on the beach. The anchor rode had chafed through. That she got over the boulders, apparently unharmed was a miracle. Still, she was a sad sight. We unloaded her, and thought of stripping her of all valuable gear, because the odds for getting her back into deep water seemed impossible. (Overland was equally impossible for lack of a decent road.)

There was three feet of water inside the boat, with everything not fastened down adrift or submerged. The uncanned food we dumped on the beach where it was recovered by the Mexicans. Miraculously, the Golden Jet had survived the onslaught. Although soaked, only the golden paint had suffered, the only gold that embellished that piece of junk! We later left it with the Mellings.

Disaster in Colnet Bay

News of the shipwreck had quickly spread over the surrounding area and attracted many Mexicans on horses and donkeys to get an idea of what was salvageable, should the opportunity arise. Each morning thereafter the same men appeared after they had camped for the night just out of sight. At night they trotted away, disappointed. We stood night watches to keep an eye on our gear that was spread outside the hut.

There! A plane! It came in low, eventually from several directions to take photographs. We watched the four-engined flying boat closely in case a message was dropped, but there was none. The Mexicans had never heard such overpowering sound, definitely not from such close range (neither had we) and they became very excited. Their skinny little donkeys acted much the same, with their long ears pricked up and rotating like radar antennas. One even managed to break his fetter. A frantic search finally located the critter in our "bedroom," where he seemed happy and content.

That plane was the last we saw of the U.S. Coast Guard. It brought to mind a favorite saying of my dear mother: "If you want to be helped, help yourself." And that we did.

Our main hope were our American friends, who had returned to the States and had insisted that they would send us help. One day we were visibly moved by the appearance of our good friend Ames Waterbury from Long Beach. He had read of our grounding in a Coast Guard report in the local paper.

Ames, an excellent boat builder, inspected *Thlaloca* and confirmed my evaluation that the boat could not be repaired except at great expense in Mexico where much of the required material was unavailable. Should we get her off (he had not the slightest suggestion how) we must try to sail her to the States. We loaded his station wagon with all the gear that had no immediate use. He was going to meet us wherever we chose to lay up.

The stationary high pressure cell remained with us. A moderate to fresh wind came up with every tide change but blew itself out after an hour or so. We were well aware that a storm from the west would be the final end of our boat.

What we couldn't afford to lose was hope, that somehow there must be light at the end of this dark tunnel. We had with us a full set of hand tools and all necessary materials to repair any reasonable damage. I spliced the mast and, after shaping it, encased the break heavily in fiberglass. It was slow work because of my chest which reacted painfully to any movement. Siggi was busy cleaning and preserving with grease our tinned provisions, all the while chasing cockroaches from one place to another.

Each day was like the next. In the morning the sun rose as a red symbol of life over a desolate land. The days were enjoyably warm, the nights shivering cold. In the evenings we gazed at the western sky where the clouds formed in wondrous sculptures at sunset, while on the beach *Thlaloca* shook her bones under the onslaught of the rising swell rolling in from the southwest. There she lay on the rocky shore, stripped of her beauty. The fiberglass was torn off in many places, the keel and rudder bent, her port side sandblasted by the continuous wash of the seas. Hope of sailing her again faded as surely as those wonderful sunsets. If only a ship would come!

☆

"Ship ho!" screamed Siggi. Sure enough, a large motor yacht had anchored just inside the point. I quickly inflated the porous dinghy and paddled out to our only hope.

On board the *Black Douglas* I met Doug and Frances Douglas, en route to the West Indies. With a stiff drink in my hand I explained our situation and asked for their help. Doug immediately volunteered to pull us off when the tide would be at its highest, early the following morning.

It so happened that high water that morning concurred with a full moon, that produces maximum height of water. A welcomed coincidence to float the boat over the boulders.

Our operation was to begin at 7:00 a.m.. Two hours before, the water was already higher than any time before, agitated by a twenty-knot wind from the southwest. A direction we feared all along. (A full moon is normally associated with a weather pattern that can be quite different to what is normal.)

All along we had a buoyed anchor out to seaward, to prevent the boat from being driven further up the beach. Siggi and I worked in the breakers to keep the bundled-up tires in place, (the Mellings had a whole pile of them) to cushion the terrifying impact. Siggi worked her heart out. A lot more than I could do with my aching chest.

"Siggi, get the .22-gun and shoot to alarm the Douglas'," I screamed above the noise of the breakers. Siggi did, but the shots were hardly audible above the roaring elements.

Siggi resisted with all her verbal strength my attempt to get

34

the inflatable through the breakers, to rouse the Douglas'. But it had to be done - and desperation did it!

Doug, not even taking time to dress, had the powerful engines of the *Black Douglas* roaring into action, breaking the relative silence of the anchorage. I rowed to our buoyed anchor with the end of a two hundred feet long ¾-inch nylon line from the *Black Douglas* and fastened it to the anchor-pick-up-line, (which we had exchanged with a ¾-inch line at low tide).

Once the lines were connected the slack was taken up. Ever so slowly, under the power of the motor yacht's three hundred horses, *Thlaloca* had no choice but to follow in a bucking manner. Siggi and I were riding the side of the hull, clutching her smooth sides so as not to be thrown off.

Gradually our little craft righted, with us creeping ever higher on the hull until we sat in the cockpit again after four of our longest days. Siggi quietly sobbed, and I felt much the same. We thanked our *Herrgott*.

We anchored the boat in three fathoms - a long way offshore. The *Black Douglas* recovered her lines and off she went. We only had a chance to say a distant "Thank you." Who would have believed that we would meet again very soon.

We must not forget to mention the exceptional skill exhibited by Doug in handling the maneuver in a most delicate manner, which in any other way could have resulted in disaster. In particular getting the boat unharmed over the large boulders, we were unable to remove beforehand.

The boat was leaking badly through the strained keel bolts, and she had to be bailed constantly. Also of concern was how to step the mast without the help of a gin pole. If this was one worry, another was how to get the boat to a yard for repair in the condition she was in.

Early next morning, I had just scrambled out of the sleeping bag to relieve Siggi from bailing the boat, when I spotted an object of great interest - a fair sized fishing vessel setting nets in the bay. It was the *Erika* from San Diego. But what interested me most was its gin pole. The speed of my approach in the dinghy was matched by skipper Al Watkins' assurance of all possible help.

Our Mexican friends got the mast through the breakers and, with all hands pitching in, we got it re-stepped. Several more trips ferried all our gear back on board, which we stowed well above the floor boards. Then we were ready to accept Al Watkins' offer to tow us back to Ensenada. They were headed that way anyway for fuel and renewal of their Mexican fishing license. Our lucky star was still with us, and the future would tell we could not succeed without it.

We said, *adios, muchas gracias!* to the Melling family and all the other friends we had made there and reimbursed them for their help and all inconveniences we may have caused. These people are the only pleasant memories of Colnet Bay.

☆

The wounds of the grounding in Colnet Bay, ours and that of the boat would take a long time to heal, and they would never be forgotten. And with these wounds came valuable lessons.

Obviously, one of the cardinal lesson was: never neglect soundings.

2.) Know the stage of the tide. If not, presume the water to be high.

3.) Never rely on an engine. Handle a sailboat in a manner that it will sail you out of trouble. If there is wind that is!

These were lessons we learned at that time. Others we picked up bit by bit in future years of travels. This is not to say that experience and all the lessons learned are sufficient to prevent mishaps. Columbus, one of the great captains, stands as a perfect example.

There was one lesson however, that mitigated somewhat the horror of Colnet Bay. It was the unimaginable strength of our *Thlaloca*. It was the confidence in her strength we needed later on when we faced the seemingly endless expanse of the Indian Ocean and the gale-ridden seas around the Cape of Good Hope.

☆

Our craft was deeply scarred, and on the trip to Ensenada she had to face turbulent seas from the northwest which opened the leaks to streams. Siggi had the worst of it. She was wet, cold and seasick. She bailed constantly, but the water still rolled into our bunks. Thanks to Al's considerate speed, we survived the seventy-mile passage with a boat still afloat. We arrived at Ensenada at noon, eighteen hours after we had left Colnet Bay. We thanked Al and his crew for their generous help. When we offered to pay for the fuel at least, Al refused, saying sternly, "We are all in the same environment. Tomorrow it might well be me who needs help."

36

Early Disaster

A couple of days later, when the forecast promised a fair wind, we set sail for San Diego. As is generally reported, it is hardly ever a pleasant trip, as in most cases the course is dead against the prevailing wind and current.

Not only was the boat leaking, the mast was unstable as well because we had lost a lot of rigging (which got kinked under the pounding keel). Instead of stainless steel shrouds, we had rigged dacron lines.

Contrary to the forecast, the wind was on the nose and blowing fresh. The seas followed suit and piled against us. Sailing close-hauled, the boat looked after herself. I took over bailing from an exhausted Siggi. Her seasickness and coping with all the uncertainties had drained her considerable stamina. The cold water splashing into her bunk made her close to a lifeless bundle. I wasn't in much better shape myself.

The rising seas increased the pounding, and the mast seemed to whip about increasingly. It gradually dawned on us that we won't make San Diego unless it moderated soon. Thus we spent a very miserable night.

The following morning greeted us with an awful looking sky to the northwest. The barometer had dropped. Not an encouraging sign. By log we had sailed forty-eight miles. Not bad considering the choppy condition and being hard on the wind all along. Still our spirits were at a low ebb. We had just about exhausted our will to press on when Siggi suggested we listen to a weather report.

Once we had left Ensenada, we had no-one to interpret for us the Mexican (Spanish) weather bulletin. Now we had to check the entire frequency scale to find a Californian station that happened to give a report. When we finally came across one, it shocked us into an immediate course change of 180 degrees, back to Ensenada. Severe gale warnings were out for the entire Californian coast.

With the wind and sea aft, the pounding diminished and so did the leaks. Half a day later we were back in Ensenada.

☆

Ensenada, then a bustling town of about five thousand and perhaps an equal number of roaming dogs, is only eighty miles south of the U.S. border, a short drive for many "gringos" attracted by the freewheeling night life and inexpensive liquors. The economy was geared to serve the tourists and appeared to be doing very well.

WEST! SAIL WEST, MAN!

Carnival week, or Mardi Gras, had just ended, but the people were still in a festive mood; a mood that seemed to us manifested in the Mexican people at birth, because if it isn't Mardi Grass, it will be something else, mostly of some religious nature. Faced with the pressing need of finding reasonable repairs for our *Thlaloca*, our mood was just the opposite.

As the boat had to be hauled out of the water, I headed towards a huge floating crane, that happened to belong to the Rodriguez Shipyard. There I talked to Mr. Arthur Yeend, the American manager, and suggested, "That big crane would be just the thing . . . "

He replied, obviously amused, "If you consider the kind of money to set this thing in operation, it would probably be cheaper to buy yourself a new boat." This hurt, and it dawned on me how dreadfully expensive the repairs would be.

"Bring your boat alongside the pier, and I will see what can be arranged," he said after an embarrassingly long silence. Back I went to get *Thlaloca*, and relieved Siggi from the job of constant bailing.

A bull-nosed crane that looked awfully tiny was waiting when we moored the boat to the yard pier. We quickly lightened her of all excess weight, including the spars. Once the lines were placed around the hull and hooked to the load cable, we climbed ashore. There I joined the half dozen Mexicans at the back of the crane to provide additional counterweight. To put it mildly, Siggi and I were very apprehensive.

Excruciating moments followed as we listened to the appalling clatter of the gears and the tearing strains of the nylon ropes, with bulging black smoke from the exhaust pipe choking us to tears. Near panic engulfed us when the back end of the crane began to lift. Calamity was averted only when more people showed the courage, including Siggi, to crowd onto the back end. We breathed a collective sigh of relief once our boat was safely cradled in the yard.

Before we had left Ensenada for San Diego, we had informed Ames Waterbury of our intention. It so happened that the gale reported to us over the radio had turned into a tremendous storm that put dozens of vessels in distress. Ames, knowing that we were at sea with an unsound boat, called the Coast Guard, which included us in their search. Three days later we were reported in the papers as possible victims of the storm.

After our return to Ensenada, ignorant of the severity of

the storm, our pressing need was to get the boat out of the water as quickly as possible and arrange for repairs. For this reason, Ames did not receive word of our whereabouts until four days later.

☆

Long hours of work followed. We patched, fiber-glassed, replaced the keel bolts, shaped the new deadwood to the keel, and did dozens of other repairs. Siggi made a special trip to San Diego to purchase all the material not available in Mexico, or too expensive. She returned with Ames and his station wagon loaded to the ceiling.

Arthur Yeend, not only found us everything we needed, but also gave us manual help. Beyond that, he picked us up in his car every evening and took us to his lovely home in the hills. There we met his family, enjoyed delicious suppers, saw the countryside, and went with him to bars to sample some of the good liquors.

Marimba and mariachi bands wandered the streets in daylight hours and made the town a symphony of music. At night the bands entered the nightclubs and bars, and for little money played and sang to requests. The atmosphere was overwhelmingly lovely, and we didn't feel like "soon-to-be-broke" sailors at all.

All along, though, with a feeling of apprehension, we looked forward to paying the bill for repairs. Even allowing for all the help and consideration of Mr. Yeend, we knew that our voyage had ended financially. But there was no bill!

One of the things we learned on our adventurous path is that a successful voyage depends to a great degree on understanding and cooperative people, Mr. Yeend, owner of a racing yacht and participant in many TransPac races, was without a doubt the one person who put us back on our adventurous road. As no final decision could be made by himself within a basically Mexican shipyard we also thanked the Mexican manager equally.

With *Thlaloca* back in the water and her wounds healed, we anchored her off the yacht club. One morning, when I was out for a breath of chilly air, I spotted a familiar yacht at one of the piers. A man was looking at me as curiously as I at him. Sure enough, it was Doug from the *Black Douglas*, which had pulled us off the beach at Colnet Bay.

The Douglas' had also run aground further south. The

39

Coast Guard had helped them off (why not us?), but they were forced back to Ensenada for engine repairs. We were sorry to hear about their troubles, but happy to have such a wonderful couple as company for the rest of our stay.

Meanwhile we had to decide: what to do next? The cyclone season to the south was about to begin. Also, the stranding had taken away much of our enthusiasm and had drained our kitty. We flipped a coin. It came up "south."

VII

BAJA CALIFORNIA

From then on we had to move fast and keep a keen eye on the weather. On April 26 we set sail to a good breeze, although dead in the eye. But once we had cleared Bahía de Todos Santos, the course was southeast, and that brought the wind abeam. An increasing wind smoothed the wrinkles in the mains'l, and a bulging bow wave gave us the sensation of exhilarating speed. Skipping away nimbly, we passed San Martin Island to our port. Abreast the foaming Sacramento Reef, a big sea began to form, and we soon were racing down the faces of towering combers. *Thlaloca* performed wonderfully.

By nightfall the fresh wind was still with us and showed no sign of abating. In the darkness those foaming seas looked frightening. To keep the boat from broaching I had to do some fancy work with the tiller.

"The mains'l has to be reefed, Sig!"

But Siggi was crouched deep in the cockpit, expecting some disaster at any moment. Needless to say, she was scared. And so was I!

A bit more coaxing got Siggi on the tiller, while I raced forward and ripped down the mainsail. Then we broached. Only then did we know how hard the wind was actually blowing . . and those seas!

With a close reefed main and boomed out jib we carried on sailing downwind. The boat was now easy to control, and we actually enjoyed the roller-coasting.

At daybreak we sighted the dark shadow of Cedros Island with its four-thousand-foot peak marking Bahía Sebastián Vizcano. We did not dare approach so dangerous a place too close without the help of good visibility, because too many vessels had come to grief there. We lowered the mains'l to slow down.

Shortly after the wind and sea lessened quickly, and soon we were becalmed. The remaining five miles to the island's settlement tested our patience for four hours.

When we plotted our run over the past twenty-four hours, we came up with an astonishing 156 miles. Truly fantastic for a boat with a waterline of only eighteen feet, six inches. A strong current must have helped us a lot. As much we tried to break this record later, we never could.

We anchored near the large wharf of the fish cannery, where a native in a dugout canoe showed up almost immediately to give us a lift ashore. At the cannery we located Vincent Martínez, who invited us to his home. Doug from the *Black Douglas* had asked us to give him their greetings because Vincent had been most helpful to the Douglas' when they ran aground nearby.

Martínez's small house was in the center of the tiny village where there was not a tree around that could have taken the sting out of a scorching midday sun. The house, being crowded with nearly a dozen adults and children, we had the impression that a party was going on, but they were all relatives, and all lived there. Vincent made us stay for a strange but delicious *champourado*, a soup they drink.

The next day we sailed out into a calm and drifted to an anchorage on the north side of Turtle Bay. Strangely, as soon we rounded the headland, the wind blew fiercely against us, and kept blowing unabated throughout the night. An all night concert by hundreds of seals and the high-pitched whine of wind in the rigging kept us awake until early morning, when we felt elated to raise the hook and escape that noisy hole.

Up went the sails, confident that the good wind would prevail. But as soon we had cleared the bay, the wind went dead. A phenomenon we were to experience consistently along the Baja coast.

We drifted far offshore in search of wind. Also, I wanted to practice celestial navigation. I had studied the subject all along and wanted practical results. There was no concern of getting lost because all we had to do was turn a sharp left to find land again, or so we thought!

For two days we drifted about in nearly total calm, and a longitude sight placed us only fifteen miles offshore. Combined with a latitude sight at noon, we had a fair idea of where we were. We set a course for Cabo Lázaro and motor-sailed for it. (The Golden Jet had been replaced with a three-horsepower Mercury.) Cabo Lázaro eventually peeked over the horizon dead on. Things began to look promising to take on the wide open ocean. But with the cyclone season almost upon us, this endeavor had to wait for later.

We entered Bahía Magdalena after dark against the usually fierce northwesterly muzzler. After two hours of hard beating, we didn't think it worth the effort to find an anchorage for only a few hours, so we came about and sailed back into the eternal calm.

Our course was east-southeast for Cabo San Lucas, the southern tip of Baja California, 150 miles away. Near our goal the seas became very turbulent, perhaps due to some mixed-up currents. *Thlaloca* rolled and pitched and jumped and lurched, the wind so feeble it did not steady her. The chilly air made us wear all available woollies.

"If this is Mexico, they can have it," Siggi mumbled, dreaming about warm weather we had rightly expected so far south.

As we rounded the steep, impressive rocky islands leading into the lovely Bay of Cabo San Lucas, the temperature changed instantly to very hot, the first indication that we had arrived in the tropics. We quickly shed our clothing and got into our swim suits. For a time we pondered over this remarkable change and figured that the topography of that part of the world must be responsible. We reasoned that the high land to the west of the bay was cutting off the prevailing westerly wind, leaving the Sea of Cortez a vacuum for the hot desert air to the northeast. Anyway, we thought this explanation made sense.

We anchored off a golden sandy beach among half a dozen yachts. Wide open to the south, the bay has a soft sandy bottom and the clearest of water. The anchor had barely grabbed hold when we dove in for a swim. We horse-played and thrashed about, happy that the coin had flipped as it did back in Ensenada. What a lovely picture our *Thlaloca* made against the background of a pale blue sky, nodding softly to a slight swell as if expressing her own pleasure.

The tranquillity of that wonderful moment was shattered instantly by Siggi's scream: "Shark!" Spouting like whales we raced for the shore. Out of breath, I took a quick dive to locate our attacker. But all I could see was Siggi's fleeting shadow over the golden sand. I surfaced and laughed. I kidded her: "Frightened of your own shadow, ha, ha!"

"Is that why you followed me so fast?" She countered.

On clearing in, the port captain told us that our papers were not in order. We either had to have them corrected by our broker in Ensenada, or have a local broker issue new ones for "Oh, just a slight gratification."

"How much would that slight gratification be worth in money?" I asked.

"Oh, hm, maybe fifteen dollars," he replied.

I telegraphed Ensenada, but the answer we received was ambiguous. Either way someone was out for a quick buck. Our demand for the return of the passports got us into a heated argument. At the end, the port captain finally conceded. The sullen looks on the port captain's and the broker's face reflected their disappointment. Later, in Mazatlán, this *urgente problema* wasn't even mentioned.

In due course we made friends from a score of boats. Our most enjoyable time was on board two tuna boats, the *Defense* and the *Marsha Ann*, both from San Pedro. We were treated to cold beer, ice cream, sizzling steaks every day, and an open invitation to use one of their speed boats for water skiing.

Ashore we met Keith Ross, an Englishman. He had sailed a small boat down the coast and had lost it on a reef some miles north of Cabo. Shipwrecked in a strange country without funds, he eventually found and married a Mexican girl. He was handy with tools and made a living doing repairs on boats. One night he invited all the yachties to a goat barbecue. While goat meat is not exactly to my taste, washing it down with a half pint of *tequila* made it palatable.

Those days were carefree and passed with incredible speed. Finally, when we awoke one morning about to face another glorious day, we decided, "Hey, this must stop," because we were already hearing talk of cyclones and changing weather.

"Why not spend the bad season up in the Gulf of California, it's nice there," was the advise of some of our friends. It was a tempting proposition, but we couldn't allow ourselves to lose momentum, knowing how easy it is to acquire the *mañana* attitude - and *mañana* might never come. My mind was set to remain on the move, rather than become a victim of complacency. It was "high noon" to get moving.

VIII

CENTRAL AMERICA

With a fair wind we had a flying start, but got becalmed half way to Mazatlán. The sickening sound of thrashing canvas was finally muted with the help of the outboard motor. But the fuel went like the wind did previously, still five miles short of the port. The light northerly wind that eventually came up did nothing more than kick up a crazy sea, to which *Thlaloca* danced wildly without much noticeable progress. It was hard work with the paddle, to assist us to an anchorage in the inner harbor of Mazatlán.

One of the more exciting things of that two-hundred-mile passage was the sighting of a shark that followed us close under the counter. A respectable six feet long, we observed the beast with awe, aghast at the sheer beauty and precise movements of that marauder as he skipped from one side of the boat to the other, followed by the ever present tiny pilot fish. With a close-up lens fitted to the movie camera, I lay on my belly over the stern and captured the spectacle, with Siggi holding me by my pants and filling my ears with advice - how not to lose the camera, an arm, my face, etc..

Exhausted from the long rowing exercise, we hit the bunks early, only to be awakened abruptly when something crashed alongside. "This bloody anchor is dragging!" announced the voice of Wes Hendriks from his yacht *Calypso*. No damage was done, so back we slipped into our still warm bunks. Two hours later the same thing happened again. "Why must this happen to us?" I exclaimed, as if not realizing that it wasn't all that unusual.

Any sailor knows that anchoring can be a touch-and-go affair at the best of times. Most of us have experienced the anchor slipping and the boat bumping into another one. If no damage is done, why should one get excited.

But there are those who simply don't care how and where they anchor. We have experienced any number of times, when boats anchor and not caring one bit about consequences. Made worse by those people who rush ashore the minute the anchor is down and leave us defending our property.

Anyway, to see the lighter side of the problem, let me recall a delightful anchoring story someone recounted to us:

A singlehander had picked up a girl for crew and companionship. She had never sailed before. When they got to La Paz, up the Gulf of California, the boat dropped anchor amongst a dozen yachts. The skipper, sure that the anchor was well set, hopped into the dinghy and sculled ashore to clear with the authorities. It so happened that in the meanwhile a squall came up, of sufficient force to bring all hands of the anchored yachts on deck to keep an eye on their positions. The new arrival started to drag clear through the anchorage with the horrified girl standing on the bow screaming, "What happened? Why are you all leaving?"

Wes Hendriks' anchor didn't drag anymore that night. It couldn't because it had fouled ours. This we found out when we wanted to leave.

☆

The Mercado José Suarez, the central marketplace, provided us with everything we needed in food. Siggi loves to haggle as much as I hate it. A fair amount of Spanish helped her along splendidly. I admired her enthusiasm more than her firm belief that she "beat them down to rock bottom."

Upon our return from the market, we rested on the pier of Heimpel's Boat Rental, when we were approached by an elderly couple who introduced themselves as the owners of a motor yacht out in the bay (a casual finger pointed to a magnificent ship, 113 feet long) They had heard of our "commendable accomplishment," having sailed our little ship "all the way from California."

"You must be short of many things that are not available in Mexico: canned food, tools, stainless steel wire, rope, blocks,

48

paint . . . ?"

Greatly humbled by so much show of wealth and consideration on one hand, and our egos tickled to unprecedented heights
by their admiration of our "accomplishments" on the other, we
answered, "Thank you very much for asking, but we don't
really need a thing." Which, of course, wasn't true at all.

As they kept prying, Siggi finally asked for a bottle of Joy
dish-washing liquid.

"Our boatman will call on you shortly," was their reply.
With many thanks we parted. That was the first of many such
noble offerings we experienced over the years.

One thing we resisted strongly during our travels was to
give the impression that we were cruising in such a small boat
to earn favors. It is true that we had very little money, and the
boat was indeed too small to entertain people to reciprocate in
kind - one of the courtesies we missed intently. However, there
was never a compromise in our resolve to make it on our own,
without elaborate support from others. Fortunately for many,
and us in particular, the world is full of good people (beginning
with Mr. Yeend back in Ensenada) with an urge to help and
who go out of their way to do so. For some, perhaps, they
were giving and helping in an attempt to be part of a venture
they had craved for themselves, but for reasons unknown were
unable to fulfill. For others, perhaps, out of true humanitarian
spirit. Whatever the motive, without them we would not have
made it.

We had asked and received help from many people - we
had to - in a measure we hoped didn't hurt. When we asked we
were always prepared to pay for with money or service. Always
conscious of our wake; we wanted it free from the reputation of
being freeloaders. We wanted people to look forward to see us
coming, not going!

Shortly after we got back aboard, a large motor launch
came alongside - as much as could - the operator, dressed in
spotless white, presented us with a jug of Joy. Because he was
obviously a Mexican, we thanked him in Spanish, of course!

We wanted to leave harbor at seven o'clock in the morning. Two hours later we were still busy getting our anchors un-
tangled from those of the *Calypso*.

"I will never forget you," Wes hollered as we finally
drifted apart. "Neither will we," we hollered back. And it
wasn't meant facetiously because Wes was really a great guy.

WEST! SAIL WEST, MAN!

Clear of the breakwater, we set a course southeast for Manzanillo, three hundred miles down the coast. We took eight days to get there. One day, with a fair wind, *Thlaloca* logged sixty-five miles, a record for the rest of the way to Panama. What a pleasure sailing is when there is wind, how miserable, though, when the sails are banging for hours and days on end. Such conditions are worse in a small boat, where there is only a tiny cockpit in which to sit under a blazing sun, with nothing to lean on or find a position to relieve cramped limbs. We doused ourselves with buckets of seawater to escape for moments at a time the unbearable heat. What we missed dearly was a well designed sailing awning - a Bimini top. There again, the boom is so low it made the thought only a dream. Instead of an awning we wore enormous straw hats with seawater soaked towels underneath, to prevent our brains from drying out.

In the chain of desirable accessories, an awning came first, closely followed by some gadget that would produce a cold drink, next . . . .next. . . ! The whole blooming misery of it all prompted Siggi to discuss the advantages of a motorboat. Although in full agreement in my innermost thoughts, I couldn't allow this conversation to go on, for fear it might lead to suggestions I wasn't prepared to accept, not right then! I retorted, "We should turn sharp right and look for the tradewind," it effectively ended the conversation right then. The truth was it was ludicrous to even consider a "right turn" with our kitty as low as it was, and the cyclone season already a threat. It was imperative that I find a job first.

Off Bahía Navidad, a huge American motor yacht approached us to within a few yards and asked if we needed anything. My immediate thought was of Heineken beer, when Siggi interjected, "yes, some gasoline, please!" Loaded up with five gallons of that "stuff" we set the outboard purring, and made ourselves comfy in the cockpit, eager to dig into the six-pack of Budweiser that had come with the "stuff" as bonus. At a steady four knots (no doubt there are advantages in a motorboat) we progressed within sight of Manzanillo. There a light breeze came up, sufficient to ripple the water.

Up went the spinnaker. But just as we settled in to relax, the show was already over. Ever-changing winds, combined with a foul tide, kept us out of the port until nightfall. When we finally got in, we hooked a mooring off the yacht club.

50

Daybreak came like any other in the past, promising continuous calm and scorching conditions. But also a beautiful panorama, so charming that for the x-time we seriously considered to remain much longer than it takes to provision the boat. Perhaps it was the lush green of the surrounding hills, the multitude of red-roofed houses that speckled the landscape that captivated our minds and stirred such strong desires to linger - something we could ill afford.

Unfortunately, the shady side of cruising is the time element; unless one is wealthy enough to ignore it. There seems to be always a deadline; a season, a weather window, some promise made lightly, even the fear that mail would be returned in case of late arrival, etc., etc..

Tied to the pier of Club Náutico we provisioned the boat, and since there was nothing in the cards that would suggest wind farther south, we stocked up on fuel more than the usual - five gallons instead of two. With deck space at a premium, it restricted living space even more.

The last evening we spent on the club verandah amongst English speaking members. Thinking of what lay ahead - calm and heat - we pumped ourselves full of cold liquids. Ice cream and Coca Cola for Siggi, while I settled for cold *cervezas*.

☆

The outboard roared into action early in the morning. Outside the pier-heads we shaped a course for Acapulco. As expected, there was no wind so the outboard kept on roaring until the tanks were almost empty. This was just as well, because the fuel could be stored safely only topsides. Exposed to the heat, the bottles expanded to bursting. The fumes surrounding us were so penetrating, we feared an explosion every time we lit the stove. Once the fuel was almost exhausted, it was back to drifting, and only a favorable current was credited for any advance.

After three days of this, *Thlaloca*'s wings were spread to a fresh following wind. It was amazing how quickly our spirits were transformed. Only minutes before we were despondent, now we were exultant, pleased to be alive in this complicated world. I heard Siggi below pumping the Primus. That meant fresh coffee, "to celebrate." In the meantime I hoisted the "tradewind rig" and made the boat self-steering.

Nursing the steaming coffee, which was fortified with a dollop of rum, we settled back in the cockpit as comfy as possible and listened to the hissing sound of water along the hull. Above us twinkled the delightful splendor of myriads of stars, a reminder of how little time we had taken in the past to wonder about what made our universe, and ponder the nature of all things so unbelievable wonderful.

Those peaceful moments were suddenly disrupted by *Thlaloca*'s sudden dash to port. The sails in a crazy angle to the wind, made an ear-shattering noise that obliged us to lower them quickly.

The rudder stock had broken. How, we asked ourselves, could a one-inch diameter steel stock break under such a light load? The abominable racket underneath the hull did not permit us to ponder the problem; like it or not I had to get into the cold water in the middle of the night, with sharks as possible company. Siggi, as usual, gave me full instruction as to the precaution I must take - precaution, if taken, would have chained me to the deck.

Below the water, with Siggi giving me light with a torch, I was relieved to see the stock had broken just inside the trunk tube. This, at least, gave the rudder some top bearing and it could not go adrift. I fastened a C-clamp to the trailing edge of the rudder and bent two nylon lines to it. Those lines we led to either side of the boat through blocks on the genoa tracks and back to the cockpit. This way we could steer horse-and-buggy fashion.

We were sixty miles north of Acapulco and twelve miles offshore, as determined by a star sight - a fix - in the morning twilight. It was my first star-fix and we hoped it was correct. The wind abated by degrees, and dawn found us drifting on a glassy ocean. This stopped all actions, rudder or no rudder. The few miles we had sailed during the night made us realize that the steering arrangements needed improvements. The way we had it rigged was fine for light conditions, but should we get a fresh wind (the first time we hoped we wouldn't) there could be trouble. We searched the boat for useful items, such as lumber. But most of what we had on board originally, had been used up for repairs in Ensenada. I dove below once more to check in daylight what I may have missed at night. All seemed O.K except that the stump of the rudder stock was stirring inside the trunk tube, and might eventually chew-up the metal, and then the wood! The optimist in Siggi said, "Well, we can always stop a ship!"

"A fat chance of that," I answered. We had hardly seen a ship during our entire voyage.

But unusual things show up when least expected, in this case the eight-thousand ton Japanese freighter *Kamu Maru* some hours later. Siggi got her attention by waving her yellow oilskins.

The ship circled as tight as she could to get close. I paddled smartly to assist. Still a fair distance off, a battery of heaving-lines came our way like streaking missiles. All missed and I had to jump into the water to retrieve one. Thus we were pulled alongside the ship and tied up for and aft.

Hollering through cupped hands, straight up a towering mass of heaving steel, I asked for two 2×4s and some plywood. There was no reaction from any of the dozen heads peering down on us. Since my English didn't help, Siggi tried it with German and then Spanish. Instead of a verbal answer, a Jacobs ladder was lowered and we were motioned to come up. This we didn't like because we feared our boat might come to harm as both vessels rolled in the undulating sea. But they insisted.

The pessimist in Siggi said, "What if they do us harm? Think about the movies we watched about the wicked Japanese?"

"In that case they should be more afraid of us, Sig, once they find out we are German," I tried to calm her.

As we scrambled over the bulwark, we were confronted by what appeared to be the entire crew of the ship, all tight-lipped. Most of them sported cameras that clicked away like automatic gunfire. A man in a white suit, obviously a steward, bowed in front of us and motioned for us to follow him. Aha, to see the captain, of course. Not so! We halted in front of a bathroom where a man was preparing a bath in two huge round tubs.

"Now we know what to do to get a decent bath," I whispered into Siggi's ear. But Siggi did not smile, still worried about these wicked Japanese.

Six pairs of slippers were lined against the wall. The steward pointed to them and in pantomime demonstrated what we should do. This was becoming a comic opera!

The slippers were beautiful crafted and decorated, the largest about size eight, just about right for Siggi. Confronted with my size 12-EE feet, another steward appeared and both rushed off. Back they came empty-handed. One of the stewards pulled a string out of his pocket with which he measured one of my feet; the length first, placing a knot there, then broadside, another knot, and off he went. After a while, the steward who remained with us must have realized that the water would get cold, I was permitted into the bathroom with my bare feet. What could have been an enjoyable bath, and we certainly needed it, was muted by our gnawing fear about *Thlaloca's* safety - the only damper in an otherwise perfect world.

We emerged outside the bathroom refreshed and ready to see a King, especially since Siggi had given the collar of my shirt a quick scrub. In the rush of things we were unprepared as to what actually happened. Therefore, our attire was not exactly par with what is expected in a civilized world.

Japanese hospitality led us to a cabin, and a table set with fried eggs, toast, butter, fruit and coffee, cigars and cigarettes. Was this real? Siggi, still in doubt whether this was a trap or sincere, worried about our baby *Thlaloca*, scolded me for my voracious appetite.

"When it comes to food, you will call the devil your friend." This wasn't exactly true, (and she knows it) I worried about our baby as much as she did. It was just that I considered it a crime not to take advantage of such delicious fare.

Anyway, to lay her worries to rest, I left the cabin to find out what was going on. Making my way along the aft end of the bridge, I was horrified to see the ship already making way, her wake stretching all the way to the horizon. Those wicked Japanese, damn!

Quickly I went to the port side. What I saw made me hurry back to the cabin to get Siggi, to confirm that this wasn't some hallucination. There was "our baby" hanging, nicely fendered, on the side of the ship, on the end of a ship's crane. Enormously relieved we went back to the "goodies," when even Siggi showed remarkable capacity of consumption; hoping that the trip would end in Tokyo or Osaka - hell, we weren't all that particular. Captain Tanaka entered the cabin and in broken English asked for our passports to take notes. We thanked him for his generosity and for the considerate handling of our boat and that we had no intention of interfering in his busy schedule. He assured us that no time was being lost, since the ship was to enter Acapulco at a scheduled time.

His mentioning of Acapulco spoiled our expected free ride

Aboard the *Kamu Maru*

to Japan. Still we were happy being rescued from an awkward situation. On deck we underwent a barrage of picture-taking and had to pose in many places and positions. My bare feet, bearded face, and less than presentable clothing made me look like a pirate and my, in every respect, much better endowed Siggi a valuable price of that hideous occupation.

Five hours later, in blazing sunlight, we entered the gorgeous bay of Acapulco. A few formalities with the Mexican authorities delayed *Thlaloca's* splashdown only minutes. On parting we shook many hands in thanks for an extraordinary experience. When I asked about any charges, the captain answered, "No penny." Later we wrote a letter to the office of the shipping company in Osaka expressing our thanks to all.

☆

At the magnificent Acapulco Yacht Club we secured a berth between the fifty-four-foot *Hotei* and the ocean racer *Morningstar*. Both we had met before. The former in Mazatlán, the latter in Cabo San Lucas. The *Morningstar* was on its way to New York for the Transatlantic Race but unfortunately never arrived there. She came to grief on a Caribbean reef. The *Hotei* was en route to the West Indies to charter. But none of the yachts in the club came even close in appeal to the towering beauty of the Chilean sail-training ship *Esmeralda* at anchor in the bay.

The club took charge of the formalities and gave us a free run of its superb facilities, of which we availed ourselves immediately, especially the showers. Refreshed and with renewed energy, we headed for the Tasty Freeze, conveniently located just across the street from the club. Forgetting for the moment that it might cost us a bundle to get the rudder problem fixed, we succumbed to some of the tasty goodies rather excessively without paying much attention to the horrendous cost. At the club I topped it up with a pint of beer. Rum and Coca Cola for Siggi.

Charlie, the crew of *Hotei*, a super diver had managed to disconnect the rudder from the skeg and brought it up. The inspection of the shaft revealed the cause of the break - crystallization. During the grounding at Colnet Bay the shaft was badly bent, and I had straightened it cold on the beach.

We searched the city far and wide for a shop that would repair our problem at a reasonable cost. Really, all we needed was a galvanized shaft four feet long and one inch in diameter, of which sixteen inches had to be welded to the rudder blade. Estimates ran from thirty to one hundred dollars. It was a steep price, but beggars are no choosers, we had to bite. When it came to paying the bill, however, only fifteen dollars was asked for!

Exuberant Siggi called for, "let's celebrate," with steaks (as thin and crooked as dried-up shoe soles) and heaps of ice cream. We paid for it rather dearly with two days of the inevitable *Turista* sickness.

Charlie got the rudder back on, and with this pressing load off our shoulders we felt free for sightseeing. We followed the tourists to a bus stop, where a fifteen-cent bus ride brought us to the ocean side, where we watched the famous high jump. A chilling experience to see those kids jump from a rocky ledge, 142 feet above the water, into the middle of a tiny cove. One could imagine the mess if anyone ever missed

To beat the stifling heat, we spent most of our time on the spacious grounds of the yacht club, amongst the crews of other yachts. Of particular attraction were the showers. They worked like any other shower, (only cold water, mind you) but on the side of a large overhead storage tank was a pull-chain, yank on it and down cascaded a "ton" of water all at once. We claim many tons of water that spilled over our hides while we were there!

From the shady verandah we observed the wonderful panorama of the surrounding country. The bay, encircled by the foothills of the Sierra Madre Mountains, abounded with the luxurious villas of high society folks. The sweeping golden beaches were studded with high-rise hotels. But only a short distance beyond that luxury was the Mexico we remember vividly, where the ordinary people only "exist" in the shadow of a posh metropolis.

We recall the disrespectful launching of *Thlaloca* with raspberry soda-pop, back in Long Beach. Subsequently, Siggi blamed that dismal performance the cause of all our calamities so far on our voyage. She was determined to give the boat a belated christening with the real stuff - Champagne!

I priced several stores for a cheap bottle of champagne. It still came to thirty pesos. This seemed a steep price for only to be dumped into the water, I bought a pint bottle for seventeen pesos. At night, when the club was silent, and asleep so we hoped, Siggi planted herself on the bow of the boat armed with the bottle, ready to commit herself to end all our miseries once and for all with a fierce blow directed against the gracious stem of our *Thlaloca*, while I stood watch ashore, to guard against any casual observer; who surely would declared us nuts. In the dark I saw Siggi's slender body moving about on the foredeck. Lying on her tummy, her chest extended past the bow, she straightened her "bottled" arm for the coup de grâce, mumbling words followed and then a short right. I heard the bang, but no splash. She worked herself some more inches over the bow for better leverage.

Again that straight arm - with the bottle glistening in the dim light like an Olympic torch - again those mumbling words, and then a huge splash, accompanied by an outburst of verbal complaints. Siggi had lost her balance and had landed in the water.

A splash of that sort, and the general commotion to get Siggi on the dock, could not pass unnoticed. It brought on deck the half-asleep, inquiring crew of the *Hotei*. The ensuing explanation, "Oh, Siggi just slipped getting aboard," delayed the rescue of the bottle until it was too late. The bottle took a decided course dead between the twin hulls of the *Hotei*, (a catamaran). We were in a dire mood. Worse, when Charlie decided to sleep in the cockpit, it was the effective end to an episode that embraced so many hopes for the future. It blew, for the time being, the chance that *Thlaloca* might taste the sensation of the real thing - Champagne. She never did!

The climax of the failed attempt came hours later, when the skipper of the *Hotei* got rocked out of his sleep a second time that night by the infuriating clatter of a bottle against the hull. Charlie ended this inconvenience with a well executed dash of a paddle, not in the least concerned that it ended Siggi's seventeen-peso-dream.

☆

Acapulco and the five delightful days we spent there remained only in memory when *Thlaloca* ghosted an offing on a course for Salina Cruz, 300 miles away. With no wind to speak of, we only drifted for most of the way. It was downright frustrating. Those were days we had reason to curse that sailboating business thoroughly, and wished we had never gotten into it. Along came a new experience that dampened our already low spirits even more - *chubascos!*

With the advancing "wet-season" these fearful storms happen like clockwork every day towards evening. It wasn't the furious wind we feared so much, rather the violent thunderstorms, that banged overhead for much too long, and lightning bolts that struck all around the boat. Bill and Marie Bodenlos of the *Nimbus* back in Mazatlán told us all about it. We sure didn't look forward to that. We now were in it.

The fury of that first storm, just as we entered the Gulf of Tehuantepec, hit us not unexpected; how could anyone misread the dark wall of clouds coming towards you? We were surprised by its severity. We scrambled to get the sails down, not easy with the boat heeling thirty degrees or more. For a few minutes we watched the fireworks of lightning around us, but prudence drove us below deck. The storm left us with the sea in confusion that made the boat hobbyhorse like a bronco, unable to make headway in the steep and short seas.

One of the many returning fishing craft guessed our predicament and offered us a tow. We didn't like to be towed since motorboat operators have little understanding of sailboat design and behavior. It is alarming to feel the fin keel and rudder quiver when the boat is torn through the water at high speed, and may cause all kinds of damage. Siggi's plea, *despacio por favor*, was answered, *si,si*, and off we went - at perhaps eight knots! Already soaked to the skin by the storm, getting more so by the flying spray didn't matter, but our poor little ship!

An hour later we were tied up inside the fishing harbor of Salina Cruz. It is landlocked and safe, but with about fifty vessels of all sizes dumping garbage, trash, oil, amidst it floated dead animals, it was the dirtiest harbor imaginable. Plenty reasons to get out of it as soon as possible. The town was as dismal. Rows of desolated houses lined the dusty roadways, where a lot of ill-fed but smiling children seemed the sole inhabitants. Trash and abandoned car wrecks were the definite markings of one side of Mexico that will take decades to erase.

The town was located at the narrowest part of the Isthmus of Tehuantepec. The town and harbor were once built with high hopes of becoming the main port for shipments between the Atlantic and the Pacific, via a railroad specifically built for that purpose. The Panama Canal put an end to that

By all accounts, the crossing of the Gulf of Tehuantepec could be a difficult passage, and we remembered well the prediction by the skipper of the three-hundred-ton *Marsha Ann* back in Cabo San Lucas, ". . . you will never make it!"

As stated in the Sailing Direction, gales blow with great fury across the Isthmus and affect the sea a hundred miles off-shore. To avoid the raging sea, it was advisable to hug the coast within yards. There, one has to fear only the blinding sandstorms.

All wonderful advice for a vessel equipped with up-to-date electronic gadgets, but worlds apart from us, with "zero" in-struments to help us. In any case, it was the rainy season, and gales are supposed to be unlikely. So we were not unduly worried.

With Salina Cruz the last Mexican port on its southern bor-der, we were forced to hire a broker, who charged us twenty dollars for a worthless piece of paper. (Be reminded that this was 1963, a time when the dollar went a long way.) If this wasn't a blow to us, the port authorities closed the harbor be-cause of an approaching cyclone. Another three dollars per day!

Next day the cyclone hit Guatemala, especially the harbor of Champerico, with devastating results. Two days later they let us go. Outside the harbor we hove-to and with *gusto* scrub-bed the heavy layer of grease off the topsides.

In the afternoon a light northerly breeze gave us a knot un-der every stitch of canvas. But like so many times before, it petered out with the setting sun. Only intermittent puffs of wind helped us to make San José, Guatemala, where we had to stop for essentials. It was only an open roadstead; a circum-stance that complicated matters.

At the seaward end of a long steel jetty, our anchor splashed into four fathoms of lucid water. The boat eventually settled with her stern some twenty feet off the jetty. With an enormous swell breaking noisily along the beach, we felt very uneasy. To be on the safe side, we set another anchor, and ad-justed the lines for the stern of the boat to rest close to the jetty. Twenty feet above us on the jetty was a gathering of lo-cals, to them we heaved a line. And on that line I worked my-self onto the jetty, taking a service line with me, on which I hoisted the empty water and fuel containers. The port official helped me politely, and with a big grin on his face, he was sure he had found a sucker who would pay twenty dollars in port fees. My refusal to pay wiped the grin off his face, and I was escorted to the port captain. Whatever he was talking about I could not follow, so I was directed to another office where I met a man who was surely an American, judging his appearance and his accent-free English. He told me to get what I needed, and get going.

A "quarter" hired a boy to carry a jug of water, with me sweating behind with a five gallon can of water on my shoulder, a paper bag with vegetables under one arm, and at the same time balancing a cone of ice-cream for Siggi. Unfortunately, the ice-cream had melted before it reached her. Another trip got us some fuel. With the lot on board we hoisted anchors and sails, and the motor propelled us past the fearsome swells.

On the next leg, to Acajutla, El Salvador., another seventy miles, whatever wind there was blew against us. It took us seven days to get there. In way of compensation, we found the officials courteous and helpful. One of the men knew Canada quite well, as he was part of a trade commission at one time. Our lively conversation may have made him forget to ask for money. We like to think of at least one port in Central America with no outrageous charges. With five gallons of fuel, and a stock of bananas lashed across the foredeck, we left the following day.

☆

The mountainous terrain that encircles the Gulf of Fonseca, between El Salvador, Honduras and Nicaragua, is very pretty, even dramatic. Particularly in the morning when the first rays of the sun kiss the highs and lows of terra firma, pronouncing the lush vegetation now that the rainy season was fully established. Full enjoyment of the spectacle eluded us, however, because the sea had too many bumps, and *Thlaloca* was too puny to drive us through. Close-hauled and with turtle-speed we held course for the southern end of the gulf, and watched the shrimpers plowing the ocean floor for harvest.

Just off Cabo Desolado a number of fishing vessels were passing us close at top speed, pointing to a gathering storm. We could not believe that such stout crafts would actually seek shelter from a storm such as we already had experienced so many times. Perhaps they were reading something we didn't, and that worried us. One of the vessels came very close and showed us a coiled line. We waved off because a gale could not be worse than being torn through that turbulent water at high speed.

With two reefs in the mains'l and the storm-jib we kept the boat going despite ever rising wind, and only surrendered when the alternative could mean destruction. The wind was bad, but much worse were the blinding flashes of lightning and thunder of unbelievable severity. Cuddled up inside the cabin, scared to death, we listened to the screaming wind, the roar of thunder, and closed our eyes to shade the brilliant flashes of lightning. It lasted for almost an hour. It was one of four of the most frightning thunderstorms we experienced over the next three years of cruising. We survived that one with shaky knees, just as we did others that popped up daily along the coast.

The truth was, that sailing became ever less a fun-game, rather a determination to get it over with soon, one way or the other. We had no clear idea what "one way or the other" meant right then, only that we were fed-up. For one thing mainly, it was the persistent calms that spelled no relief from the burning sun and temperatures up to 120 degrees, and humidity nearly as high. We felt like sitting ducks on a glassy pond - only that we sat there for days on end. Also, it was lonely. South of Acapulco we had not seen a single pleasure craft - none at sea, an anchorage or harbor. And talking of harbors, they were filthy and full of bureaucrats who saw in us only "cash-cows." It was best to avoid them, unless absolutely necessary. How it all differed from our dreams back in California, where the least we expected was wind!

How did it look farther southeast? The Pilot Chart placed us in the doldrums, an area along the equator notorious for conditions just described. Where we were, this belt extended over fifteen degrees in latitudes - 900 miles!

To sum it up, had we understood how to interpret the Pilot Chart correctly, we would have chosen a different path. Then again, we would have missed the true meaning of misery!

For each twenty-four hours of sailing, we had averaged around twenty-five miles over the two thousand miles so far. The coast to port was for the most part a yellow-red, burned clean of any vegetation. By no means unattractive, but viewed from a stationary craft for days, not an exciting picture to feast your eyes on. Farther on, with the advancing wet season, the coast was basked in mangroves of jungle-like density. The only cheering moments were the ever-so-pretty sunsets and the starlit nights, that kept up our hopes for wind - tomorrow maybe?

Since leaving Acajutla, El Salvador, we had sailed 175 miles in twelve days, and we were approaching Corinto, Nicaragua. It was imperative we procure water and vegetables. Siggi was opposed to putting in because of the horror stories that circulated about the place.

"Gosh, what if they fine us? We are broke now!" she said.

"Think of it, Sig," I said, "the next harbor is 200 miles down the coast, and we need water." Adding a bit bravado, I said, "Well, the worst that can happen is the firing squad!" I was convinced I could talk myself out of that. Above all, I bet our last $11.67 (Siggi had just counted) on her terrific smiles that normally melt away any die-hard's resolve.

From a distance, the harbor of Corinto looked inviting, with new warehouses prominent. The coastal vegetation was a healthy green, growing profusely in the wet season. It was late afternoon when we entered the long buoyed channel, hardly moving against the ebbing tide. When we saw the familiar cloud formation of an imminent *chubasco*, we turned the boat quickly, intent to face the storm in open water. But too late. The wind took control of the boat, and there was nothing else to do but drop the hook. Driving rain soon blotted out the landmarks, making us suffer a hair-raising half-hour fearing that we would be driven into the shallows should the anchor slip. Once the storm was gone we raised anchor and sails and, with motor power to assist, proceeded against the still foul tide. Within the harbor we spotted a mooring buoy. Siggi grabbed the pickup chain with the boathook, unfortunately it slipped through the hook, as there was nothing on the end of the chain that would have prevented it. The strong tide had taken us back a fair bit before I had the motor restarted for another try. Straight ahead was a concrete seawall, on it a lot of people, all shouting and gesticulating, and giving us all kinds of confusing signs. Attracted by their enthusiasm, which we took to be a rousing welcome, (modest people that we are) we paid only scant attention to our progress.

That something wasn't quite right dawned on us when the boat listed all at once to port. We were hard aground. With the help of natives we pushed hard to get her off, but to no avail. The bottom was too soft for proper footing. Siggi unshackled the main halyard and tied it to a spare anchor rode. I swam it ashore and handed it to the people to pull on. It heeled the boat and decreased her draft, and with us in the water pushing, the boat cleared without much effort. Immediately the strong tidal current carried the boat toward a broken-down concrete pier which ran diagonally across the current. Before I even managed to get back aboard, the boat pounded hard against the pier where the rigging got entangled in protruding re-inforcing rods that spiked the entire pier. It took all our effort to prevent the boat from being sucked under the bridged pier. Fortunately, there was plenty of local help, and all seemed under control. We had only to await slack water, two hours hence.

But all wasn't right, judging by the sudden roar from the crowd. We first ignored it because we were too busy - Siggi fending off and me trying to get the blasted motor started. But when I felt warm liquid splashing on my back, I looked up, meaning to give the offender a blast. (I was sure that one of the guys on the pier harbored a grudge against gringos and was peeing on me).

Suddenly all was dark around me. A warm, sticky substance slushed over me and soon covered the aft deck, and the entire cockpit area as well. (Later we found out that a factory that was producing brown tar was located inland. Pipelines provided links to the harbor for pumping the tar into ships. The heat during the day had built up excessive pressure, causing a break in an eight-inch pipe. It was our "luck" to be at a spot at the wrong blooming time.)

With great effort - even harder since most of the locals had fled - we succeeded in clearing the rigging, and someone "up there" must have understood our plight and prompted the motor to start. I had recovered the stern line but inadvertently left the end of the line hanging over the stern, it got into the prop, busting the gear. The boat robbed of its propulsion, again became the helpless victim of the tidal current and was carried smack under the bow of a Japanese freighter tied to the pier. It is practice of ships to drop an anchor seaward to facilitate maneuvering on leaving port. The chain hung straight down from the flared bow, leaving a large gap between the bow and chain at the waterline. In the direction of this gap drifted our *Thlaloca*.

We raced to the bow to fend off and somehow got hold of the chain. For a brief moment the boat came to rest broadside against the chain. By applying our last ounce of strength, we managed to make the boat slide off to seaward. The other way would have been a broken mast. Eventually we freed the anchor and kicked it over the side. Thus we came to rest in the middle of the channel.

WEST! SAIL WEST, MAN!

Even in the darkness, illuminated only by a faint moon, we could see the terrible mess the boat was in, and by daylight it would look a lot messier. It didn't seem real, it was like a bad dream. Siggi, luckily, was spared the brunt of the dousing as she had worked more amidship, fending off. And speaking of luck, all the hatches were closed; we normally have, to bar the entry of cockroaches.

With the boat anchored, there was time to reflect. I concluded, that in my life there had been low moments, and with Colnet Bay still vividly in our minds, nothing could be more devastating than this. How could we rid the smeary stuff off the deck and hull, the cockpit, ropes, sheets, etc.? What really shocked us was the look of the sails. They resembled oily rags, the folds loaded inches thick. Thanks to my splendid mate, I snapped out of my frustrated mood. To her nothing is impossible, and I was first in line at the receiving end of her determination.

I was covered from head to foot, the stuff hanging in various densities all over my body. My head made me appear like some Draculian monster. The top of my head received Siggi's radical cure, shearing it bare with a pair of tinsnips; they seemed to work better than regular scissors! A final scrub down with gasoline transferred me back into a human-like creature.

We scrubbed, we scraped, we washed, with me cursing our "luck" throughout that night. Dawn was breaking when we dozed off, Siggi in the bunk, I in the cockpit.

The pilot launch bumped hard alongside and startled us out of a deep sleep. It towed us to a mooring buoy to await the officials. And being a weekend, we had a long wait.

Past noon a cramped boatload of local officials pulled alongside the *Thlaloca*. They were dressed in sparkling white uniforms, except the commandant. Being a military man, he wore khaki. He was a short, stocky man with the strong features of an ape. Mr. Gorilla we named him, who convinced us instantly we were in trouble.

And trouble there was! I went aboard the launch and, under questioning through an interpreter, I stated the reason for entering the harbor: that we intended only to fetch water and food. Further, I told them of the awful accident and the resulting damage to our boat, which they could see for themselves. As a last trump card, I exposed my tormented scalp, which was still sprinkled with tar. This caused the only grins during our conversation.

They stuck their heads together, squabbling in Spanish I could not follow. Finally, the interpreter announced that the harbor dues came to eighty dollars and that we were not permitted to remain in the harbor. We should leave immediately.

At that moment we heard a weeping cry that penetrated the launch's crowded cabin. Drained to exhaustion by the ordeal, plus the present demand, Siggi burst into tears. The good-natured interpreter pricked up his ears and stepped outside, comforting Siggi with the words, "Señora, please don't cry, tomorrow is another day."

This pathetic episode did not shake the commandant one bit. We were convinced that only dynamite would rock his authoritative composure. Nevertheless, I contested the unreasonable charge with a modest appeal to their conscience, saying that we were not wealthy, that we had to work for a living as much as the local people. Furthermore, that water and food are essentials, and our boat too small to carry large stores, that we must enter every harbor along the way. "Surely, you don't want to punish us so severely for reasons I just stated?"

"Pay or confiscation", was the final verdict.

Sure enough, the next morning brought "another day," as the interpreter had said to Siggi. Señor Vasalli, the local shipping agent, sent us a note that we should see him in his office. Very influential, he was the man of the hour, and a very fine man at that. He promised help in a very precise manner. Apparently the entire local administration was to receive a cut from the eighty bucks; we did not even have!

Señor Vasalli had spoken to the doctor already who said he wanted no money. He assigned his interpreter (the same one we had on the launch) to us, and with him we visited six different offices: immigration, municipal, mayor, agriculture, customs and the *comandantura*.

Each head of the departments received us with utmost courtesy in their individual offices, stocked with massive furniture and national and provincial flags. The kind interpreter stated our case, and each man nodded his understanding of our desperate situation and waived his demand for money, except the customs. He asked if two dollars was too much. We gladly handed him the two bucks.

At the *comandantura* we were prepared for the coup de grâce. As expected, "the gorilla" sat placidly behind an enormous desk. What was different about him was that he wore a deep grin all over his wrinkled face. We liked that grin, for we knew we were winning. He dismissed us cordially with a handshake.

When we went back to thank Señor Vasalli for his help, he suggested we call on Mr. Titman, manager of an American shrimp company in town, who might help us earn some money. His company was based in Brownsville, Texas, and had a dozen vessels operating out of Corinto. Mr. Titman offered us a berth for the boat and a job for me.

The tar incident had already made news around town, so Mr. Titman was quick to offer us half a barrel of Varsol (similar to kerosene) to clean the boat with. Over the coming weeks we made an all out effort to do just that. Still, the end result was nothing to resemble her former self. It took months, actually years to clean all crevices, and replace what never could be cleaned, such as lines, etc.. As for sails, they retained a permanent tarnished look until we had them replaced.

The promised job was converting an old whaleboat that was propped up in the yard into a lobster boat. Once I had removed the rotten planks, there was less boat left than what Slocum found in the original *Spray*. And what first appeared to be a quick project turned out to be building basically a whole new boat. The amazing thing about the yard, it was unbelievably primitive. The shop had not a single power-tool except a half-inch drill. The rough lumber was stacked in a standard thickness; that of the shrimpers' planking. Any variation required was whittled down by hand plane. All ripping was done by hand as well. The work was exasperatingly slow and cumbersome, completely against any work-ethic we northern people are used to. The quality of work, however, was first class. Add to this the scorching heat and high humidity, it was enough to drive a person mad. Only the prospect of revitalizing our finances made me hang on.

On the whole, I did some deep thinking about the effects of certain climatic conditions on people, because we northern people are quick to condemn the apparent indolent behavior of our neighbors to the south. Solely through my experience in Corinto I had every reason to change this attitude drastically.

WEST! SAIL WEST, MAN!

Corinto is the chief port of Nicaragua on the Pacific. The large pier and warehouses were almost new, built with American-aid dollars. It is a rather marshy spot. The large lagoon was very shallow for the most part, and only the turning basin and a channel for the shrimp-boats were dredged for deep draft vessels. It did not take us long to know the entire town and many of the inhabitants. It seemed that everyone knew us. We made lasting friends with a family by the name of Quiros, who had three lovely children, everyone of them stunningly beautiful and cute. Señor Quiros exercised the job of an assistant port captain, and on the side ran a swap-shop. With these credentials they represented the upper class of people. By our standards this would require a certain amount of noticeable luxuries, but not in Central America. There it is sufficient to own a decent dwelling, and what is most important, wear a light complexion, drastically in contrast to the major population.

The Quiros' spoke only limited English, and us very little Spanish; with Siggi, though, catching on fast. Their main topic was history, and we had to admit our ignorance of Central American affairs compared to their in-depth knowledge of ours. Nicaragua confirms the fact - much as it is in the entire world, as we came to know it - that people of a nation however small and insignificant, take it seriously that the world revolves around them. Skirmishes of basically local character are exaggerated to world-shaking events. This in case of a national holiday, commemorating a 1856 battle between Nicaraguan forces, equipped only with pitchforks and stones, and an American legion, fifty-six strong, but with up-to-date weapons. It ended with an American defeat. It is a good story and gives a small nation the pride of a superior spirit. Considering our own effort in this direction, we must concede to their right to blow their own horn as well, I suppose. Ultimately, what counted most was not casualties, but the splendid fun we had.

The people who toil the land live the simplest life imaginable, in desolate houses, even earth-holes. They were poorly fed and dressed in tattered clothing. The people still hauled their goods with oxen and on carts with solid wooden wheels, and none seemed disturbed by the wealth of American or European luxury cars passing frequently.

One place to study local life was the open market place. As in Corinto and other towns we visited, the business was con-

67

ducted along the sidewalks, next to the filthy and stinking gutters, the breeding ground of flies and mosquitoes. Business along the sidewalks was exclusively handled by women, all blessed with a flock of children. These children were shockingly undernourished and crawled about the rough boardwalks with blown-up bellies. Only the baby had mother's close attention, for it was under the table hemmed in by a piece of burlap nailed under the table top cradle-fashion. To squelch the baby's cries the busy mother rocked the contraption with her knees. This may sound cruel, but we believe that these women were excellent mothers, just that the men were nothing but a bunch of crap! They either drowned all their earnings in cheap liquor or spent it on other women. In fact, it was considered highly *macho* for a man to brag about how many children he had with other women, and nothing was thought of to cry it out in the wife's presence.

Every Thursday, a mass of people queued in front of the government warehouse for whatever the helping hand of the U.S.A. had to offer. How shocking it was for us to see that much of the merchandise, paid with American tax dollars, was not even appreciated. Many pounds of first class milk powder and shortening was sold to us for little money, because people did not like it. Most of that food was bought up by the storekeepers and sold with a large profit to the more affluent people not eligible for help.

While we were in Nicaragua, the country resembled an armed camp. Every square yard of strategic important area was guarded by the military, armed to the teeth. Real eerie. Our inquiries produced many reasons that justified such powerful demonstrations of armed might, but never the real cause, namely the tension between the Somoza government and the dissatisfied people in general, who eventually united under a socialist banner (and in later years exploded to a full-scale guerrilla war). It was interesting to observe the fear of people even to talk about it, being afraid of consequences. And the consequences were demonstrated vividly one morning while I was sitting in the barber's chair, when a brawl broke out in the market square. Suddenly a shot rang out, and the crowd dispersing in all direction. One man remained - dead!

The soldier who shot was obviously a thug, and the people cowards. The cowardliness was expressed by the people in the shop, who only managed an embarrassed grin - no outcry, no debate, nothing! These undisciplined soldiers (or shall we say, highly disciplined?) in their tattered uniforms were a tough lot and we made a detour around them whenever possible. Still, Nicaragua is a lovely country and rich in history. Managua, the capital, and León, to name only two cities, are well worth a visit. Numerous monuments, parks and beautiful churches of Spanish architecture told us of a once proud past. Only we found all of it dreadfully neglected.

Already mentioned, the lagoon was huge, but only the turning basin and a channel was dredged to any depth. There was no room to anchor anywhere. Moreover, we had orders to moor the boat in a way it could be observed at all times. The only place to do so, was to moor Med-fashion - anchor over the bow, the stern tied to shore. In our case, the stern was tied to a barge. Unfortunately, the barge was used to unload the harvest of the shrimp boats. The shrimps were dumped on long, narrow stainless steel tables, to be skinned and cleaned by about twenty women. The finished product was packed and stored in huge refrigeration units, for the eventual shipment to the U.S. market. One can imagine, that by midday, when the sun beat down hard on this slaughter, the stench was penetrating. Our boat, lying at right angle to the barge, called for good maneuvering by the skipper of a shrimper. All that was needed, really, was normal caution, and this we took for granted. Well, there are good skippers and some are not so, and some that take chances. It so happened, that a fierce *chubasco* was blowing when a skipper thought he could get away from the barge. He cleared the barge all right but was driven by the wind into our anchor line. His prop caught the line and ripped the cleat with back-up-block clear out of our deck and also broke the stern lines. The boat caught by wind and current was adrift. Luckily, I observed the calamity from a distance and was at hand to recover the boat before it was blown into the lagoon. This incident made us realize how desperate we were to get away from this place. The whaleboat I had finished, but we still awaited a new gear for the outboard motor from the U.S..

Not only was our precarious mooring the cause of our resolve to move on, worse were the cockroaches that had a ball amongst the grease and skins of the shrimps. With so much food present the roaches grew huge - a special breed perhaps, but some of them measured a good two inches. It gave rise to a standard joke: Coming back from shore and the boat had a list, caused by wind or current or both, one of us would say, "Well, Sig, (or Hein) there again is one of the critters resting in one of our bunks!"

Once the motor parts had arrived, we prepared for leaving. The Quiros' invited us for a farewell dinner. The menu stated a suckling pig. Cooked in beer and topped with prunes, pineapples and squashed egg yolks, it was *muy delicioso!* What followed was an emotional parting from people we truly loved.

IX

THE LAND OF
ETERNAL SPRINGTIME

We set sail from Corinto in early October. All our friends were there, as well as a lot of people we didn't know, for a last "good-bye." Towering above the crowd stood "Mister Gorilla," the man we feared so much at the beginning, but who seemed had mellowed since.

Thlaloca, somewhat disgraced by her tarnished sails, gathered momentum in the ebbing tide. She floated well down on her lines, loaded with every essential to reach the Panama Canal nonstop. Becalmed outside the harbor, I tried to start the motor - it wouldn't. A bad start!

The low, sandy shoreline dropped away slowly. We were strangely elated now that we had cleared the land, compared to other departures when we had felt sad. But truthfully, Corinto had little to offer beyond its splendid people, with the Quiros family occupying a special niche in our hearts.

"Hein, Hein!" Siggi called urgently, I jumped out into the cockpit, where Siggi's finger directed my disbelieving eyes at a point less than one hundred yards away to seaward where huge seas were breaking, with broken water just off our starboard bow. There was hardly enough wind to give *Thlaloca* steerage way, and with the motor on the blink, we had no chance to take evasive action. With our hearts in our throats and pudding in our knees we mumbled a silent prayer. Inces-

71

santly the long Pacific swell piled up a good ten feet and broke with fantastic roars. As *Thlaloca* inched away from the danger I quickly had a closer look at the chart. Sure enough, there was a tiny encircled area indicating a shoal, with the note, "Not examined."

A breaking shoal should certainly be visible from a distance - but perhaps it had only begun to break, when the tide fell to a critical level.

With only the daily *chubascos* to drive us on, we realized we had to shorten the passage. Instead of the Panama Canal, we decided on Puntarenas, Costa Rica, as our goal. Encouraged by advertising of it as the "Land of Eternal Springtime," we could hardly go wrong.

Mucho viento, is Spanish for much wind, which the Gulf of Papagayos is notorious for. We did not have to wait for it long. A fierce northeaster battered us to bare poles. Before we could tackle the jib, the clew had ripped out. We were disgusted and cold that made us retreat into the warm cabin. But after the wind lessened and steadied, we were able to sail many miles before we found ourselves becalmed again. We made a note that it was the first time since north of Acapulco that we had wind for any length of time.

Back to watching the bubbles along the wake that gave some indication of movement. We concluded that the devil is in the wind, and he sure didn't favor us. We drenched our disappointments with drinking coffee - gallons of the "stuff." Our imperfect mathematics came up with the result that we had consumed more gallons of coffee than we burned fuel since we left California!

By sundown on October 14, our plotted position put us two miles west of Cabo Blanco, the western entrance into the Gulf of Nicoya, with Puntarenas only about twenty miles to the north. It was dark when we rounded the point, and immediately encountered a fresh wind from the north. We tacked against it, until a *chubasco* forced us to heave-to. During a miserable inky night filled with thunder and lightning, we watched the light on Cabo Blanco becoming progressively dimmer, until it was gone altogether. It was sad to admit we were losing every yard we so frustratingly had conquered the day before.

Once the morning sun had wiped the haze away we were able to take cross bearings on the high mountain peaks. They placed us eighteen miles southwest of Cabo Blanco. Surely it wasn't the wind alone that worked against us, an unfavorable current was also present. Up to that point we could always count on the help of a current that propelled us in the right direction; apparently this had changed.

A council was held to decide whether to by-pass Puntarenas or not? Our water situation urged "go for it!"

Just then, a Nicaraguan ship, the *Managua*, passed us close and we cheered each other vigorously, for we had met before in Corinto. The ship brought us luck, a lively breeze from the west, to which we hoisted the spinnaker. Progress was slow, however, against an obvious opposing current. But we were moving in the right direction, that raised hope we might reach Puntarenas before nightfall.

Darkness came with the inevitable *chubasco*. Instead of striking sails and drifting with the wind, we held on with shortened sails. In the eerie darkness, lit up by the foam of breaking waves, we kept a sharp lookout for dangers; and the main danger was floating logs and trees we had seen during the day. Sure enough, there appeared something unusual, obviously a submerged log but visible only by a fat branch sticking out of the water like the periscope of a submarine. We tried to tack, but the boat got into irons and fell back. Within seconds we ground to a halt alongside this subterranean monster. Pounding against the log with sickening regularity, it made us weep in anguish. What if the log has broken branches, it will pierce the ½-inch cedar planking of the boat in a short time?

With the spinnaker pole we sounded several feet of water over the log - as nearly as we could determine with the boat bouncing up and down like crazy. Why didn't she jump over it? She had to be helped. We untied the reef-points in the mainsail, and with both of us working from the leeward side, we sweated up the mainsail. Some awful bumps followed, but we were free.

Half an hour later the storm had abated, but the scare of the incident left us in no mood to take full advantage of the fair wind still blowing, instead we only crawled at a snail's pace until daylight. By then the wind had vanished. Taking bearings on landmarks told us that a fair tide was with us. But once the tide had changed, we dropped the anchor in fifteen fathoms, to prevent us losing ground.

With every cat's-paw we upped the hook and sails, and thus worked ourselves close to the beach. From there into the estuary, where the yacht club is situated, we needed a fair wind or a motor. While waiting, I worked on the latter, but soon found that it required more than a screw driver and a pair of pliers to fix the corroded piece of iron.

Siggi busied herself preparing a hot meal against my veto, because the heat was stifling. How often in the past (and the future) did I have reason to admire this wonderful person - my wife. A true lady. Like all women she likes the beautiful things life offers. No doubt, she would have preferred her own secure home on *terra firma*, family and kids - dreams reduced to essentials, . . .we need water . . . food . . . when, she must have wondered, will this end! A team, husband and wife, soon becomes meaningless if it isn't supplemented by a sense of camaraderie. Siggi is just that, a wonderful comrade! At all times considerate towards the well being of crew and boat. Forever caring that the cramped cabin reflects the appearance of a home. Once anchored or tied up there came out of hiding little knicknacks to dress it up, accentuated by a couple of vases with artificial flowers. She was first to grab brush and soap to clean the boat before entering a harbor. At the end of many hard passages she would forgo earned rest to make certain that there were clean clothes to go ashore in. And both of us share a strong sense of duty towards our national ensign, that we present ourselves in a honorable and decent manner. I'm so very proud of Siggi, and so very happy that she is my lovely wife.

We asked a passing fishing vessel for a tow into the harbor. The way led up a river where to our starboard sprawled a colorful waterfront. Abreast the custom house we cast off the tow, and the tide helped us to a rough landing alongside a barnacle encrusted jetty. It took some elaborate fendering, as the pilings were widely spaced, and the boat rocked to the wakes of passing traffic.

While Siggi kept a close watch on our precarious position and entertained a crowd of people, I made off for the customs house. I returned with four officials - gold braided, and the blooming lot that goes with it. Real high class. Apparently, the customs official couldn't decline a thorough inspection in the presence of so much brass. He reluctantly mounted the slimy ladder leading down to our boat.

He was a fat man with a pencil-thin mustache under his stubby nose. He lowered himself laboriously, his meaty paws clutching the ladder tightly, until he flopped into the cockpit with a resounding thud. I opened the lazaret for his inspection. But since he was unable to bend low enough on account of his bulging gut, he directed his attention forward by sticking his head into the cabin. Obviously daunted by its smallness, he withdrew quickly and was about to reach for the ladder for a fast getaway, when his superior on the jetty intervened, and ordered him to check inside.

Fair to say, that it wasn't easy to enter the cabin for a person not used to it - and almost impossible for a person as clumsy as he was. Mainly to protect our property from structural damage we demonstrate "how" to anyone determined to get inside. "Stand on deck, bend down and place your hands on each side of the hatch coamings. Hold your weight while you stick your feet inside the cabin and slowly lower yourself until you find footing."

Since the customs official had already demonstrated an awkward behavior, I thought it best to remain inside on standby, just in case.

Here came two stubby barrel-shaped legs pumping wildly like a cyclist on the end run. A panicky quibble followed, a crash, a scream - the eagle had landed!

The poor fellow lay twisted and moaning on the galley floor. As soon as I touched him to help he screamed like a stuck pig. Indeed, I thought, he might have broken a bone.

Siggi immediately called for help, which brought four young locals to the scene. They should have brought a crane because it was almost impossible to get a handle on him in the cramped space. Also, the guy lashed out like a snapping turtle to anyone who came near him. Meanwhile an ambulance (an ancient beaten-up van with a red-cross symbol) had arrived which carted the fellow to a hospital, we suppose. *Thlaloea* had again proved her toughness.

Her toughness was even better demonstrated a short time later, when a flat-bottomed vessel with a load of human cargo crashed alongside her to unload. With the tidal current running strong, the skipper had to use a lot of power to keep position, while dozens of people loaded with all kinds of luggage trampled across our boat, and in their wake dragging a goat that resisted every effort to be treated like . . . a goat, I guess - the lot up the slimy ladder!

Lucky for us, there was a Señor Batista who pushed himself through the crowd of onlookers, and in perfect English offered us a berth alongside his vessel, which was moored fore and aft midstream.

Night comes quickly in the tropics. When darkness drew its curtain around us, peace and quiet settled over the waterfront. It was wonderful to sit in the cockpit and listen to the unfamiliar sounds of tropical wildlife in the dense grassy marshes opposite the waterfront. A late arrival, one of the peculiar vessels so well fitted to carry any cargo, human and otherwise, coughed her way up river against an ebbing tide. Past the huge, solidly constructed *mercado*, the vessel slackened her speed. The muted engine-noise was suddenly drowned by the sound of dozens of squealing pigs, as they were driven from the boat into the water. How smart these pigs were, they swam to the nearest land; how stupid though, because it was the slaughterhouse!

A flood-tide helped us sail up river to the Costa Rica Yacht Club. We anchored in front of it. It is a lovely club, and as far as we knew, the only club between Acapulco and Panama (1963). Everything was there to enjoy life thoroughly, including a swimming pool. For the first time since Acapulco we met other yachts - five local, one foreign. The foreign boat was the American yacht *Little Tramp*, a forty-eight-foot ketch, skippered by Truman (the only name we ever knew). It was wonderful to have someone to talk to in a language we know. He offered us to treat his boat as our home for the length of our stay - an offer we did not refuse.

The *Northeast*, a thirty-eight foot fiberglass ketch, was a yacht we greatly admired. It was owned by the Gaston family, who operated a large meat packing plant in San Josê, the capital. Subsequently, we got to know the family very well, and even spent a week with them in their villa up the mountains. Their life story intrigued us very much, and it should be interesting to read about:

The Gastons hailed from Germany, where they owned a butcher shop. Discouraged by crowded living and high taxes it was decided to sell the lot and find an uninhabited island in the South Pacific, and be happy ever after. With the business sold, they bought an old fishing vessel, thirty-five feet long, built of steel. Although a motor vessel, to make it sailable, it received a mast and a centerboard. Some of the bottom plating was so porous that daylight shone through it. But since the boat needed ballast, several tons of concrete, with boiler punchings mixed in, filled the voids and strengthened the weak spots. Rivers and canals carried them into the Mediterranean Sea. In Marseille, they were joined by a couple with the same interest - seeking paradise.

The Atlantic crossing went well. But trouble developed on the Pacific-passage to the Galápagos Islands - the centerboard pin had gone adrift, and with it the board. Where to repair it? Costa Rica to the north was closest, and Puntarenas the logical place to find what was needed. A costly repair made them think of self-sufficiency. They bought a pig and made sausages. Invited guests spread the word of an excellent product. It not only paid for the repair, but earned them money to spare. A small shop first; then a large production facility. Within ten years Tega Productos de Carne had developed into a large business, with export all over Central America. A formidable success story, which made it easy to forget an envisioned lonely life on some South Pacific island.

Theo Gaston, the owner of *Northeast*, always shy on crew, had no trouble finding willing hands in the Zenkers. We looked forward with excitement to sail in a much larger craft - and magnificent it was. There was no lack of space in the cockpit even for three pairs of legs, and how comfy it was to lie stretched out on six inches of foam-rubber cushions. It was heaven, a feeling strong enough to breed envy. That afternoon saw us anchored off a sandy beach, where we skin-dived among multicolored reefs. There was enough *wurst* and beer aboard to conclude a memorable day.

Homeward bound, within the estuary, we ran aground. Unable to kedge her off, we spent the next five hours on the boat heeled sixty degrees. This slight inconvenience did not deter my able mate from preparing a fine meal on the gimbaled stove that was balancing way above her head.

We got off at high tide, but were sitting on the next mud-bank fifteen minutes later. Theo Gaston was in tears - with us close to it, thinking of another uncomfortable night. Quick action with the dinghy and its six horsepower outboard motor, tied to the end of the main halyard supplied the leverage to free her. The rest of the way home saved Theo from further embarrassment.

Bob Law and his beautiful wife Marge were another fine couple we got to know well. Bob was flying his own aircraft and was "spotting" for the American tuna fleet. At the same time they were building a thirty-five-foot Piver-designed trimaran. For a week I helped them step and rig the mast. Leisure time, and there was plenty, we spent sitting on their well-shaded patio, sipping cocktails and spinning yarn. Over the following days, Marge destroyed my reputation as a master cribbage player. (I still think she cheated a lot.)

Siggi's recollection of Puntarenas is rooted in two unpleasant experiences. One involved a monkey the Laws had tied up on a long chain. Siggi made the mistake and passed the animal too close while carrying a bundle of bananas in her arms. She was jumped on and bitten on arms and legs. The bites had drawn blood and should have been treated against tetanus - had we known better. For the rest of our visit we made a large detour around the unpredictable beast.

The next incident exhausted Siggi's faith in animals. We had been invited aboard the *Holly*, a large sailing yacht at anchor down river, The owners, a Swiss and his petite French wife, kept an ocelot as a pet. We were assured the cat was tame. Yet we felt uneasy in its presence, and the cocktails acquired a bitter taste as a consequence. It was eyeing us with it's head through the skylight. Every time it yawned it exposed long needle-sharp teeth. This gave us the shivers. A fantastic leap landed the cat in Siggi's lap, gashing her leg. Blood ran profusely. We immediately doused the wound with vodka. Before any of us even realized what had happened, the cat had leaped back through the skylight onto the deck. We left with Siggi's leg heavily bandaged.

Not every day was unpleasant, though. We had ample opportunity to explore the country. Like most of Central America it is very mountainous. A high rate of precipitation generates an abundance of tropical vegetation, and fertile soil. Coffee is particularly abundant and is the base of the country's economy. The dazzling beauty of the countryside was somewhat dimmed by thousands of tons of ashes, discharged by Volcano Irasu. *Thlaloca's* deck was covered each morning with a layer of this rather annoying substance. We suffered, as did the entire country. All major industrial plants and transportation came to a standstill, as every air shaft and engine got choked by ashes. Indeed, it was considered similar to the greatest disasters that have befallen different countries in one way or the another.

Costa Rica left us with one more unpleasant memory. The three months we were tied to a barge in Corinto had infested the boat with the sailor's pest - cockroaches! We had more than enough to give us a case of bug-phobia.

Killing the visible ones to get rid of the pest is fruitless. A magazine article I had read mentioned that a couple multiply by three hundred thousand a year. Another article in a different magazine proclaims that a female is pregnant throughout her life. One thing is certain: one is too many to live with. An effective method had to be found to erase this evil. Our friend Truman on *Little Tramp* had the answer, a treatment he guaranteed emphatically - fumigating with sulfur.

According to him, old sailing ships did it, and what was effective then should work today. What made his suggestion even more attractive was that he gave us a bag of the powder, a leftover from his own treatment. What he failed to mention was the safe amount that could be used.

Determined to do a super job, we loaded half a dozen empty coffee cans, carefully dividing the powder equally. Once lit and smoking nicely, we placed them all over the boat. We left the lot in place for three days, while we had a splendid time on *Little Tramp*. Every time we rowed by *Thlaloca* in our dinghy, we spotted a trickle of smoke rising from the vents (tiny openings that weren't taped completely). The impending extermination of this repulsive vermin aroused in us a remarkable delight.

Delight in killing the roaches changed to consternation when we opened the hatches. Although the cockroaches had suffered a total defeat, it also nearly wrecked our adventure. The sulfur had affected every metal part in the boat. The radio was oxidized beyond repair, as well as our precious watches. Every chromed item severely pitted, all the paint had bubbled. All clothing and foul weather gear was discolored, the zippers gone and the lot so brittle to be useless. Worse, it had taken the mercury off the sextant mirrors, and the frame was a mass of corrosion. It even had affected the luff wires in the sails, and discolored the sailcloth more than the tar in Corinto. These were the major items affected. To name the lot would fill a whole page. "I didn't tell you to use all the powder!" Truman exclaimed. He was right . . . he didn't, but could have!

Despite the unpleasant mishaps, Puntarenas held us captive for seven weeks. We had grown fond of it because it was rightly considered the best country Central America had to offer. But we could not afford to tarry any longer.

WEST! SAIL WEST, MAN!

The bright early morning sun was casting extravagant shadows on the beautiful mountain panorama around us, and that grandiose sight cleared our gloomy minds of monkey bites, cockroaches and sulfur damage. We felt relieved to be at sea again. We settled into our sea routine, which never deviated much from the usual, namely, watching the bubbles drift by the hull slowly or not, and enduring calms and the daily squalls and darn thunderstorms. Crossing the Gulf of Dulce, we became aware of a current that was setting us toward the northwest. It forced us to use the motor and most of our precious fuel to gain a position where a favorable current helped us drift in the right direction.

A light wind eased us around Punta Burica and into Panamanian waters. Off the penal island Coiba, three hundred miles from Puntarenas, we lay becalmed for two days. The intense heat clobbered our brains. Again and again we pondered why there is so little wind in this world. Much would we have liked to jump into the water to cool off, but a blasted shark was circling us and apparently had no mind to leave. When he was real close under the stern I tried to stab him with the boat-hook to give him a scare, but I misjudged the distance every time. Occasionally, it would come racing straight towards us as if to land right on deck, scary enough to make us retreat quickly. For entertainment, there is hardly anything more exciting than watching the sea life. We normally lay on our bellies, heads prodruding over the stern and watched the performance.

The following morning, the shark was still around us. Coiled paper or stale bread failed to make him snap at it. When I knotted a 3/8 inch nylon line to the stainless steel wire leader of a shark hook that Charlie had given us in Acapulco, Siggi voiced her absolute opposition.

"Just to see what he will do, Sig!"

"You are not going to do a foolish thing like that." She meant it, and that was the law.

During the course of the day, when Siggi went below for some errand, I could not control my temptation, I flipped the hook overboard. There is no telling why the shark went for the hook at once, perhaps the glitter of it had him fooled.

With the hook wedged between his jaws, he raced to the end of the line and thrashed around wildly. His powerful movements yanked *Thlaloca*'s stern from side to side. Siggi, alarmed by the commotion (she knew exactly what had happened) emerged from below with a knife and cut the line against my mild protest. It was the last and only time I challenged a shark - on grounds of simple economics!

The same day at sunset, a zephyr of wind from the northwest rippled the water. Up went the spinnaker to help us pass through the narrow Canal de Afuera, between the island of Coiba and the mainland. Amidst a fleet of Panamanian fishing boats the wind died, the spinnaker collapsed, with it all hopes of a good sail. The pattern of perpetual calm haunted us until we finally drifted past Morro Puercos Light. There, wind came up from the north, sufficiently strong to force a reef in the mainsail. We intently hoped that the breeze would hold and propel us around Punta Mala, and into the Gulf of Panama.

X

THE POWER OF
OCEAN CURRENTS

Punta Mala Light, the gateway to the Panama Canal, loomed to windward. The powerful lighthouse, built massively on a sandy spit, sheds its blinking light twenty miles seaward, to guide shipping to and from that important waterway.

Ninety miles left to go to reach the first of our goals, the Panama Canal. It was only a small fraction compared to the thousands of miles already traveled since our departure from California, almost a year past. We should be snug in Balboa tomorrow - if there is wind. (had someone hinted that it was to take fifteen days, we would have keelhauled the person.)

Once around Punta Mala we expected a strong south-setting current, as indicated in the Pilot Chart. This current we hoped to escape by hugging the coast as close as possible. Two things, however, were against us from the outset. One, that we approached Punta Mala in the middle of the night, therefore unable to judge the distance offshore. Two, that we didn't have a depth-sounder that would have given us in depth what we lacked in vision. What we lost next, was our coup de grâce - the wind!

The coast so near only hours ago, had faded to nothing. It confirmed the wisdom of the Pilot Chart. Indeed, the current had become the master of our destiny. Unless a fair wind came up, we were powerless.

WEST! SAIL WEST, MAN!

The swift Humboldt Current, which originates off the southwest tip of South America, sweeps north along the coast in a broad stream. One branch is diverted towards the Galápagos Islands, and from there is named the South Equatorial Current. The other branch retains its northerly course and enters the Gulf of Panama. Still following the coast in a stream thirty miles broad, it completes the half circle of the gulf when it re-enters the Pacific main at Punta Mala. It continues its southern flow to about latitude five north, where it is diverted back into the stream going north. Thereby it completes a full circle. This was the situation we were faced with.

We thought it a waste of time even to consider sailing against the current. We evaluated our chances to be more logical if we sailed east, towards Colombia 108 miles away. Knock off thirty miles - the width of the favorable current flowing north - we had to sail only eighty miles and we would be in a current that would carry us to Balboa without sweat! A fresh northerly wind that had come up, made the decision easy. The good wind held throughout that day and night, we expected a landfall at any time.

At noon the following day we had sailed seventy-two miles by the Walker-log. A latitude sight placed us on a latitude thirty miles south of Punta Mala. We were not unduly alarmed by this shocking revelation, as we were certain that land was near to the east. In fact, we should be close, or already in the favorable current flowing north.

Our sextant, that had taken such terrible abuse during the fumigating process, I had repaired, first by cleaning it very thoroughly. Repairing the mirrors posed a problem, because I know how to take things apart, but reassembling such a sensitive instrument I was ambivalent about. But since I had no parts left over assured us of a job well done. Anyway, to get reflection back in the mirrors I utilized the foil of a pack of cigarettes, that I placed behind the mirrors. Unfortunately, our radio and all our watches were all beyond repair, therefore we were without the benefit of time, so necessary to plot a longitude - a fix!

Night fell with no land sighted, instead we endured a teeth-rattling thunderstorm. In the ensuing downpour we managed to catch a couple gallons of water. With the wind blowing so fiercely, we were glad to catch even that much. After the storm, the wind held good from the northwest and *Thlaloca* on a broad reach sliced ahead at five knots towards the northeast. We kept a sharp lookout, for the coast must be near. When the new day cleared the horizon, there was no land even though we had sailed another ninety-six miles by log over the past twenty-four hours. A noon sight confirmed that we had lost a further twenty-seven miles on latitude. Thus we suspected something was terribly wrong, but still were not worried much about it. Hell, what is another day - there must be land tomorrow for sure.

The wind had freshened even more from the northwest, how wonderful. In addition to mainsail and genoa, we boomed out a stays'l to windward. Now or never!

Tomorrow had come, and as much we strained our eyes, there was no land anywhere. From then on we had reason to worry, no doubt we were in the grip of something incomprehensible. In the past three days we had sailed 286 miles by log, mainly on a northeasterly course, but still lost ninety-four miles in latitude.

Siggi took stock of our provisions. Accordingly, we had food for ten days being frugal, and three gallons of water. Things did not look hopeless.

The four days following were one big nightmare. No land, no ship, no life at all. At times we were amidst huge fields of floating logs and entire trees, reminiscent of the Gulf of Nicoya, when we were driven onto one of the trees. As then, we were now deadly afraid of colliding with one, especially at night. A real miracle that we didn't.

Very low in spirits by all the uncertainty, weakened by insufficient food and water, we became irritated and unrealistic. Unwavering in my belief that land must be near to the east, and whatever the obstacle we must be headed that way, I imagined land in every cloud bank at dusk. Siggi was never convinced of my weird sightings. Nevertheless, we plugged on with renewed hope for the next day.

In six days we had sailed 422 miles, and had lost 148 miles in latitude. For hours we studied the charts and books to find a way out. Already we had plotted a course for Ecuador, but discarded the idea as quickly. The Galápagos Islands seemed a better goal, again the whole prospect seemed as gloomy. I murdered my brain to find a way to determine a longitude, but without a time piece Bowditch had no suggestion. The truth was, we were absolutely helpless and at the mercy of the elements. Only God could help us now.

Could it be that the sextant gives us a wrong reading? Sure I had fixed the problem with the mirrors. That was easy enough, but had I reassembled and adjusted the instrument correctly? Another worry - we were greenhorns, mind you!

What caused untold frustration was the fact that we were not adrift in a helpless liferaft, where the elements have total command, but in a modern sailcraft, handled by two characters not always up to par but quite capable of giving direction to whatever destination we choose. Yet, without the slightest indication of ever succeeding.

Each passing day reduced our limited supply. Macaronis cooked in seawater tasted horrible, impossible to get it down. A 50/50 mixture with fresh water tasted bitter but tolerable. Hardly did we speak a word, as any discussions as to "what can we do?" were exhausted. We sat under the blazing sun, awed by the magnitude and the power of the sea around us. We succumbed to our last resort, laying all our hopes into the "power above."

Presently we had three colorful bonitas around the boat, but all declined interest in any of the two permanently trailing hooks. The cause may be we are lousy fishermen, but hardly possible that the fish knew of it. I sharpened a stainless steel welding rod I had found in the tool box, and tied it to the boathook, to use it as a spear. It did not catch a thing.

A fresh southerly wind made up. What shall we do? Pursue our northeast course? It hadn't helped us in the past, so lets try something else, sail north. Exactly against the cause of all our nightmares!

Under a bulging spinnaker *Thlaloca* accelerated to six knots. The reward we harvested at noon the following day - we had gained an astonishing eighty miles in latitude! Here we experienced the crux of this confounded piece of ocean no one can predict, and what haunts motorless crafts today, and had for centuries past. Basically, it is the confluence of many ocean currents in that particular part of the world, and weather conditions that may strengthen or weaken a particular current. On the whole a confusing issue and anyone trying to make sense of it is lost, as we were!

If this wasn't enough to raise our spirits to unprecedented heights, it was a ship that was steaming over the horizon that made us belief in the "power above."

The Power of Ocean Currents

The ship's course should bring us close. To mark our position, and to indicate we needed help, we lowered and raised the mainsail. In addition, Siggi waved what was left (after the ordeal in Puntarenas) of the yellow oilskins.

The *Cristal*, a banana freighter out of Miami, was a small ship, but she gave us all she could. We rigged a high-line between the two vessels, and along it we received five gallons of water and a large box of food. The sea was running four feet high, and the maneuver required careful engine work by her skipper, Captain Foster. To keep the line taut we ran the outboard motor. Also he gave us our position. Accordingly we were seventy miles south and twenty miles "west" of the longitude of Punta Mala. Although the latitude conformed with our observation, the longitude was a knockout. What it meant, that we had sailed 422 miles towards the east from the longitude of Punta Mala but in fact found ourselves twenty miles west of that longitude.

The "rescue operation" completed, the *Cristal* made up steam, and soon disappeared behind an ageless wall of heaving ocean. After a hungry week we ate so well that we almost needed another ship to supply us. With a pint of water each we toasted the generosity of Captain Foster.

Next day we raised land near Morro Puerco, a promontory we had passed twelve days ago. There the wind lost weight, but remained light from the north. By nightfall it changed to fresh southwest. Checking on landmarks, we were making excellent progress with no apparent current to hinder us. When Punta Mala Light bore south of west I handed the tiller over to Siggi. I drifted to sleep hearing Siggi's beautiful voice singing Christmas carols. After all, it was Christmas Eve, and we were exuberantly happy and elated.

Plenty of shipping surrounded us all at once and we wondered where they all came from, as for almost a fortnight we hadn't sighted any, except the *Cristal*.

The wind, now blowing from the north, made us sail tight on the wind for the Perlas Islands. Twenty miles south of it, the wind increased to gale force (in connection with the tradewinds, these winds are called "intensified trades") which forced us down to a storm jib and a close reefed mainsail. Even this little bit of sail seemed to overpower the boat. The strain on sails and gear gave us a mental fit, but we really had no alternative - except to heave-to and perhaps be driven out of the gulf again. The boat pounded ahead bravely through the gray mass of ocean, while we huddled in the cockpit wrapped up in sails, as substitute for our useless foul-weather suits.

Throughout that unpleasant night we watched the sails for any indication of the slightest tear, that would have prompted quick action to lower them, and the heavy traffic which was passing either side of us in endless procession. Our envy went out to those big ships with their massive power, their comfort, their cozy cabins, while we balanced precariously on the verge of sanity.

It had moderated in the morning, and the rising sun soon burned the wind to a whisper. Close to the Perlas Islands we hauled onto the other tack, on which we made Tobago Island. There we anchored off an inviting sandy beach, on December twenty-seventh, 1963. On balance we had sailed 470 miles from Puntarenas to Tobago Island in twenty-four days. In reality, though, we had covered more than a thousand miles.

With the boat securely anchored, we impulsively fell into each other's arms, fully aware that we had escaped a great peril that could easily have cost us plenty, even our lives.

Looking back and evaluating the 3,500-mile voyage from California to Panama, we conclude that it was continuous misery, caused foremost by perpetual calms and those dreadful thunderstorms. Perhaps it was an unusual year, we don't know. Next the smallness of the boat which did not permit transport of large stores, especially fuel which we rightly considered far too dangerous to have on deck in lightning storms. And let's face it, the port officials were a nuisance and only interested in money. However, it was not without benefits. Foremost, we had gained valuable experience for a much greater adventure that lay ahead. We started out as total greenhorns - apprentices who had advanced to journeymen. A real benefit was the fact that I had lost a lot of weight - thirty pounds. Even Siggi was down in size to that of a reefpoint.

Another point I like to make with emphasis: What Siggi, as a woman, had gone through over the past year was unquestionably astonishing. She could have bailed out at any time. That she didn't proves her sense of loyalty to me and *Thlaloca*, far surpassing what is expected in a marriage. It is camaraderie, a higher sense of values that was called upon.

Our arrival in Tobago Island brought a visitor, a pleasant old Indian in a dugout canoe, who offered his services. I collected some cans for fuel, and he rowed me ashore. Also I wanted to call the Balboa Yacht Club, to hear if a club member was available to pilot us from the quarantine anchorage to the club, only a very short distance. Exactly what Bill Bodenlos had suggested back in Mazatlán. It would save us $4.50 per foot of draft, over twenty dollars! The law of the Canal Zone was simple: No one was permitted to operate a vessel without a permit. Residents of the Canal Zone had it, visitors not.

Unfortunately, no one was at the club. Besides fuel, I bought bread and a large cone of ice-cream for Siggi. The little time I was ashore convinced me that this was an island of outstanding tropical beauty (we explored thoroughly at a later date). I handed the Indian some coins, he acknowledged with a touching smile on his wrinkled face.

A dead calm made us motor the ten miles to the quarantine area, where we remained adrift amidst many ships awaiting transit. The yellow flag in the rigging alerted one of the dark-blue painted launches. It pulled alongside to discharge a man with a briefcase. He handed us papers to fill in while he measured *Thlaloca* for tonnage-dues. Once finished we were told to wait for a pilot. He left unacknowledged my plea to proceed under own steam.

One hour later a launch unloaded not one but two pilots. Captain Haff and a trainee. Expecting something like a 30,000 ton cargo carrier, the captain stood on deck and shook his head in disbelief. After he was assured that this was the ship he was to pilot, he carefully balanced his six-foot-six frame and 225 pounds of weight behind the tiller. The trainee was placed forward the mast besides Siggi. Thus the trim of the boat was maintained. I coaxed the coughing motor to give a good show for the next two miles. Being different to the usual, the captain got a tremendous kick out of the whole deal. Impressed by our story he promised to arrange to be our pilot through the canal, as long we let him know a long time in advance.

As we secured *Thlaloca* to a mooring buoy at the Balboa Yacht Club, a man from a nearby yacht hailed,

"Hallo, do you know anyone around here?"

"No," we replied.

"Well, you know someone now, " he answered.

We had truly arrived.

XI

PANAMA

The club's launch ferried us ashore, and there we got to know Mr. Campion, an Air Force colonel (actually the man who gave us the first "halloo"). He invited us for a belated Christmas dinner at his house. The invitation included all our laundry, which we packed in a hurry and off we went.

At his home we met his wife and daughter who had the table already set with all the food a real Christmas dinner encompasses. While the laundry was in the automatic washer and received a total transformation in color and fragrance, we spent the next two hours eating and talking. Adventurous people they were, their plans for the future were similar to ours. Soon to be retired from the service, the dream was to roam the South Pacific in their neat little ketch, and many preparations to that end were already completed. ((Thirty months later we had arrived back in the Canal Zone, having completed a circumnavigation, but they were still there. An example how elusive dreams are.) Stuffed with delicious food and carrying a couple of sailbags of salt-free laundry we returned to *Thlaloca* for the first undisturbed sleep in a month.

The following morning we met Bill Arbaugh, the vice-commodore of the Balboa Y.C. For the past year we hardly had contact with people of the same cultural background and similar interest except in Costa Rica. Not that we had suffered, quite the contrary. After all, the essence of cruising is a desire

91

meet people of different cultures. Still, it is wonderful to converse with someone fluently in the same language, exchange ideas, share dreams, drink a beer or two, and enjoy fun and laughter as we all do. Bill Arbaugh and his wife Peggy are the sort of people we wanted to meet. Both of them remain to this day some of the outstanding people we had the pleasure meeting during our voyaging - and some we are still in contact with.

Broke and disillusioned by past year's tribulations, we wanted to end the voyage as quickly as possible, somewhere on the east coast of the U.S. or Canada. While I discussed with Bill the transit of the canal, he was far ahead in considering the difficulty we may have sailing against the tradewinds during the height of winter, he repeated one particular slogan: "Sail west, man!" Words that inflamed my tortured mind.

We had dinner that night at the Arbaugh's home. After we had consumed half a dozen cans of "Buds", Bill was singing Hillbilly songs, and suggested going to the New Year's dance at the American Legion. Granted that this was a smashing idea, our concern was our mildewed clothing, or whatever was left of it. "Well! What about clothing? We've got plenty." Bill exclaimed.

Bill and I were about the same size, no problem there. It was different with Siggi. True, Siggi was down in size to a reef-point, the trouble was that Peggy was less than that. This slight inconvenience delayed our attendance a couple of hours until necessary alterations were completed. At any rate, we entered the party well dressed, in a fabulous mood, and enjoyed it thoroughly.

☆

We made arrangements for the transit of the canal three days in advance. At the same time we informed Captain Haff of our intentions. At the port office we paid twenty-three dollars for the two-mile piloting from the quarantine anchorage to the yacht club and - read carefully - $1.79 for the 35-mile transit! We asked for center lockage (we were told was best), with two lines on either side taken ashore, to hold the boat in the middle of the lock chamber.

Eight o'clock sharp on a Sunday morning Captain Haff boarded *Thlaloca*, and settled down on a piece of six-inch thick foam (just bought to keep him happy) and took control of our magnificent ship. With the outboard motor roaring we approached the Miraflores Locks, doing five knots, our maximum speed. We were to join a fleet of Panamanian fishing trawlers. We pulled alongside one of them, it eliminated a lot of line handling. The crew of the *Pedro Gonzales*, a rather filthy tub, kept a close eye on us during the turbulent locking operation. The ease of the operation contrasted sharply to some accounts we had heard and read about in the past. Our fears of pulled out cleats and smashed hulls lessened. Perhaps we were just lucky to have Captain Haff with us, who seemed to have a lot of pull in arranging things. We remained with the trawler into the next lock, while the "mules" (small electric locomotives which run on tracks along the lock chambers) transferred the vessels from one lock chamber into the next. Once clear of the second tier of locks we raced across the mile-long Miraflores Lake towards the Pedro Miguel Locks. From there on we had some thirty miles towards the giant Gatun Locks, on the Atlantic side.

When the last of the Pedro Miguel Locks opened its massive gates I uttered a silent prayer, that the outboard motor might continue its roaring performance, and not demonstrate its hardheadedness of the past - quit at the wrong damn time.

It so happened, that no prayer or curse would make the thing go. The trawler's diesels roared into action and dragged us along. Once clear of the lock we were dropped aft on the end of a long line.

The motor was flooded, and I had it going soon, a fact our patient pilot could well hear, but I could not refrain from announcing it.

"Stop your bragging and get rid of that noisy beater. We are doing fine as it is," was the surprising answer. Surprising because, as far we knew, it was unlawful to be towed privately. But who am I to judge? I gladly left it up to the pilot.

Shortly after, we passed one of the extraordinary engineering feats of our time, the Gaillard Cut, so named after the man who defeated its challenge. Here the canal slices the steep grades of the Continental Divide. This mountain range had proved an almost impossible obstacle to complete the canal. Many lives were lost due to landslides and all kinds of tropical diseases. The only reminder to suffering is a plaque that pays tribute to the victims.

Still under tow we entered the man-made Gatun Lake. Reading out of a brochure it mentions that an ocean to ocean transit draws fifty-two million gallons of water out of the lake. The area is also a wildlife preserve, a welcome distraction from the drudgery of reading *Pedro Gonzales, Panama* in front of us. To keep Captain Haff in a happy frame of mind, we had rigged a bed cloth over the boom, that funneled a breeze nicely through the gap. Beer, soft drinks, cake and sandwiches were all there. Hell, even ice. We weren't cheap!

Late afternoon we motored under our own steam into the first tier of the Gatun Locks, and easily slipped alongside our adopted friend. Siggi took the opportunity and handed the skipper a six-pack of beer to show our appreciation. Descending in the locks presents far less danger, as the water escapes from the chambers without a ripple. For lack of anything else to do, we watched the "mules" doing their job dragging us from one lock chamber into another.

Out of the last lock we headed for the Cristóbal Yacht Club, to tie up alongside the *Holly*, our old acquaintances from Puntarenas. Remembering the ocelot, we first made sure it was not visible. Over gin and tonic we traded highlights of the past months. Apparently they had taken the cat ashore on Cocos Island, and it had escaped. More likely, the beast had become a liability to be kept aboard a boat.

Of particular interest to us was their attempt, beating against the winter trades out of Panama to the West Indies. The *Holly*, sixty-five feet long and a 300 horsepower engine to assist, pounded against the seas for a week, until a cracked mast forced her back to harbor. "Don't be a fool and try it with your dinghy," the skipper advised. Sobering advice we meant to check out thoroughly.

Harold Sweeny, whom we befriended, had a car, and never tired of taking us to the ocean side to check out the real thing, rather than depending on the weather forecasts we mistrusted. Daily we listened to and read the expression, "intensified trades," it made us sick and restless; quite in contrast to the couple aboard the *Holly*, who enjoyed their nightly cocktails with no apparent worry in the world, while we were sitting on edge. But, if the *Holly* had reservations about going, we would be fools to try. Bill Arbaugh's slogan: "Sail west, man!" moved ever closer into the forefront of my mind. Convincing Siggi in this direction was a hard nut to crack.

The winter months are notorious for the tradewind to blow strongest. According to the weather bulletins posted at the club's blackboard, the wind averaged twenty-five knots over the past week, and nothing less could be expected soon. Siggi's argument, "it must get better eventually," dwindled with every forecast. As did our money, to a point that drastic action had to be considered. My argument, that it is better to be moving, rather that than being frustrated by that confounded wind blowing into our faces day after day. Only reluctantly did Siggi come around and saw it my way, "Let's sail west, downwind!" Words I had waited for a long time.

It had not come lightly to her because of the lousy trip we had down the west coast of Central America that had disappointed us greatly, and she had counted on the conclusion of it 2½ thousand miles to the north, in Canada, in not too distant future. The "long way around" was at least thirty thousand miles, and only God knew what was in our cards. Sure, we had a good boat to go anywhere, but still very small, an oversized doghouse, (she had to rub it in) to be home to us for years to come.

"But, Sig, (using the same argument I had used before) a doghouse all right, but in the South Seas you don't live in it, size is immaterial, our playground will be the water, the beaches - the dreams of millions of people.

"What about money?" she asked. "Well, hm, surely there are jobs in this world, no problem!" said I.

Before Siggi changed her mind I raced to the telephone and called Captain Haff, to find out whether he was willing to take us back through the canal. A long pause convinced me, that his first thoughts were he was dealing with a couple gone nuts, but he eventually promised to look into it, he would call us back.

He called us back on a Thursday, saying that Sunday morning would be perfect because we would lock through with two Jamaican coastal freighters. Unfortunately, he was unable to be our pilot, unless we preferred to postpone it until he could? I decided on Sunday morning; nullifying any change of heart of my magnificent mate!

The owners of the *Holly* volunteered for the trip, in addition they offered us the use of their 9 hp Johnson outboard motor - as compensation for the cat-bite, as they put it.

This time, the locking operation differed, as we were asked to center-lock, meaning no tie-ups to the freighters. Instead we had to bring out four lines to shore, two on each side. We also learned the concerns of other reports, for the water on the uplift was so turbulent, that we feared for our cleats indeed. To be on the safe side, we tied short pieces of rope from the cleats to other solid structures of the boat, such as the bow fitting, in case a cleat let go.

Once the locking-through operation was completed, we celebrated with a dance on the foredeck. After two eventful weeks, we moored to the same buoy we had left that long ago, at the Balboa Yacht Club. When Bill Arbaugh spotted us the following day, he couldn't believe his eyes, "What are you up to now? Sail west, eh?" He felt tickled that we finally were following his advice.

☆

Many preparations were necessary for the long haul across the mighty Pacific. Foremost in my mind was finding a job, to pay for the essentials - a reliable clock and a radio that receives time-ticks were most important. Bill, the good friend he is, solved some of our needs. First he gave us a very good clock, next a job that earned us a radio, in exchange for putting a new transom on his motorboat.

A birthday present from my good mother took care of Sailing Directions, charts, etc. - the last items alone dug a hole in our kitty fifty bucks deep. It dawned on us, that in sailing the only thing free is the wind. That even has a price-tag attached; the cost of sweat and disappointment too many times.

To buy all these things, Cristóbal is the proper place with its large duty free shopping area, the Free Zone as it is referred to. To get to it from Balboa, one has to take a delightful train ride. Subsequently, we took the train many times and never tired of it. Back from the shopping trip, we found the radio inadequate for what it was intended, it wouldn't receive clearly on the frequencies important to us. We meant to exchange it the following day.

News of a violent riot by Panamanians canceled the trip and any further shopping. The apparent cause was the so-called "Flag incident." It was a dispute over which flag, the American or the Panamanian, should be hoisted higher on the masts. The Americans insisted on a loftier display, and the shooting and looting started. Our first thoughts were of the thousands of charts and publications in the Hydrographic Office Building, the very building that was fire bombed and gutted first thing. Considering that we had turned every dollar twice before buying the minimum, and along comes a nut who destroyed in seconds what we couldn't afford, seemed ironic. The situation remained critical for several days, confirmed by shooting we heard day and night.

When calm returned I ventured to exchange the radio, well aware of serious warnings, not to stray outside the Canal Zone. The question was, how long must we wait? We had things to do to get us moving. Before I boarded the train, Siggi pushed a hard object into my hand, saying, "Better take this to defend yourself;" a miniature pocket knife with the picture of a Canadian Mounted Police on it. It used to embellish the key ring to our car. I sincerely hoped, my would be attacker would see it before doing anything foolish; preferably amuse himself to immobility.

The train stopped short of a blasted out section of track and a burned out train station. Buses were waiting nearby to shuttle the passengers to town. Although apprehensive being the only gringo in a crowded bus, I was treated as if not there, and this suited me well.

The crowded streets of Colón wore the face of contempt and hate. On the sidewalks, four or five young militants would block the walk, waiting for me to bust through. Instead I stumbled along in the streets, taking my chances with blaring automobiles and ox carts, what I considered as better odds of survival in that hostile world.

With the radio exchanged, I managed a quick retreat into the security of the Cristóbal Yacht Club, to settle my strained nerves with ice-cold beer. My eyes fell on a beautiful British yacht, the *Kochab*. Drooling with envy I walked her length when a distinguished looking gentleman emerged from below,

"Franklin Evans, my name, please come aboard!"
West Indies rum was his favorite drink, and no time was lost we indulged in it freely. With amazement I observed through my fogged-up eyes that the scantlings of his frail physique had received much stronger fastenings than mine. Mine had eroded after the third drink, and I only managed a rather inglorious departure. We were destined to meet many more times in the future.

Thinking back of the enjoyable weeks at the Balboa Yacht Club and the fine and lasting friends we made there, we remember one person in particular, old Nick Carter. Part of the reason we remember him so well, because he resembled so much our good friend Charlie back in Long Beach. Nick was old in years, like Charlie he lied about his age, he said he was seventy-four. His former crew recalled a seventy-fourth birthday party four years earlier. Whatever, he was young at heart and in better physical condition than most men half his age.

A New Zealander, Old Nick had celebrated his fourteenth birthday on an ancient square rigger rounding the Horn. He was a tough old bird and he could hold a drink. Never lost his composure and always spoke a precise English no matter how many drinks he had under the belt, "I never let go of the bottle that was forced into my mouth after birth, only the contents changed." Nick exclaimed. An extremely talented storyteller with an unbeatable humor, "That helped me survive the Spanish Civil War."

In England he had bought the old cutter *Matuko Moana*, and with a couple of hands, one a girl, sailed her to Panama. After transiting the Panama Canal, they were bound for New Zealand. Old Nick had not been home since he had left as a teenager, and he had promised himself to return only on his "own bottom."

His first "own bottom," the *Matuko Moana*, ended as a wreck soon after. Badly in need of a haul-out, arrangements were made to haul the yacht ashore with the help of a crane. While anchored off the beach awaiting the crane, a sudden southerly gale had caused the anchors to drag, that drove the yacht onto a rocky shore, severely damaged.

This man, who in his lifetime had rounded the Horn a dozen times, and as a soldier of fortune had served four foreign armies loyally, stood by his ship equally loyal.

"I owe it to her for the splendid deed she did saving seventy men off the beach at Dunkirk," he once told me over a cup of coffee.

The ship lay gutted with a broken backbone on a lonely beach, a none salvageable wreck. Not one of his many friends expressed true opinions in the face of this faithful old man of the sea, for fear of losing his friendship. It was heartbreaking to see him work all kinds of menial jobs to earn money that he pumped into his only true love - his boat that would never float again. The U.S. Navy, no doubt, saw the boat for what it was, but to their credit offered help; perhaps only to make Old Nick face reality. When the crane lifted the boat it fell apart. The tragic end of a valiant boat and an old man's tenacious dream. (Much later we heard that Old Nick was still working in Panama and saving for a new boat.) We think of him many times in fond memory, the fine specimen of a true Kiwi - too bloody stubborn to fly.

Nick and I landed a job, stepping and rigging the mast on the 48-foot yacht *Chicatica*. Peggy Poor-Allen, a freelance writer, with her husband built the yacht in Costa Rica and made a fine job of it. They had motored the yacht to Balboa to fit her out. Once the crane had stepped the massive 60-odd-foot "stick", we busily cut the rigging to proper length, attached the end fittings and secured them to the chainplates. With the end in sight it became apparent that somebody had to climb the mast to release the crane. I, the youngest guy around, was the obvious choice. Of all the people present no one doubted - not even Siggi - that I was the fellow most capable. When it was time to release the hook, I busied myself on a bottlescrew, true to the advice of my grandfather, the old war-horse of 1914-18 vintage, "never, ever volunteer."

After considerable time had past, suspicious of the fact that I wasn't called, I looked up. There was Old Nick, agile as a squirrel, half way up the mast already. Ashamed of my devious game, I made a feeble attempt to stop him, "Vat de hell are you doing up der?!" When the "old man" stood beside me, I had reason to admire him even more.

Before departing, there was one more important errand to be made, securing visas for the Galápagos Islands and French Polynesia. The difficulty was not in getting them, rather how to get there and back unharmed with the hate still smoldering in Cristóbal and Panama City. Most taxi drivers refused transporting gringos for fear their car would be stoned. We were lucky in finding a willing hand. Five of us, Doc Evans (Franklin Evans) and Dick Pohe from *Kochab*, Ron Russel from *Gannet* and Siggi and I squeezed into the taxi. At the French embassy we asked the driver to wait, making sure of return transportation without having to search for it. After a long delay, to the delight of the taxi driver, we received our visas for a fee of $2.50 each. We got back to the club unscathed.

Rumors circulated about high fees for Ecuadorian visas - as high as fifty dollars apiece. We called the embassy. The answer we received sounded ambiguous: "It depends . . ." With other words, whatever the traffic can bear.

We knew that the two boats had received their visas at the Cristóbal consulate for five dollars apiece. Back we were on the train across the isthmus and into the fangs of a militant crowd.

The office occupied the basement of a building and was run by a very pleasant gentleman and his secretary. The consul not speaking English, we conversed through our driver. We were taken aback by the first question, "Would you like a drink?" Before modest Siggi could express her favorite, gin and tonic, the driver added, "Coca Cola, Pepsi or Seven-up?" Even that was appreciated in that stifling hot office. His next question lured us into making a booboo, "Where is your yacht located?"

"In Balboa!" There was no way he could issue a visa to a vessel stationed in Balboa. It is under the jurisdiction of Panama City. From this point on it was up to Siggi to argue the case; and no doubt in my mind that she would be successful.

"*Señor, por favor* . . . think of how precarious the situation is after the riot . . . taxis won't take us for fear of getting stoned . . . *muy peligroso!*

Much would we have liked to listen in on the phone conversation the consul had with his superiors in Panama City. At last he dropped the receiver and fell back on his chair exhausted, using his handkerchief freely to cope with the perspiration running down his face. We received our visas. We certainly appreciated what the good man had done for us, and we thanked him sincerely.

Thlaloca was put on the slip, and it was amazing to see so many barnacles that had found a home on such a small bottom. We scraped, we checked and finally gave her three coats of antifouling - at five bucks a gallon we could afford to be real good to her.

The day before our departure date we had a quick drive to Old Panama City, which the notorious pirate Henry Morgan plundered and burned back in 1671. As an added tourist attraction, the band of the local fire department gave concerts every Saturday, while young native girls danced and showed off beautiful embroidered costumes. It was like a festive fashion show which we enjoyed thoroughly. As of Old Panama City, there is not much left to see, but certainly worth the time to check it out.

XII

TO THE

ENCHANTED ISLANDS

Early in the morning of a windless February the 5th, we disengaged *Thlaloca* from her mooring, only yards off the main fairway, and secured her to the jetty of the Balboa Yacht Club. It was the day of our intended departure. We filled the plastic water bottles, as well as any container at hand, which brought the total capacity to 45 gallons. This was fifteen gallons more than the normal we used to carry so far. The reading of different accounts of cruising sailors plus our own recent experience on the inward passage made us extremely cautious. The Sailing Direction in particular gives stern warnings to motorless sailing vessels, and even names the stretch of water between Panama and the Galapágos Archipelago "the most difficult in the world." The culprits of all these uncertainties are powerful ocean currents (as mentioned in a previous chapter). As in all endeavors it is luck one must hope to be on your side. And not only there but on the whole, that gets you anywhere.

The fact that we were not alone facing the problem, made the burden of anxiety easier to carry. There was Frank Casper on the thirty-two foot cutter *Elsie*, from Miami, bound to circle the globe. Jean Gau was well into his second circumnavigation with his thirty-foot *Atom*. Ron Russel on the twenty-two foot

WEST! SAIL WEST, MAN!

Gannet was bound for New Zealand. He had left the U.K. a year before. Also there was the benevolent old sea-dog Dr. Franklin Evans with his beautiful yawl *Kochab* (my acquaintance from Cristóbal) bound also for New Zealand. All the boats, except the *Gannet* and us, had power, therefore were less concerned with ocean currents and foul, or no wind.

After we had taken on water and stowed the last items we had bought the previous day, there was still no wind. Strange, because for the last six weeks it had blown strong across the Isthmus, to a point we cursed it for it made the anchorage bumpy and living aboard uncomfortable. Now that we needed wind there was none.

Bill Arbaugh dropped by with the suggestion: "No wind, why waste time, better load up on cold beer!" A suggestion impossible to refuse, and even Siggi hailed it as a great idea. Minutes later we sat in the cool of the verandah sipping beer with disgusted looks on our faces about that persistent calm spell. Acquaintances came by for a chat. Instead of making some intelligent remark in the face of a dead calm, they would inquire, "How come you're not on your way? Or, "Did you change your mind about leaving?"

Shortly before noon we had enough of it. We boarded *Thlaloca* and set sail. Only a few hundred yards up the channel lay the Tahiti-Ketch *Adios* to a mooring, with Tom and Janet Steel the owners. This fine couple had already a circumnavigation to their credit and we had spent some delightful evenings aboard. Janet's vivid description of the life and beauty of the South Sea Islands had raised such hungry gleam in our eyes that we could hardly wait to get there. During my conversation with Tom about general navigation among islands, quite incidentally he dropped the remark, "Never pass an island on its windward side!" This remark did not impress me, but still lodged in my memory bank as being something important to be recalled - subsequently almost too late!

Normally we met Tom and Janet towards evenings at the club, except the last few days, so we missed saying "so long" to two fine people. As we drifted clear of the jetty, we spotted their dinghy alongside *Adios*, meaning they were home. Paddling desperately we did our best to get close for a handshake but the unrelenting tidal current carried us into the Gulf of Panama.

By late afternoon we were still becalmed, and only the

102

ships steaming to and from the canal disturbed the water. A motoring ketch drew alongside, people we knew from the club, who handed us two cans of cold beer. Six hours after our departure we were still drifting soundlessly on a silent sea and all our hopes of a fast passage were fading with the setting sun. Tobago Island, we had visited in the interim and found it so beautiful, lay conveniently to starboard, we decided to anchor there and wait for wind. Just then a light northeasterly wind sprang up to which we hoisted all appropriate sails. The gurgle of water around the hull now assumed a definite rhythmic sound, rising and falling with the undulation of the sea. By degrees the wind freshened rewarding us with a gorgeous sail all through a starlit night, and some of the major stars perfect guides to steer by.' After six eventful and hectic weeks ashore, the sea was most alluring, and it was wonderful to be moving again. "Allow yourself a month to the Galápagos Islands, it is a tricky passage," Old Nick Carter had warned us. He himself, with his *Matuko Moana*, had tried for 58 days to get there. Running low on stores they had returned. (Subsequently to be wrecked). But his bitter memory was not to be heeded as *Thlaloca*, surging along under her enormous load of food and water, tirelessly kicked off the miles on the register, "It will not take that long," her bow-wave confidently whispered.

A meridian altitude at noon the next day shortened the 900 mile voyage by eighty. The wind had fallen light then, and slowly veered. But with a favorable current under her bottom *Thlaloca* stood well south for the Line.

Sitting in the cockpit of our tiny craft I fully realized that my adventurous dream of sailing around the world was slowly becoming a fact, for right then was the beginning of a circumnavigation. One would think that sailing out into the wide open ocean ought to have raised doubts and fear in our minds. It is only fair to assume that we should have questioned our navigational skills, or whether our sailing experience was really up to the job. Perhaps there were lingering thoughts, but decisive was my intent to reach for the goal and prevail. Siggi, to be truthful, expressed many doubts, until she was convinced that our navigational department was able to produce a landfall - one we had actually aimed for! After that she shared with me the same confidence. Finally, it was the faith in *Thlaloca* and in ourselves that started us on the voyage, and we meant to see it through whatever obstacles may linger in the way. Quite frankly, though, had we known how huge the world really is, and with how much hardship we would have to pay for ignorance - lack of experience - our aim would not have been that far reaching. As a dear friend once remarked, "Had I known beforehand what to expect, I would never have started out!"

So, what is it like to push off into the unknown? Not too different from leaving on a day or weekend cruise to an offshore island or cove along the coast, just plenty more of it! For days, and even weeks on end, there are the heavenly bodies as a faithful guide over an endless expanse of heaving ocean with us suspended in the center of a complete circle. One day is much the same as the next, with food to eat and books to read, and watching the dolphins leap to the music of the bow-wave. Then one day this daily rhythm is broken by something rising gradually above the horizon - an island. A great relief and satisfaction overcomes the navigator, having made, over hundreds of miles, his first landfall.

The wind had fallen to a light southeast when we spotted Mapelo Island - a sinister inaccessible pile of rocks, some 300 miles out of Panama - partly hidden in a rain squall. Its vicinity is marked by swirls of hissing water, caused by the meeting of several opposing currents. Fortunately we passed that area during daylight. At night it would be hair-raising, as the sounds and looks of cascading water is terrifying even in daylight.

With the wind very light, we were swept towards the island until it was close enough to grab it with a spinnaker pole - had we tried it. But drastic actions, such as getting the outboard motor from under a pile of miscellaneous stores in the lazaret, was avoided when the wind increased enough to drive us out of danger.

Since the wind was too fluky and unsteady in its direction, it was not worth the effort to make the boat self-steering. Therefore, Siggi and I took two hour watches, and it was wonderful to sit there at night with only the gurgling sound of water to remind us that we were floating on the mightiest ocean in the world. Captain Slocum called it, "the misnamed Pacific Ocean." He continued: "The Pacific is perhaps, upon the whole, no more boisterous than other oceans, though I feel quite save in saying that it is not more pacific except in name."

For us at the time it looked like smooth sailing all along, and we had not a worry in the world. In the middle of a dark night we crossed the equator without Neptune's permission.

Apparently he did not mind, as we sailed into the "Southern World" unscathed.

On my watch, towards morning, I sighted the navigational lights of a ship to starboard. It was coming close rapidly. To avoid being run over, I directed the beam of the flashlight onto the mainsail to achieve maximum illumination. Surprisingly, the ship immediately changed her course and came bow-on towards us. For seconds I had vague imaginations of a pirate ship or the like, until it dawned on me that it is the twentieth century we are living in. Still the ship kept coming until it was close - too damn close for my liking!

It stopped broadside to us, and at once opened up with a barrage of searchlights. Although it was almost impossible to keep my eyes exposed to such a volume of light, I recognized a typical Japanese fishing trawler. The crew, which appeared to be thirty strong, cheered and waved their caps vigorously, I cheered back. Alarmed by all the bright light flooding the cabin, Siggi awakened and came on deck to check out the commotion. Her appearance silenced the crowd for seconds, apparently amazed at the courage of a female on such a nutshell, then the cheering renewed, "woman . . . woman!"

The closeness of a live female to men at sea for months is bad for the morale, and the ship's captain must have realized it, because the trawler quickly accelerated its engine and soon disappeared from view.

The morning of our ninth day at sea broke bright and clear. A southeast wind of force four had *Thlaloca* sailing beautifully, while for the past hour we had our eyes glued to a particular spot on the horizon. Of all the days at sea, that day had particular significance, for it would prove or disprove our navigational accuracy. When the bluish mass of Santa Cruz and Chatham, two islands of the Galápagos Archipelago, rose from the sea, there was elation and jubilation aboard our ship because we had brought her there where we wanted her to be, entirely with the help of heavenly bodies.

From then on it was a race against time. In Panama we were informed about an overtime charge for half a day on Saturday and the whole of Sunday. We piled on sails to make harbor before noon. By eleven o'clock we were off the northwestern end of Chatham Island, with twelve miles still left to go to Wreck Bay, the Port of Entry. The wind had abated close to nil, when we finally realized we couldn't make it.

WEST! SAIL WEST, MAN!

Disappointed we shortened sails, and cautiously stole shorewards in search of a suitable anchorage. We found one about five miles short of Wreck Bay. The water as dark as ink, we proceeded slowly to find depth suitable to anchor, all along entertained by the sea life the Galapágos Islands are famous for. There were seals galore, all frolicking around the boat. Our anchor splashed down in five fathoms.

To beat the time, we occasionally mustered enough courage for a dip into that frigid water, one at a time. As soon we spotted one of the large bull-sea-lions taking to the water, we quickly scrambled back aboard. Whether they are harmless or ferocious, we had no desire to find out. We are convinced that they would take a nibble if given a chance, because they are so-o big!

Overnight we had two fishing lines hanging over the side, baited with flying fish we had collected off the deck. Monday morning we still found them untouched. We recovered the lot, set sail and headed for Wreck Bay, the Port of Entry.

Two hours later we sailed through an opening of a reef, and came to anchor in front of a broken down steel jetty. Along the shore we noticed some scattered dwellings, one of which we recognized as the building of the *commandancia*, solidly built on a slab of stone.

A boat with four officials drew alongside *Thlaloca*. After a courteous greeting they demanded our passports and our final destination, (a very significant question as it turned out later). We stated it as New Zealand. We then learned that overtime charges had been eliminated some time ago - news which heartened us little after having spent two nights in a rolling anchorage.

A short time later we sighted a sail, and we wondered who it could be. It was the *Kochab*, which had departed Balboa three days after us. Doc Evans really must have put the coals to her, for the passage was made in seven days. But we did not feel too bad having taken 9½ days. The twenty-two foot *Gannet* even made the passage in nine days. Yet, all three cases are extraordinary in the face of a truly difficult stretch of water, and the reason for this must be found in the splendid wind conditions we all enjoyed.

Along with Doc Evans, Dick Pohe and Rod Paul - the latter two were young New Zealanders and the crew on *Kochab* - Siggi and I rowed ashore to test our sea-legs and to check out

106

To the Enchanted Islands

the availability of fresh vegetables. We secured the dinghy to the rusted steel jetty and had a short walk among the houses. We quickly got tired of so much desolation and retired back aboard to discuss future plans; and plans were, to visit the capital of the Archipelago, a town called Progresso, located five miles up hill.

A beautiful morning saw us strolling along an exceptionally good road by island standard. With the rising sun came the heat. The air became oppressive and turned the climb into an ordeal. We soon blamed each other for a stupid idea. Siggi and I were quick to suggest a shameful retreat, but Dick and Rod refused to comply. In truth, both of them feared Doc Evans' pointed remarks should they fail.

Along the road grew extensive patches of orange trees full with fruit. Unfortunately, the oranges were one month short of being ripe; still, the odd ones that were came handy to squelch our thirst, and they were absolutely delicious. We discovered that they were never attended to. We could imagine that such rich harvest could benefit someone. Apparently not. So it was wasted, a shame indeed!

Progresso frustrated all our imagination of hamburgers and ice cream. Nothing was there except a few houses with thatched roofs, an ancient Dodge truck parked at the side of the church-yard, and an old man in rags having a snooze in the shade of a ruin. Progresso was a town in name only. We marched back.

The descent so much easier, it gave pause to admire the impressive view of the blue ocean in which nestled the islands of Santa Cruz, Charles and Hood, some of them on our itinerary for future visits.

Returning to the beach, we found Doc Evans in one of the huts, all smiles sampling cactus-brew. The room was hot and stuffy, and the filthy glasses beset with flies. To be a good sport amidst those happy-go-lucky natives, I caved in to their prodding and downed a couple drinks that burned my throat and tasted horrible. I was a sober man in the hut, but the minute I stepped into the open my legs buckled, and my eyesight went haywire. With Siggi in near panic, I was carried into the din-ghy and onto our boat. Doc Evans, the medical doctor, was still gulping down home-brew and never noticed a thing what was going on. At the time I swore this to be my last home-brew. But all the good intentions faded as time went on.

A light pleasant sail brought us to Academy Bay, on Santa

107

WEST! SAIL WEST, MAN!

Cruz Island, where we anchored among local boats. The settlement that stretches around the bay is small, but the largest in the Galápagos Islands.

Over the past decades, great effort has been made by the Ecuadorian Government to attract settlers, but with only small successes. Most came from Europe, mainly Norwegians, who tried hard to make a living. Nearly all failed and went back. The few hearty ones that stayed must be a special breed, accustomed to a lonely life, in complete absence of any social activity, living in isolation from one another.

The Angermeiers, four brothers from Germany, had settled in the islands in the middle thirties. It seemed they had cornered the market - and the only market was the UNESCO, which had established a scientific station in Academy Bay. With scientists visiting from all over the world to study the exceptional wildlife, there ensued a demand for guides and other services the islanders could perform. Consequently, the Angermeiers seemed well established - much to the dislike of many people! We spent some delightful evenings in their company, and could not understand the animosity directed against them. Of course, we did not live there either!

Another couple, also German, we came to know very well. Again it is the memory of pleasant evenings with people that we remember folks so well. He was a dentist, very young with a flair for adventure, and of considerable wealth in Germany. Attracted by romantic magazine stories, television commentaries and personal interviews with traveling islanders, his family (wife, baby and three in-laws) settled on Santa Cruz Island. They had come with two prefab houses, a twenty-six foot motor-sailer and a complete dentistry.

"It cost me a fortune to move here. Another to move back," he said. They were awaiting the next supply ship to escape their growing disappointment.

Dick and Rod from *Kochab* were again the brains behind the next fiasco - a wild pig hunt. Ron from *Gannet* and I followed. From the outset the going was rough over jagged lava flows and through stinging cactus bushes. Our light canvas shoes were no match for that kind of abuse, and soon fell apart. Our socks were even less resistant. It reduced us to hopping about like kangaroos, in an effort to miss the spiky outcrops. Up to that point we hadn't seen a living creature of any kind. Gaining altitude, the vegetation increased to jungle-like density, and the air became moist. It had softened the ground, and made walking less of an ordeal.

Entering a clearing, we came upon what could be interpreted as a mirage, a beautiful house surrounded by a gorgeous flower garden. For orientation, and advice on how to hunt blooming wild pigs in this confounded jungle, we approached the house where a snarling dog barred our advance. It brought the lady of the house on the scene, who immediately invited us inside for a glass of cold milk, fresh from the cow.

The family had come from Norway thirty years ago. They were a happy lot. Crowned by success, they were some of the few who would not trade their homestead for anything in the world.

The advice on hunting was disheartening. It was essential to have dogs. Also they expressed concern that we mistake their own pigs, which were running free inside a large enclosure, for wild ones. It ended our pig-hunt, instead we spent the bullets shooting at the occasional empty tin can on the way.

Overnight we camped in a clearing amongst some shacks. The friendly villagers gave us wood to keep a fire going all through the night. We cooked our bully-beef and ate whatever we had brought with us. Sleep was impossible, and despite the fire we nearly froze to death, with only a shirt and shorts for protection. We desperately awaited daybreak to set our shivering bodies in motion.

Back at the beach, at Bud Devin's Tavern, we drowned our disappointment with a quart of good Ecuadorian beer, and endured the needling fun Siggi and Doc Evans were poking us with. We decided to visit other places in the group of islands.

Although we had enough staple provisions aboard to last us many months, finding water in the islands was like looking for a needle in a haystack. Help came from the scientific station, that offered enough water to fill our tanks. At the same time we were given the opportunity to observe the research they were doing on all kinds of animals.

About to leave Academy Bay, I went to the commandancia and asked for clearance papers - I was refused, *caramba!*

If my Spanish was half as good as I thought it was, I gathered that in Wreck Bay we had stated as our destination New Zealand. This did not even allow us to be in Academy Bay - what amounted to a violation of the law. We should sail back to Wreck Bay and have the matter cleared up there without delay. This demand I found unacceptable considering that the trip was against wind and current. Worse, with our plans to visit other islands, we could not chance to ignore the demand. If caught, it would be costly.

What now! Siggi!!!

She was the person capable to get us out of this mess. For a strategy meeting we retired to Bud's Tavern for a "quart," to sound the opinions of our friends.

That very same morning an old rusty gunboat had anchored in the bay with the district commandant aboard. Presently he was sitting with Rolf Wittmer, a born islander, and some naval officers, opposite us at a table drinking beer. Weighing the situation carefully we thought the time perfect to approach the man. And Siggi eager to do just that.

She confronted the dignified gentleman with the case of the "clearance papers." He was a gentleman no doubt, but also intent that the full weight of his authority be well registered all around. It took time before he realized he was facing a very dogmatic German lady not accustomed to take NO for an answer. When he did notice he promised help, and even jumped from his chair when Siggi departed. At the commandancia we were handed a piece of paper that had no value beyond the sight of a gunboat.

Rolf Wittmer is the son of a family which had settled on Floriana Island, the next island farther south, decades ago, and that Island had made exciting news at least twice in this century.

An Austrian Baroness was the cause of the first mystery. Apparently she had come to the island with two male companions, and lived among the settlers harmoniously for a time, when the Baroness developed ambition to reign as the Queen of the Galápagos Islands. That's when harmony turned to jealousy and hate. One day she had disappeared along with her lovers, never to be found again. What happened is a mystery, and the subject of many books. The second mystery is more dramatic, and it happened only two weeks after our departure. It involved the brigantine *Yankee*, in which Irving and Exy Johnson had circumnavigated the world several times. The *Yankee* was eventually sold to a charter company. She was on the way around the world again, when she anchored off Floriana Island. The passengers had been ferried ashore to stretch their legs. Two elderly ladies disengaged themselves from the crowd, for a walk in a different direction. One of the ladies complained about an obstruction inside one of her shoes. While she removed her shoe, the other lady walked ahead slowly. When she looked back a minute later, her companion had disappeared.

The following days saw hundreds of people searching for her. Navy personnel from American and Ecuadorian bases on the mainland joined, but failed to find the unfortunate woman. A mystery indeed!

We parted with the friends we had made in Academy Bay, and a leisurely sail brought us to the Plaza Anchorage in the late afternoon. The anchorage is deep, between two long, narrow islands, which are separated from Santa Cruz Island by only a narrow channel. We had difficulty making our anchor stick on what appeared to be a smooth rocky bottom. But it concerned us little at the time, as the weather seemed settled, and the anchorage well protected.

Only the southern island has a suitable landing on a strip of low shoreline. Immediately beyond, the island rises abruptly to several hundred feet. Every square foot around the landing area was occupied by seals basking in a hot sun. Around the boat were others, visible only as lightning flashes speeding through the water for fun or prey. Some stuck their heads above water and greeted - or despised us with the sounds of "oo-oo-oo." A big one surfaced close by, and as it roared menacingly, Siggi remarked, "Surely a mean bull!"

We landed in the middle of their odoriferous camp. The seals nearest to us slid into the dark water, some grudgingly gave way and resumed their *siesta*. The young ones generally looked at us with big bright eyes as round as golf balls. The long whiskers around their mouths and inquisitive expression on their faces, we thought excruciatingly funny. It encouraged us to move close for snapshots. A move not at all appreciated by mamas, or the bulls we thought to be mean b-----ds. They sent us running away many times. In the water we would not like to confront any, but on land they were no match against a set of speedy legs.

Further along the shore, protected by lava boulders from their deadly enemy, the sea lions, were brightly colored fish darting about in great numbers, and also an abundance of crabs of a reddish hue.

The island is completely barren except for some cactus shrub. Needle-sharp lava crags furrowed the high side of the island along its entire length. At our feet the rock wall fell steeply several hundred feet down to the sea, creating the impression that this part of the island had simply slid into the ocean, sometime in the past. Frigate birds and boobies, two magnificent flyers, were sweeping the windward coast continually in search of spoils, and they had their nesting places somewhere among the rocks in the steep wall.

The following day we sailed to Bartholome Island, just off the east coast of mountainous James Island, and found one of the few anchorages in the islands which can boast of a nice sandy beach. It was occupied by some enormous sea lions. The *Kochab* and *Gannet* were with us, and Dick had caught a Mahi-Mahi on the run. It was our evening meal aboard the *Kochab*.

Dick and Rod, taking advantage of the beautiful day and the clear water of the bay, swam a cable length to shore - the easy part! Siggi and I were content with swimming and diving around the boats. Their presence ashore infuriated the sea lions. What followed was one of those amusing battles of wits between humans and beasts, and one that went decidedly in favor of beast. Every time the two entered the water to swim back toward the boats, the sea lions would come charging. It made them hurry back to shore. Other times the sea lions allowed them to swim a fair distance and only then slithered into the water. It resulted in very close calls. Finally they sneaked all the way to the other side of the bay unnoticed, they thought, but as soon they entered the water the sea lions were there to greet them. So the battle waged on, prolonged by Doc Evans, who remarked, "Just let them fry a bit longer!" It left two exhausted characters stranded on the beach - and would still be there had we not launched the dinghy and rescued them!

A fair wind had *Thlaloca* moving well the next day. Once around the spectacular top of James Island, appeared in the misty distance the massive hulk of Albermarle Island, which reaches nearly 5,000 feet into the sky, the summit shrouded by low white clouds. We anchored in James Bay, a crescent-shaped bay on James Island. The water as black as ink. It was our intended jumping-off place for the Marquesas Islands, 3,000 miles to the southwest. Having used up several gallons of precious water over the past days, we hoped to find a source ashore to replenish the loss. It was important to start a long voyage with the maximum we could carry, about thirty gallons.

One could ask, why not forty - fifty? Well, the main disadvantage of water is its weight, about ten pounds a gallon. Thirty gallons, 300 pounds. A lot of weight for a boat already overloaded with other essentials. An overloaded boat decreases speed and reduces buoyancy, an important safety factor. Also, the storage capacity of a small boat is very limited. Whatever, with insignificant restrictions, such as cutting out teatime twice a day, thirty gallons should be ample to last forty to fifty days for two persons being frugal.

Ashore we followed a long dusty road that led to a camplike concentration of timber shacks, with men about doing repair work on machinery. In our best Spanish we asked for the manager, and we were answered in the best English where to find him. The manager presently came driving down the road in a Land Rover. He introduced himself as Mr. Egas, an Ecuadorian of smart appearance and good English. As of water, he offered us all we needed from a homemade desalination plant. We doubted its quality, but four weeks later it was still good. With a pressing problem solved so quickly, we took our time to look around. Mr. Egas invited us to observe the operation of a salt mine, which was his domain.

The mine was located at the bottom of a large extinct volcano crater, accessible over a winding road along the crater's wall. The mining operation was simple: a mechanical shovel and a Euclid truck, the only power equipment. The rest was done by manpower. The men were contracted from the mainland and worked twelve hours a day, seven days a week. The production was said to be 20,000 sacks per month. How this figure compares with up-to-date operations, we don't know. To us it seemed a huge amount of salt.

With the *sucres* (Ecuadorian money) we had left, we meant to buy a gallon of fuel, and we asked Mr. Egas if he could spare it; knowing well that supplies are scarce in the islands, with only one supply ship per month. Surprisingly, he gave us five gallons, and told us to keep the *sucres* as a souvenir. It was plenty of fuel, we had to find room for. We lashed the bottles around the base of the mast, where they could do little harm. Later on, the fumes became so annoying and dangerous that we chucked most of it over the side in mid-ocean.

On the way back to the beach, we came upon two penguins perched on a spit of lava-rock. Apparently they are the northernmost and smallest species in the world. We regretted that no film was left in the camera. Sensing our presence, they dove into the water.

Back aboard we checked our gear, making sure that all was in order for the long ocean passage. That morning, *Kochab* and *Gannet* departed, and we agreed to meet in Hiva Oa, one of the Marquesas Islands. Siggi and I spent the rest of a glorious day swimming for exercise in the dark water of the bay, with some brightly colored Portuguese man-O-war as company. We were careful to keep adequate distance away from a potentially uncomfortable creature.

We had always wondered why these creatures are named as they are, until we came across an interesting report on studies made at the University of Miami's Institute of Marine Science. Amongst other things it mentions: "Three centuries ago, so the story goes, one such fleet was sighted by English ships off the Portuguese coast. To sailors on deck, the *Physalia* (its scientific name) which is the Greek word for bladder, looked like miniatures of the Portuguese galleons that once ruled the seas, so they named the creatures Portuguese man-O-war." To us they looked harmless, but there is another side to it, as the report mentions: "Like an iceberg, there is far more mass and menace to the man-O-war than meets the eye on the surface. Trailing away beneath each float like streamers is an array of murderous fishing tentacles that slowly writhe and reach as much as a hundred feet below for prey. These deadly fishing lines are studded with thousands of stinging cells that contain a poison almost as powerful as a cobra's venom. That poison is deadly to small fish once they are stung. So powerful is the poison that even beached *Physalia* is dangerous - a false step on the dried, blue strings will cause an excruciating hotfoot. People have died of *Physalia* stings but common rubbing alcohol seems to neutralize the poison and is used as a standard treatment. Natives in the Bahamas have developed their own treatment - they wash the infected area with strong detergent. If none is handy they use urine."

At the time we had no knowledge of the danger. Had we known we would have lost out on some refreshing exercise. Again, if we paid attention to every harmful creature in the ocean, we would be better off staying out of the water altogether thereby renouncing our greatest pleasure.

In the morning we were off. The weather was fine and the blue sea rippled from a light southeast wind. At dusk we rounded the low, rugged northern outcrops of Albermarle Island, and before us lay 3,000 miles of open ocean. At the end of that passage lay the South Sea Islands. We were hugely excited.

☆

Past the headland, the wind headed us from the west. We tacked throughout the night. In the morning, Albermarle Island stood as massively in the back of us as it stood before us the previous day. We tried hard making southing, but an apparent strong current prevented it. As a result we crossed and re-crossed the equator several times. The weather remained bad. Thunder and lightning was followed by dead calms and fierce squalls. Typical doldrum weather. We had estimated a month to cover the distance, but if things don't improve we are in for a long haul.

There seemed no end to this adverse weather - "This wonderful life in paradise," Siggi would remark rather cynically. Up to that point it was senseless even to make the boat self-steering. Thus we had to man the tiller around the clock, taking two-hour watches.

On March the seventh, at last, we plotted a latitude which gave us the assurance to be south of the Line for good. (It wasn't crossed again until twenty-five month later, on the run to Barbados Island, in the Atlantic.)

Again we got becalmed in a jumble of a sea a squall had left behind. For the x-time I studied the Pilot Chart which said we should have southeast winds. In disgust we took to reading books, written by fellow cruisers, to find out about their experiences in this part of the world. It was a disappointment! Siggi's book reported gigantic waves and colossal squids sailing through the air with outstretched tentacles, ready to snatch any moving object on deck. Matter of fact, it was not advisable to be on deck at all. Siggi, the avid reader, never read past those pages, in fear of something worse. My book revealed a desperate battle with a shark that had jumped into the cockpit and threatened to smash the boat. No encouragement there!

There! A light wind had sprung up from the southeast. Doubtful at first, was it real? Or will it change to some other direction shortly as in the past?

When the wind raised its tempo and tore up the ugly gray blanket above us, to reveal a pale-blue sky and a warm sun smiling, we knew it was the real thing - the tradewind!

WEST! SAIL WEST, MAN!

From then on relentlessly, *Thlaloca* followed the path of clumsy square-riggers and magnificent clipper-ships of a past era. As if she sensed it, she was forging ahead with a bone between her teeth, with her bow chasing the waves which only seconds past had so menacingly overtopped her stern. This was grand sailing, the sort we had dreamed about since we had started out, so long ago already; the sort that makes one forget any misery of the past. It was the first time we hoisted the "trade-wind-rig" on an ocean passage, and we were anxious to know how it would self-steer the boat in a sea with all its wild motion.

To make our *Thlaloca* do just that (wind-vane devices were not on the market in 1963), we set two staysails of equal size, their tacks to eyebolts on the bow one foot apart. They were boomed out by eight-foot spinnaker poles, the heels attached to the mast. We led the sheets outside the shrouds through blocks on rails alongside the cockpit and lashed to the tiller. We sheeted the staysails so that the chord of each was somewhat forward of athwartships. Thus we obtained a dihedral effect with the two sails. If the boat yawed to starboard, the port running sail assumed a much finer angle with the wind. The loading became heavier on the starboard sheet than the port and the tiller was pulled to starboard, to bring the boat back on course. Similar occurred if the boat wandered off to port. It worked marvelously for us, though it was a lot of work to set it up. Finer adjustments were made on the tiller with heavy rubber bands - cut from a tire inner tube - increasing oder decreasing pressure on the side necessary.

Amidst the giant circle of heaving water and blue sky we were overcome with a feeling of great satisfaction. It was the beginning of a wonderful life away from the dictates of society, free as storm petrels or the flying fish around us. The two of us with our *Thlaloca* the sole inhabitants on a steadily shifting circle of ocean. We sat in the cockpit of our little craft and watched her tireless motion, never a complaint, forever forging ahead to a new land without much effort on our part. My mind drifted back to a distant shore where mathematical minds put her down on the drawing board; a sterile blueprint that Siggi and I converted into something with a soul - *Thlaloca* - which in the following years would be an integral part of us, floating us safely and willingly over many thousands of miles around the world.

The weather remained truly excellent day after day. Every morning dawned with moisture laden heavy clouds moving slowly across our masthead but would disappear with the rising sun. The wind blew a steady force 3-4, and on rare occasions to five. The blue sky was sparingly dotted with puffy trade-wind clouds, and heavier ones lined the horizon north and south. Occasionally a black cumulus cloud would darken the sun for minutes. It was our worst weather. Some of the remarkable sights were the magnificent sunsets, reminiscent of California and Mexico. We had chosen this time for our evening meals, and nothing was more awe-inspiring than the red ball of fire, producing a multitude of colors which sank slowly beneath the sea. When the "great show" was over we already wished for more the following day.

Although bread and potatoes had run out after a week at sea, the meals Siggi produced on the one-flame Primus were something else to look forward to. The meals were simple but very tasty, and my ravenous appetite made Siggi doubtful whether our lockers were sufficiently stocked. Truthfully, though, our hold was crammed with all kinds of foodstuff, and just as well because had we relied on a fish diet, we would be dead. Despite trailing a hook day and night, we never caught a fish. These damn critters had a collective dislike toward us!

A cup of steaming instant coffee and some biscuits brightened all our mornings. A variety of food, such as pancakes, eggs, canned fruits, canned fish (not a joke) kept us going through the day. The main meal consisted mainly of fried canned meats, vegetables and rice, and normally different canned fruit for dessert. The latter, no doubt, was our favorite each day.

At noon when we crossed the latitude sight with the morning sight for longitude we added another circled-in dot on the chart, and discovered how little advance a hundred mile run is on a chart that encompasses an entire ocean.

By log, the boat sailed a consistent seventy to eighty miles per day. A powerful current boosted the total to anywhere between one hundred to one hundred and twenty miles. This is not much to a person accustomed to ocean liners and jet aircraft, but a hundred-mile average for a small sailboat, eighteen feet on the waterline, is very good. And the nicest thing of all, it doesn't cost a penny!

As this was our first ocean passage, the question foremost

in our minds was how much sail can we carry and still be safe? We felt vulnerable that something might happen if not careful - losing the mast, breaking the rudder, etc. - that would maroon us in the middle of a giant ocean. Besides that, with the ropes to tiller setup for self-steering, any sail-change would have required rearranging the whole. A lot of time consuming work we were reluctant to do. So we ambled on with no particular hurry to get anywhere fast. Only gradually did we gain the self-confidence, and faith in *Thlaloca* to burden her with everything we had on sails - and too many times too much for our own good!

A lot of reading material occupied our spare time during daylight hours, when we lay in our comfy canvas bunks with one leg braced against the mast to steady our roll. Paperback books were in great demand those days. Siggi's favorites were Perry Mason exploits, while I loved to read Micky Spillane. We like reading and had with us books on all kinds of subject; most of them too serious and lengthy. The best reading was the Readers Digest and the like - brief, action-packed stories.

Not so pleasant were the long nights. Once the sun had set, darkness followed quickly. With no lights in the boat (except an inadequate kerosene lamp) we were practically chained to the bunks for at least twelve hours until daylight broke. Of course, there were numerous checks on the rig and the compass. Any minor wind-shift was compensated by sliding the rubber band along the tiller - increasing or decreasing the pressure on the side necessary.

"Hein!" Siggi called from the cockpit. I was out there in five seconds flat and gazed in the direction Siggi was pointing. Seconds later we saw something long and shaped like a rocket cone flying a short distance through the air. It plunged back into the ocean with a loud thud. Shortly after, once more. Then we knew what we had heard occasionally during previous nights, when the impact had frightened us a lot. We guessed it to be giant squids. Hell, in that case we should not be on deck at all - isn't that what the book said? We retired below for more reading.

On the 27th day at sea, gannets and frigate birds were out en mass to alert us that land was near. We had our eyes glued at a particular spot on the far horizon where our navigational department had computed we could expect the nearest island.

But the day wore on and on with no land sighted. Siggi did

not say a word but exhibited that pronounced doubtful expression, that never failed to make me feel extremely uncomfortable. I rechecked the star-fix of the day before, the morning position line, the afternoon position line, and all added up to within fifteen miles of Hiva Oa Island. Perspiration was running down my body and my heartbeat on the increase - damn, what if we missed the blasted island? Thank God there was Australia several thousand miles to the west. We may miss islands, but not an entire continent!

Not long after, Siggi's jubilant voice cried out, "Land-ho," I felt the relief right down to my toes. When I did see the speck of land myself (for reason unknown, I was always last to recognize land) I could hardly believe it. We had been at sea for nearly a month with nothing to break the horizon, only the water and our small world to live with, and today, a day like twenty-seven others, there is a dot of a bluish mass distorting a perfect straight line of horizon - indeed "our island" had risen from the sea.

It was our last sunset on that passage and we watched it filled with emotion. This called for a good cup of coffee, laced with a shot of rum, "to celebrate!" That evening we were unable to follow the sun beyond the horizon for she disappeared behind the island of Hiva Oa, our destination. We hove-to ten miles east of the island to await daylight to guide us to an anchorage in Traitors Bay. Shortly after, a glorious full moon rose out of the sea, a spectacle so dramatic it had us gazing in total amazement, because the moon was as large as if it stood only yards away from us. The night remained wonderfully clear, lighted by the moon and millions of twinkling stars, and our island always a lovely sight.

With daybreak we made sail and soon closed with a steep-to coastline; around a headland and there was the opening to a narrow bay with two boats anchored in the middle, the *Kochab* and *Gannet*. We dropped our hook between them after a voyage of twenty-eight days.

☆

Ron from *Gannet* bumped alongside with his dinghy, and we all had a happy reunion on *Kochab*, where we exchanged all the extraordinary little happenings of the long passage. After that, the lot of us went ashore.

On the northeastern corner of the bay is a little pebble beach where our dinghy ground to a halt. From there it was only a short but rather steep walk to the village of Atuona, conveniently built in the shade of tall palm trees. These were necessary to shade the villagers from the oppressive heat in the open. Also, there seemed to be a lot fewer no-no-flies; a sort of fiercely bloodsucking blackflies that swarmed about us the minute we entered the bay - and we thought we had entered paradise!

The village held three immediate attractions: Siggi's mouth watered for the delicacy of freshly baked bread; mine for a cold beer; and we both were eager to collect our mail.

Mail first. We bought a stack of picture post cards, and lost no time in letting the outside world know of our "epic voyage across 3,000 miles of storm-swept ocean!"

A white man by the name of Charlie approached us. An architect by profession he hailed from San Francisco. Being on vacation he had visited many islands to study local architecture and interior design. Not only was Charlie a pleasant chap, he was also a born linguist. The short time he'd been in the islands he taught himself fluent Polynesian.

At the "Chinaman" store we bought two quart bottles of excellent Hinano beer. As it was not permitted to drink beer openly, we dug behind a low hedge, and among snorting pigs consumed the contents. The bakery lay handy across a small pasture. There Siggi and I indulged to satisfy our cravings.

Since Hiva Oa was not a Port of Entry, we expected to be asked to leave at once for Nukuhiva for clearing into French Polynesia. We ordered a dozen loaves of bread double baked - double baked extracts more moisture, therefore longer lasting.

One thing became obvious from the beginning, that nearly all business was conducted by the industrious Chinese. The reason may be that the Polynesian people live off the land, where everything is plentiful and free for the taking. With the intrusion of outside forces much has changed. If plenty of food and free love, and unbounded gaiety might still be the predominant stimulus by which their lives were measured, there were signs that a capitalistic lifestyle was not unattractive to them, as many low-powered Japanese motorbikes and transistor radios were abound, which underlined that kind of evolution. Unfortunately, to acquire that kind of wealth one must work and save, not easy for anybody, but a lot less attractive to freedom-loving natives, who even bought boiling water for tea or coffee from the "Chinamen."

A winding trail led us to a hut where an elderly native woman awaited us with a basket full of papayas, bananas and breadfruit. Of the multitude of fruits we had tasted so far, breadfruit was new to us. We retired to the beach, collected coconut husks and made a fire to fry the fruit. Along came a young native man. Our negative reply to his question, "You have meat?" had him running towards a long, low building a hundred yards away. He returned with chunks of fried tuna in a frying pan. Thus we met Mahine.

The taste of breadfruit did not excite our palates - the tuna yes! History tells us, that the purpose of Captain Bligh's voyage to Polynesia was to pick up a load of breadfruit plants, to be replanted in the West Indies, to feed the slaves there. The natives of the West Indies reject the taste of breadfruit to this day. We don't blame them one bit!

Mahine was helpful in many ways. Actually a native of Moorea, one of the Society Islands, he was brought to Hiva Oa to serve a nine month prison term. With other prisoners he was supposed to do roadwork eight hours a day. Normally, though, Mahine was found anywhere else but his workplace. When we collected our bread, he was fast asleep on one of the bread tables in the shop. Ask him for something, he delivered, for us it was a stock of bananas. Surely, the man wasn't much of a criminal, for he was entirely free during the day, and only locked up over night. Big, strong and well built he was popular with the *vahines*, which may have landed him in the coop.

The most remarkable fruit Mahine fetched for us was pamplemouse, or grapefruit as we know it. It was the most delicious kind we ever tasted. They come big, as much as a foot in diameter, juicy and very sweet.

The two boats had left for Nukuhiva Island to clear in. Why we were not asked to do likewise, we don't know. A couple of days later we cleared for Tahiti with the Chief of Police, when he expressed a desire to pay us a visit with his family that afternoon. The ensuing conversation was not exactly fluent as Siggi and I speak very little French. We conversed in a mixture of French, English, German and Spanish. It is always surprising that despite all these handicaps a conversation is possible - and this goes more to the credit of Siggi who never tires to extract the last detail.

Before we leave our first South Sea Island, it is only appropriate that we briefly touch on the turbulent history of the

WEST! SAIL WEST, MAN!

Marquesas Islands; which, in effect, was the tragic consequence of most islands around the world that was in contact
with white men.

Upon discovery it enjoyed a sizable population of a strong
and healthy race of people. Tribal-laws and cannibalism in particular were ruthlessly exercised until well into this century.
Whaling ships came to refill their depleted larders, and let their
tired crews recuperate. With them they brought venereal diseases and tuberculosis which almost wiped out the whole population. Only modern drugs saved the natives from total extinction. Very slowly the population was again on the increase.
And on this encouraging note we shall leave.

On a southwesterly course we stood for the island of
Rangiroa, one of the eighty-seven islands of the Tuamotu Archipelago. The day was sunny with not a cloud in sight, except
those deep on the horizon. The wind whined a gentle force
four, and *Thlaloca* under every stitch of canvas slithered ahead
at five knots, with a school of dolphins frolicking on both
bows. The wind held its promise only to nightfall when it
dropped to a breath, not even enough to work the self-steering.
Reluctantly we manned the tiller. It turned out to be a wonderful night, though, as the sky remained clear and Orion, that
brilliant constellation, accompanied by myriads of stars sparkled above us. The wind kept light as we progressed, our daily
runs however were excellent, indicating a good current in our
favor.

An almost dead calm prevailed the morning we expected to
raise the island. The sea was glassy and had an oily look, with
a haze lying over it of equal hue that totally obliterated the true
horizon. We were faced with a situation of which the Sailing
Direction gives stern warnings to mariners. With a far less vantage point compared to a ship, it meant for us to exercise increased caution. Despite a lively lookout we were unable to
sight the island. The visibility being what it was, an altitude
sight on the pale sun could never be relied on even though the
resulting position line cut right across the coral island, where it
ought to be!

Helped by a dollop of wind from the east we sailed along
the position line. Gradually the horizon cleared, but still no island. While Siggi checked the clock against a time-tick on the
radio, I crawled up the mast to the first set of cross-trees for a
better view. Unsuccessful in what I hoped to find, we decided

rather reluctantly to forget about the blasted island. It was an ugly blow to my reputation as a crackerjack navigator. But prudence dictated a course-change, directly for the island of Tahiti. Later, glancing in the direction of the island one more time, I was certain that my mind was playing tricks, I saw a long row of palm trees floating upright in the water, like a marching column of men on parade. There was our island, at last. Our gloomy spirits underwent a drastic transformation. The least it restored my reputation. We brought the trees dead on *Thlaloca's* keen bows which sliced the water at four knots, now that the wind had increased to a lively sailing breeze.

It was our first encounter with low coral islands and at once we realized the potential danger they represent. The Tuamotus Islands in particular are a classic example of the whole of the Pacific. The seventy-eight islands of that group with its far extending reefs and unpredictable currents constitute a huge trap line. The bleaching hulks of many a fine ship are constant reminders to never relax vigilance. And in spite of it, it will happen as it did to our good future friends, Bob and Nancy Griffith. They lost their fine sailing yacht *Awahnee* to a submerged reef there, only a couple of months before we met them in Papeete. A total loss. What made it even more tragic, that they were searching for a missing yacht!

Under full sails *Thlaloca* entered the narrow Avatoru Pass. We felt tense when suddenly the coral bottom reached up to us and we expected a grounding at any moment. But the crystal clear water had us fooled in the true depth of more than ten fathoms.

The anchor splashed down four fathoms and buried itself in the coral sand of the extensive lagoon. The temptation to follow was almost irresistible, but the report of an abundance of sharks within the lagoon had us scared off. Instead we accepted the invitation from a very dark-skinned native to step into his outrigger canoe, to be ferried ashore where there was already an assembled crowd of natives that greeted us reserved. A dignified old native stepped forward, and bowing gracefully he mumbled some words in English. We guessed him to be the chief. For a while we chatted over trivial things, when a boy approached and handed the headman some sea shells, and he in turn handed them to us. The were a fine collection, which put us at a loss of how to adequately show our appreciation. We were fortunate that Siggi had grabbed a couple packs of cigarettes on leaving the boat. Those, she handed to the good old man. This gesture produced more shells of every description, and also green coconuts. We had received so many shells that later on we had to give most away to find room for other gifts.

Two hours later we retreated back aboard where we stored the more valuable shells securely. We had to agree, that a welcome of that sort is worth every bit of tricky navigation. And it was only a modest beginning.

We had an all exciting day. We felt content but also very tired. But before we retired into our bunks we sat in the cockpit for a long while and inhaled deeply the intoxicating scent of Polynesia, while Sirius sparkled over our heads, and close by glistened Canopus, another great star of the south. The Southern Cross, then rising, was visible over a tight cluster of gently swaying palm trees. Never before had we had such satisfying feeling, now that we had brought our little ship amidst the splendor of true coral islands, to the gate of our dreams which, when it was all in the past, would enrich our memory for the rest of our lives. Siggi's definition, comparing *Thlaloca* to a "doghouse" and our lifestyle as less than that of a "dog's life," was the result of all the unpleasant experiences of our first year in sailing. From then on she believed the word "paradise" most appropriate.

☆

Sail was raised early one morning. Sailor's Eldorado - Tahiti, the magic pearl of the Pacific - had pulled persistently ever since we left Panama. The morning was glorious, the sort that make people happy to be born in our complicated world. Once the pass was cleared we performed a dogleg to port, a course that skirted the sandy coast of the island for several miles. After checking the chart, making sure that no unpleasant obstacles lay across our path, we settled comfortably in the cockpit to enjoy the sights of Polynesia.

Sailing only a cable length off the sheltering coral bulwark, the sea was as smooth as a pond. The water beneath the keel a deep blue, indicating great depth, was furrowed astern by a white wake as broad as our little ship is long. Only the hum of wind in the rigging and the gurgling sound of water along the boat's hull broke the deep silence around us. Above us was the sky in a color considerably lighter than the ocean blue, interspersed with puffy trade wind clouds as tender as fluffy cotton balls. Man, this is sailing - this is life. Grandiose!

To the Enchanted Islands

Once we had drawn abreast with the island's western perimeter, our course changed to southwest. With the change of direction, the weather changed also. Dark cumulus clouds gathered and crowded together to a solid mass. With it came squally winds that had us scrambling to reduce sail. This condition lasted throughout the night, and neither did it change much the following day. We got a lucky break when the dark clouds lifted for a fleeting moment and revealed Makatea Island only about two miles to our port. This excellent fix put Tahiti just "over the hill."

Down sails, up sails, was the call of the day. A couple of times we missed and that laid the boat on her beam ends. We finally let the reduced sails stand and let *Thlaloca* stumble on between the squalls. Night fell with no end of the bad weather in sight. It didn't deter us however from having many hours of good sleep.

Dawn came and the first rays of the rising sun enlightened our view with the spectacular "Pearl of the South Pacific". Still tinted in a bluish haze but changing to its true colors with every yard of progress. Soon it revealed deeply cracked hills and mountains, all blanketed with lush tropical vegetation. We could well imagine the impression of the early explorers when they spotted an island of such magnificent splendor.

The closer we came to Venus Point, the more the wind increased, as if to hurry us into the womb of eternal paradise. Sailing to within yards of the fringing reef on which seas broke incessantly, we sharply bore to the right on a course parallel to the reefline, where we hoped to find the pass into the lagoon and the harbor of Papeete.

The wind piping to twenty knots and better, *Thlaloca* was virtually flying under the press of the spinnaker, in the grandest of fashion. Matter of fact we had grave concern about how to get the chute down before we had to turn a sharp left into the lagoon. This thought was not even completed when the range markers were already upon us. Bringing the wind abeam, *Thlaloca* staggered under her enormous load of canvas, making the foot of the sail drag water to leeward. It was a grand finale to a 5,000-mile voyage from Panama.

Once in the silent water of the lagoon, the rocking-about stopped, and so did the wind. The creeping progress towards the harbor proper was utilized to clean the boat and ourselves. Encouraged by Siggi to make the best impression, I hacked away on a two-week old beard as stiff as a wire brush with a couple of old rusty razor blades. With everything under control we manned the paddles and headed towards a cluster of yachts neatly tied up to the seawall, that ran along the Main Street.

Soon a pilot boat bumped alongside. A casually dressed official with a bundle of papers under his arm jumped onto our deck inquiring, "Where do you come from?"

The usual answer and question period followed. After that we were helped to a mooring; squeezed into insignificance between two giant yachts, the 65-foot American yacht *Barlovento* and the almost as large French ketch *St. Briac*.

The arrival of an overseas yacht in Tahiti was always a special event, and never failed to attract a huge crowd along the pier. And no time was lost in meeting the people of other yachts. They stood waiting to introduce themselves, and to offer help and advice. There were the Wrights of the *Barlovento*, the Deprets of the *St. Briac*, Chris Christopher of *Hinano*, the crews of *Europe, Seawife, Paisano*. And there was the family Griffith - Bob, Nancy and Riedi. The family that had lost the *Awahnee* on a reef in the Tuamoto Islands. Lovely Nancy met us with a broad smile; a smile so sincere it instantly conveyed a deep feeling of camaraderie.

A homecoming could not have been more pleasant. Between introductions we positioned and fendered the boat, to be safe for the weeks of our intended stay. Once more I was called ashore to satisfy the questions of the immigration officer with the name of Gigi. One of the forms demanded a list of all the stores aboard, I answered with "Nil," and this was as close to the truth as I could.

Next came reporters who wanted the highlights of our voyage so far. Next day's papers read in headlines:

Tour Du Monde Sur Un Bateau 20 Pieds.

Then it was time to grab one of the water hoses lying about and rinse the salt off our hides and the boat. It not only cleaned our bodies but also rejuvenated our spirits to digest in full all the wonderful things for which Tahiti is famous for.

The sun was setting like a fiery ball in the western sky, and the lively Tahitian night life already in full swing, when we rushed off to a party on the *Barlovento*. What a treat to sit around a large cockpit, well cushioned on six inches of closed-cell foam, among a crowd of a dozen people. The cocktails and snacks harmonized splendidly with the amplified recorded music in the background. The two Chinese waiters wore running shoes to satisfy the thirst of the assembly. This party continued the next day on *St. Briac*. A pattern that repeated itself nonestop.

Only a short walk separated us from Quinns, a notorious nightclub with a shady reputation. But anyone worth his salt could not miss a visit at least once. It was the hangout for the French Legionnaires, whose pugnacious attitude was mostly rewarded with an all-out fight. It so happened that one of the *vahines* chose the time of our presence to tell a large audience her intimate exploits of the previous night she had with a Legionnaire by the name of Hugo; a mighty big Italian who was sitting beside me. When she graphically mimicked the action, he became increasingly irritated and finally jumped at her and slapped her face. His action made us all jump in a desperate leap for the door. Chairs were flying, tables turned on edge for protection, and everybody pounded away on somebody. Anyone with sense beat a hasty retreat. It included Siggi and me.

On another visit we sat around a table, with leis of Tiare Tahiti slung around our necks, and single flowers displayed on every prominent part on our heads; nearly everyone exhaling huge clouds of smoke into the dense bluish murk. Occasionally we swung our rusty sea-legs to lively music. Only a faint idea we had about the proper display of flowers. Frankly, we cared very little about it in the exuberant mood we were in. Apparently, the custom is to wear a flower behind your left ear when single, the right ear when married (or vice-versa, we forgot). Presenting flowers behind both ears signified married but still available. A category I represented! That something was contrary came to light when one of the amorous *vahines* clung herself dangerously close to my side - Susi-no-pants her name - ignoring completely the poisonous arrows Siggi was piercing at us. To keep the peace in our closely knit family I chose to treat the girl indifferently, and invited Siggi to a swinging dance.

Another native girl of ill repute was Fani, very beautiful and with scantlings just perfect. The only blemish of an otherwise perfect appearance was her gaping mouth with not a tooth in it. It was said, that an American had fallen in love with her, and to bolster her looks he furnished the money that put a set of teeth into her mouth. When the fellow had to attend to business in the States, he extracted from her the promise to remain faithful to him. When on his return he learned of her failings, he simply removed the choppers and said "good-bye".

With another fight in the offing, we retreated aboard the *Hinano*, where a party was in full swing. As any newcomer to the island, we were given the traditional welcoming song, sung by three *vahines*. It went something like this:

" Hallo captain, how are you?
Hallo captain, we are yours!
We love you,
Yes, we do,
Goddamn son-of-a-bitch what's the matter you?"

Hilarious laughter followed, we joined with equal enthusiasm. The sun had already broken a new day when we stumbled back aboard *Thlaloca*, to gobble up strength for the next round.

The next day we were all done up Tahitian style. With the crew of the *Windsong* and Bob and Nancy Griffith we ventured out into the hills, on the outskirts of town, to mingle and dance with a large native crowd. There we met happy and laughing people who expected you to smile with them, charming girls with their intermixture of blood - French, Polynesian, Chinese. This was Polynesia, conquered not by missionaries, but rather by love of life.

Gaiety and easy going are the trademarks of the islanders, and it has an immediate effect on its visitors. We yachties have it all over the normal tourists, simply because we have the means to hang around for a long time, free of the burden that pertains to those who are dependent on commercial transportation shifting from one island to another. In most cases the normal tourist has a time schedule far too short to explore in detail "Gods little acres." Whatever it may be, it's the little floating home - our doghouse - that makes it so convenient. Cramped and sticky it may be at times, nevertheless it is there after a grueling day of sightseeing, etc.. We are free at all times to pursue whatever our fancy dictates without being encumbered in finding suitable lodging. Once an island has exhausted its charm, it is a simple exercise to break the hook and search for another haven perhaps even more fascinating. Time looses its meaning; what is another day, a month? As long we have fresh water in our tanks, we are self-sufficient with an abundance of fish crowding the water, and local grown food available almost anywhere, at a reasonable cost.

Ouch! Don't take the last literally because French Polynesia

Between the *Barlovento* and the *Saint Briac*

Above: Tahiti Waterfront. Below: Haul-out on the *Fernstar*.

can be blooming expensive. We recall that the cost of a pound of potatoes in California was three cents (1963). It was fifteen cents in Papeete, and similar differences prevailed on every item. Once we ventured outside the tourist-traps, the prices became more reasonable.

When alone, Siggi and I converse much in German, and so we did one day promenading along the row of yachts tied to the seawall, when an elderly couple approached us with the words: *Nun, wo kommt Ihr denn her?* (Where do you come from?) Thus we met Eric and Lulu Heyer, perpetual travelers from Malibu, California. Promptly we received an invitation to tour the island in their rented car. It suited us perfectly.

That day was certainly the highlight during our stay in Tahiti, for we saw much of the island's four hundred square miles of lush, green foliage, cascading waterfalls, gurgling creeks, strange black and dazzling white beaches under whispering palm trees. The whole island seemed to be ornamented in acres of fragrant flowers - frangipani, purple and red bougainvillea, hibiscus - a symphony of color and fragrance. Occasionally we parked to cool off in the water of a motionless lagoon. At Faaone, the island split in two, connected only by a narrow isthmus. The smaller part of the island is called Tahiti-iti (small Tahiti).

Back in Papeete after dark, we concluded the day with a steak dinner at the gorgeous Matavai Hotel. We parted with the fine couple in the knowledge that we had found lasting friends, who from there-on took genuine interest in our voyage.

The following day found Papeete in a festive mood, more pronounced than any day previous. The news had spread that the New Zealand cruiser, the *Royalist*, was about to enter harbor on a visit. Sure enough, soon after, the gray silhouette of the man-O-war was crawling along the outer reef. This caused a mad rush towards the proposed mooring site, to witness the traditional welcome display by wildly swinging *vahines*.

When the *Royalist* moved slowly towards the pier, there was no tug to assist the ship in her labor to get alongside the quay, true to the tradition of British Navy ships to moor unassisted in foreign ports.

Half a dozen of us boarded *Barlovento*'s Whaler and motored to a good vantage point from where we could watch the ensuing festivities. With the last line secured ashore, the music was on. The tamure dance was performed by a couple of dozen dusky island maidens and their male counterparts. Grass skirts shook to the frenzied rhythm of wooden drums. The beat increased to a crashing crescendo, as the girls' hips circled slowly at first but gained momentum to sheer incredible speed. It all looked very pretty and created much excitement. It sure brought home to us the thought how hard it will be to part with this place.

The *Royalist* left harbor several hours later, with a very sour crew we imagined, having been stirred up and not given a chance to take advantage of all the exciting possibilities. Curse the bloody navy!

Next was the liner *Mariposa* that entered the harbor, and all the gaiety and dancing repeated itself. What really shocked us was the appearance of the passengers. The cruise originated in California. Compared to the generally tanned local people, the passengers looked like walking corpses. It was difficult to imagine that we ever looked that sickly ourselves.

Every morning began with an unwritten ritual. First a few minutes in the cockpit to inhale the fragrance of Polynesia - Tiare Tahiti and vanilla. Then we jumped from the boat into the "main street" (the pier was practically in one with the main-street) to hose ourselves down. After that, about 6 a.m., Siggi strolled leisurely to the market, to collect a couple of French-sticks freshly baked, and any other food that was needed through the day. By the time Siggi returned I would have the coffee brewed, and we had a simple breakfast.

It differed one fine morning, when a mass of people rushed towards the end of the quay and the moored yachts. "What is it all about?" we asked.

"*Valrosa* is coming, *Valrosa* is coming!" Who or what is *Valrosa,* we asked ourselves. Judging by the effort that was made in crowding together several yachts, it meant a yacht of some prominence was expected. It was custom, that any vessel approaching was reported to the authorities by the lighthouse keeper on Venus Point. (It should be remembered that many devices that are taken for granted today were unavailable in those days (1963) such as a VHF radio).

The *Valrosa* was a large French schooner, that soon appeared off the outer reef. That's when the mood of the natives stirred to a feverish pitch. The ship was old, but so lovely. The brass and the brightwork sparkled over every inch of her one hundred feet. The crew must have worked hard to bring her up to such high standard. She was a graceful ship. The ornamented wheelhouse sat squarely on the bleached teak deck. Her tall varnished spars reaching far towards a cloud-speckled sky. She certainly had the potential to give us all a super show had she left her sails standing. Instead, the skipper chose the easy way, blowing a cloud of diesel smoke. Still, it was exciting. The one-legged skipper and the large crew were all dressed Tahitian style, and the moment contact with the shore was established, lovely *vahines* rushed aboard and laid leis around the crew's necks, and the hugging and kissing continued for a long while. To the disgust of some envious characters ashore! (A few months later, *Valrosa* was lost on a reef).

One after another our sailing friends we met in Panama drifted in; somewhat less spectacularly though. The *Kochab* was first, followed closely by *Elsie* with Frank Casper. Next came the *Atom* with that indomitable Frenchman Jean Gau. Jean had made the longest passage. Intending to call on Pitcairn Island, he was unable to land there on account of bad weather, Papeete was his first harbor after Panama, after seventy-two days.

That evening the reunion was celebrated on the *Kochab*, where Doc Evans grilled a dozen steaks on a charcoal hibatchi, mounted over the stern of his yacht. This being a special occasion, Doc opened the bilge to bring to light several jugs of excellent Mount Gay Rum, still from the West Indies.

As yachts came in from every point of the compass, there were also some that left, but our little community of overseas yachts never dropped below half a dozen and never more than ten. *Paisano*'s turn to leave came first. John Hazelhurst, the owner, had just married a very beautiful Tahitian girl. Half the island's population had congregated on the pier, crying their eyes out as the yacht gained an offing. Next was the *Europe*, a big ketch, which had Princess Grace of Monaca as her Godmother. They were on a picture and film-making tour around the Pacific.

"Darn," said Siggi, "I like it here more every day, we could make a living here, couldn't we?" A highly significant statement I had listened to in many places since we parted from Long Beach, and would in many more beyond. I hurried to get *Thlaloca* ready for the sea again, or be doomed to never cross the world. No doubt, Tahiti was another place in the world so easy to throw in the towel - at least as easy as it was for the many who did.

Just then the Griffiths had bought a French yacht, the *America*. She was seventy years old and needed a lot of TLC to get her anywhere near in condition so she could face the southern ocean in the winter. They had plans to sail her to New Zealand. Bob asked us to lend a hand. The prospect of making a few dollars delighted us, and perfectly fitted Siggi's desire to hang onto Tahiti a little longer.

We did a lot of work to that old lady, but in the company of Bob and Nancy, work was pleasure. In New Zealand the Griffiths wanted to build a new *Awahnee*. In fact, we decided to sail to New Zealand in company, as much as that was possible.

With the *America* operational, Siggi and I had one more job, cleaning *Thlaloca*'s dirty bottom. The prospect of getting hauled in Tahiti looked grim, as the boatyard had a long waiting list, and the cost of a haul-out outrageous. All we could afford was to take her to clean water within the lagoon and scrape the bottom by diving on her.

A much better solution presented itself in the shape of two Norwegian Merchant Marine officers who were walking along the row of yachts and were talking to the owners or crew. Our *Thlaloca* impressed them enormously, we invited them aboard for a drink. As we mentioned our itinerary, leaving for points west as soon we had scraped the bottom of the boat, they offered us a haul-out on their 8,000 ton *Fernstar*.

The slings were around *Thlaloca*'s hull the following morning, and up she went, no problem! Even though we had our own excellent Balboa paint, the officers insisted on the much superior Norwegian paint. No problem there either! The seamen got a tremendous kick out of it, and there was more help around than *Thlaloca*'s small bottom could accommodate. We were pushed aside to act as supervisors. The ship's "chippy" even had his tools handy to shave down the wood fairings on the keel. In no way were we able to adequately repay their kindness. We did it with two cases of Beck's beer, which we bought out of the ship's store

Next day, before dark, *Thlaloca* was back in the water, and we motored back to her mooring. We noticed that she moved ever so lightly, eager to tackle a few more thousand miles before the next haul-out.

On May 15th we made our rounds to say so-long to the

many new friends. On the way we paid the bill: Pilot fees, water and mooring for six weeks came to $2.85. We did not complain!

Loaded with leis around our necks we boarded *Thlaloca*. A light wind blew us clear of the outer reef, where we, as is tradition, placed the leis in the water, to be carried by the waves back to shore, which sealed our pledge that we would return someday.

Returning from *Fernstar* (Photo by Nancy Griffith)

From Venus Point, with Moorea Island in the distance

XIII

ISLAND-HOPPING

Ten miles to the northwest sprawls the small but very impressive island of Moorea, by many seafaring folks judged the most beautiful island in the Pacific. A fair wind blew us to within a mile off Cook's Bay, when the wind stopped suddenly. But *America* was close at hand to throw us a line, on which we entered the pass into a dazzling bay, passing close to a French man-O-war that got wrecked there many years ago.

The Griffiths who had visited most of the Society Islands previously still with their *Awahnee*, knew exactly where to go, a small indentation, called Robinson Cove, at the far end of the bay. With deep water right up to the palm-studded beach, *America* moored with the anchor over the stern and the bow tied to a palm tree. Thus we were able to get ashore without getting wet, via *America*'s bowsprit. But who had any desire staying dry with so much tepid water around us, and so inviting. Diving around for shells, we noticed *America*'s bottom totally covered with barnacles. Industrious Bob made immediate arrangements to scrape her. With hardly any tidal actions in that part of the world, there are two ways to do the job. One is to skin or scuba dive to scrape, but less strenuous is careening - haul a vessel down on the mast until she is lying on her beam-ends. And that we did.

After removing a score of miscellaneous items from the boat and piled them up ashore, the old lady was grounded

135

softly. With heavy tackles rigged from the masthead to convenient palm trees, we began to haul her down. She did not come easily and muttered some awful grunts, but with six hands pulling on a couple of six-part tackles, she didn't have much chance to resist and soon was lying on her side, ready to be attacked by scrapers and brushes. After one side was completed, we swung her 180 degrees and the whole procedure was repeated.

The following day we took some photographs while sailing within the bay. Later we celebrated Nancy's birthday, for which Bob produced a bottle of champagne to toast the occasion.

The nights were lovely, and everything was quiet and serene. The stillness was only broken now and then by the gentle swish of the anchor line when it was tightened by the undertow. The heavy surf on the outer reef was as rhythmic as if some subterranean giant was breathing. And from ashore one could hear the occasional "thump" of a fallen coconut.

One evening we spent with a family Kelly, who lived in a charming home a short walk from the cove. They had been living on the island for much of their lives, and therefore had many stories to tell about yachts that had called there over past decades. There were many we had read about in books, and which had inflamed our desires.

Very early one morning we cast off the lines for the ninety-mile sail to the next island - Raiatea. Lack of wind prompted the use of the motor. The hideous noise it caused roused the birds to leave the bay. Some mustered enough courage to investigate what in their opinion had to be total idiots, since no one in their right mind would show so little respect to neighbors this early in the morning. Sorry, birds! Should there be a next time for us, it will be a quiet little diesel, you won't hear a thing!

Once in the open, we picked up a nice easterly breeze that had us in a close race with the *America*, sailing half a mile to leeward. By nightfall we lost sight of each other, and we made the best of a wind that had fallen light. By sunrise we lay becalmed just south of Huahine Island, in a sea as flat as the pancakes Siggi was preparing for breakfast. The pancakes were delicious, well seasoned with margarine and syrup, all still left over from Panama. The lot we washed down with a couple mugs of lukewarm Nescafe. It was a meal that would please a king!

Island Hopping

To help the digestive process, we lay on our bellies on the after deck, heads protruding past the stern, and watched the fish swim by. Also we waited for wind. Tired of waiting I reluctantly manned the paddle. Soon we noticed bubbles along the waterline that made us very happy because it meant progress. Siggi's mathematical conclusion averaged four bubbles per yard of advance through the water. I thought this to be a lot of bubbles and did not hesitate to clock the speed at ½-1 knot. This my nit-picking mate did not agree with. To prove it she got a wad of paper and the stopwatch. The piece of paper she diligently chucked over the bow, starting the watch. Hurrying aft - a totally unnecessary exercise - she had a long wait for the paper to arrive, and to be clocked. Thus equipped with irrefutable data she went below. Her computation gave us three-tenths of a knot. Disappointed, I "boated" the oar!

Cat's-paws helped us to within two cable-length off the fringed reef guarding a large lagoon wherein lie the two principal islands - Raiatea and Tahaa. The town of Uturoa is the main settlement on Raiatea, where we had to report in with the gendarmerie to clear. Also it was our meeting place with the *America*. Unfortunately, all we had for a guide to find the pass and the town, was a pencil drawing a fellow cruiser had given us in Tahiti. He had neglected to indicate a single bearing. No matter how we rotated the blasted piece of paper it didn't match the locality.

"Hold on!" Siggi exclaimed, "there is a motorboat headed our way." It was racing full bore along the reef-line, impossible to miss us, so we could ask for directions. When the boat was near we motioned to come close, instead he pointed towards the sky behind us and never even throttled down.

Not sure about the significance of his motions - disappointed about his neglect - we looked behind us and we knew what was meant, an ugly looking line-squall was bearing down on us.

To face such a black mass of evil out at sea is nothing to get excited about, but crowded against a deadly reef was enough to turn our stomachs sour. We grabbed the paddles to gain a few yards away from the reef, and we stopped only when the storm was upon us with great fury. The water dropped on us by the tons, to be picked up by the wind and driven horizontally in sheets, blotting out any visibility. The weight of such a tropical downpour is so heavy that we doubt it would ripple the water more than six inches high. No denying, we were scared while it lasted, and fearful of being driven into danger. But a storm of that sort is short lived. Once the sun was back, there was no indication that we had moved significantly.

The squall had left us with some wind that helped us to attain a safer offing for the night. We hove-to and anxiously awaited the following morning.

At daybreak the sun peaked over the horizon large and clear, indicating little wind. With the tiny bit that was, we worked ourselves close to the reef-line again in search for the pass. When we finally found something that resembled the drawing we turned in, at the same moment Riedi (the son of the Griffiths) was sailing towards us on his surfboard. They actually had observed us from the deck of the *America*.

Now that we were united again, we all walked to the gendarmerie to be cleared. On the way we decided to push on to a little motu off the island of Tahaa, which promised good diving and fishing.

We followed the *America* in tow, as the wind was nil. The passage through acres of multicolored reefs turned out to be very exciting. The Griffiths with years of experience in reef navigation took some of the most intricate channels we would never have dared - at least not at that time. By late afternoon both boats were safely tied up to palm trees off the tiny motu.

One yacht was already there, the 38-foot Australian ketch *Windsong*. They had left Tahiti several days before us with destination Hawaii. It seemed they were not in a particular hurry.

The crew of the *Windsong* was out spear-fishing, while Bob and I dove for shells in about two fathoms. As a total greenhorn, I had no idea of what to look for to find shells on the ocean floor, and I'm grateful to Bob that he taught me the essentials. By nightfall we had a fire going with dried coconut husks as fuel, to fry the freshly caught fish and some huge steaks the Griffiths had bought in Uturoa. Some natives joined us later, and danced and played guitar straight into our hearts, under a night sky of tropical splendor. Old Captain Walker, the skipper of the *Windsong*, who had spent most of his life at sea, gave the evening a special note by relating some fantastic tales from the past. His yarn was heavily spiced with expressions like "fair dinkum" and "not a word of lie." Nancy, of course, one of the best storytellers we know, gave some of her best. It all contributed to an indelible night.

The *Windsong* finally set sail for Hawaii, while we sailed the short distance to Tahaa, and there secured our boats to palm trees again in a bay of outstanding beauty. The skipper of the American yacht *Seawife*, whom we had met in Papeete, had given us the name of his native friend there, Meteta, who actually had sailed on the *Seawife* to New Zealand and back. He was a very handsome young man, powerful and built like a statue. The small plantation he worked with his wife occupied the ridge of a steeply rising hill. Taking advantage of his invitation to meet his family, we walked the pleasant soft and moist ground under a solid umbrella of tall palm trees for a quarter of a mile, when we came upon a typical island hut, built mostly with bamboo sticks and palm fronds - the family's home.

Mrs. Meteta, in the process of frying platanos for the midday meal, received us like old friends, followed by an invitation to be part at the dinner table. Siggi and I recalled that we tasted something similar in Central America and we didn't fancy it. It was surprising how good it tasted now. Perhaps it was the ambiance that gave it the spice needed to make it more palatable.

Meteta was anxious to show us his land where there grew a profusion of fruit - yams, taro, papayas, bananas, coffee, etc.. We were given the choice to pick anything we wanted. Gradually the pickings accumulated to a sizable heap, when finally we had to decide on how to get it all down the steep hill, which since last night's rain had become as slippery as ice. Bearded Bob, with an enormous stack of bananas balancing on his broad shoulders, was the first to chance the treacherous trail. Ten seconds later we watched as two separate bundles cascaded down the hill. It looked so comical that we developed stomach cramps from laughter. I was next with the same result, exuberantly applauded by the gang still up the hill. Bob and I had our revenge when we watched the two girls came tumbling down screaming their heads off. Only Meteta made it without a problem, at the same time collecting the spilled fruits from an area that looked like a war zone.

Besides the fruits and vegetables, we were given a bag full of green coffee beans and bottled homemade sun lotion. We were told that it was made of coconut oil and Tiare Tahiti extracts. Whatever it was made off, it smelled quite good and did its job well.

We invited the couple aboard, where we rewarded their generosity with items of great demand - clothing, custom jewelry, fish hooks, etc.. The Griffiths who had sailed all the islands before several times had the boat loaded with presents of that sort and therefore contributed most. All we could do, was to give what we could spare out of our meager supply.

Young Riedi, nine years old, was really a wonderful chap and one of the best all-around hands one could wish for. Long years of sailing, and almost continuously exposed to the company of older people gave him a knowledge and understanding much beyond his years. All on his own he stood watches in any kind of weather. He handled and trimmed sails, and he was a good cook. For the short run to Bora Bora it was agreed he should sail on *Thlaloca*, a boat more to his size than the 53-foot *Awahnee* or the 43-foot *America*. Siggi appreciated the chance to sail on a boat more her size for a change.

The *Thlaloca* left first, with *America* to follow later. The sun was still too low for spotting underwater dangers, and as there was no wind, it required the use of the outboard motor. I was aware of an underwater reef that extended for a considerable distance from a spit of land we had to round. Motoring along the reef for a long while, I was sure it was safe to make the course-change to starboard. Riedi was just hoisting the mainsail when he spotted the shallow reef ahead. He was petrified and couldn't speak a word, but the bewildered look on his face made me cut off the motor - at the exact instant we hit the reef. Rocking the boat and pushing with the boathook, we managed to get off. We backtracked carefully, and minutes later we were back alongside the *America*.

Checking the inside of the boat, there was water all over the shallow bilges. I cursed my lack of proper caution. And to be sure, nothing is worse than a leaking boat that needs constant attention. Moreover, for the next several months, on our planned track, there was no haul-out facility available,

Bob and I dove to check the impact, which was easily found on the fin-keel. Lucky there! Therefore, the leak could only come through strained keel bolts.

In the meantime my industrious mate was busy mopping up the water, and by so doing had the marvelous idea to taste it.

"It's sweet water," she exclaimed. That had Bob and me

140

looking at each other incredulously. So much for the all-knowing so-called experts!

Well, it is not only Riedi I consider the best hand around a boat, but there is that little gorgeous lady of mine, she is the greatest. Well deserved to carry the title "Admiral" from then on. Pass the bottle!

What had happened, a five-gallon plastic water container had tipped over from the impact and had blown the spout.

Both boats left the bay together, with Siggi back aboard *Thlaloca*. She and I needed her more than ever, because she is our lucky star.

Out on the ocean, only the lightest of wind gave us steerage way. At snail's pace we crept along a seemingly endless wall of reefs, on which the long Pacific swell broke furiously, giving us a fantastic sight. Those combers were huge, spewing spray a hundred feet up in the air. Somehow we felt uneasy, perhaps in the knowledge that one would have no chance to survive if caught in such fury. Yet, some do! As Bill Proctor did at Wallis Island. He was sailing a sister-ship to ours out of England, and one night was caught by the swell and thrown clear into the lagoon. That time he was lucky. The next time it happened (no-one knows what did) he was dead, never to be found! Perhaps it is skill to survive the oceans. More likely it is luck, in our opinion!

The *Malis*, a charter yacht out of Tahiti passed close by, and we exchanged greetings. Little did we know that we just had exchanged greetings with two popular fellows in the music field, the Beetles. A third member we later met at Bora Bora. There, people were surprised that we hadn't heard about this pop-group. We realized how much contact we had lost with the outside world; and people could not comprehend how lucky we considered ourselves having missed it all!

The pass into the extensive lagoon is broad and we had to use the motor to buck the strong out-flowing current. Such a current is present in almost every pass, and is caused by the volume of water that is thrown over the fringed reef - what goes in must go out - it is that simple!

We tied up to the government pier, where we corrected *America*'s steering problem. Later we shifted to a small jetty off the Bora Bora Hotel. Aside from Tahiti, Bora Bora is probably the best known island in the Society Group. At least to the tourists, who come en mass on regular passenger liners,

WEST! SAIL WEST, MAN!

the *Mariposa* and the *Monterey*. With no port facilities available, the ships anchor and then shuttle the passengers back and forth. In this way, a tourist gets perhaps a more lasting impression of a tropical island, than Tahiti for instance, where it is more convenient. Of course, no island will escape for long the vast advancing commercialism, and with the potential of Bora Bora, it would not have to wait long.

At that time there was only a small airfield with regular flights to Tahiti. Tourism was still low key.

Bicycles were the only transportation available, and we rented two for a round-trip of the island. What roads there were, were excellent by island standards, and these were built by the American Seabees, who held a large base there during World War II. Not only did they built roads but contributed wholesomely in the production of blue-eyed Polynesians!

The following day we sailed about the bay to explore the shoreline and perhaps find a good anchorage. Fronting a village there was a small jetty to which we tied up for the last night in Polynesia. Tomorrow the ocean would call again.

We called at the local bakery for bread too early next morning, we were told it wouldn't be ready for another two hours. The Griffiths decided to wait for it, while we pushed off. With very little wind in the forecast, it wouldn't take them long to catch up, by using their engine.

The wind so reluctant to show itself the past two weeks didn't behave differently that morning. By sundown we had sailed barely five miles. With darkness falling quickly in these latitudes we were worried that we may miss *America* - our bread! But just then they hove in sight at the precise instant the impressive skyline of Bora Bora disappeared in the darkness.

We were sad to leave those wonderful islands. We looked back many times, perhaps we were granted one more glimpse of what soon would only be memories of places and friends that now were reduced to addresses in our logbook. What is cruising really? But a process of constant parting with something or somebody we had become accustomed to love.

The *America* motored close by, for Nancy to hand us the eagerly awaited bread wrapped in a plastic bag. Fresh bread, fried eggs on "bully-beef" were our evening meal that night. No doubt, we were living high on the hog! Throughout the night we sailed within sight of each other in variable light winds.

By noon the next day we had advanced sixty-four miles

142

towards the island of Mopelia. There we intended to skin-dive on the wreck of the *Seeadler*. This German vessel was a square-rigged sailing ship. During World War I she was equipped with guns and sent out to raid Allied shipping. Chased by the British and badly in need of a refit, especially the bottom needed cleaning, Count Felix Luckner, her skipper, decided on the isolated coral island Mopelia as a likely spot to work undisturbed. It all ran smoothly until a tidal wave set the ship hard aground on a reef, where she eventually broke up. Several months later, the entire crew ended up in a prisoner-of-war camp in New Zealand.

During the day, both yachts drifted off in different directions in search of wind. As none was found, *America* joined us again late in the afternoon for the night. Nancy's call for "chow-chow" we answered with heaving a line over to her, to draw both boats together for us to jump aboard the big boat. After that we set *Thlaloca* adrift, to avoid bumping together while we were below eating. We could not help but take to the deck often, making sure she didn't escape, and to observe her from an entirely new perspective. She looked so tiny but so unbelievably lovely, rolling gently in the long Pacific swell, nodding her bow reassuringly, as if promising her loyalty forever. This she proved more so by always crowding in on us instead of falling off. Siggi and I felt so proud to be part of her.

Indications were that the night would remain calm. To keep in touch, Bob handed us one of his walkie-talkies. He also was going to display a powerful pressure lamp.

A good sailing breeze sprung up shortly after, to which both yachts hoisted every stitch of sail. With *America* forging ahead fast, we struggled to get the "chute" set, but in the darkness we got hopelessly tangled up in lines, we had to call it off. Bob's message over the radio was, "Well, folks, this is it. See you in Mopelia!"

The light on *America* had gone, but also the wind. What was left of it gave us, by my estimate. half a knot - the Admiral's far less! When the light on *America* became visible again, I manned the paddle to close the gap, and by four o'clock in the morning we were even. Satisfied with that, we turned our attention back on the fouled-up "chute," and had it up shortly. Drawing poorly, still, we had overtaken our friends by at least a mile before the break of dawn. What happened next is what Nancy told us later in Rarotonga.

She had been on watch and seen us sneaking by. Bob, unaware of this, emerged from below stretching his sleepy limbs, sure of good progress while the wind lasted, looking aft he remarked, "I wonder how far back *Thlaloca* is?" To which Nancy replied, "Don't look aft, look forward!" We had the feeling that Bob never really forgave us for that,

"You never showed a light!" But we really did, only it was far less powerful than theirs. Anyway, the calm prevailed, and we hitched a tow to within sight of Mopelia Island. It was late in the afternoon when we arrived off the narrow pass, only about thirty feet wide. The water was boiling from an outgoing current and it looked very treacherous to us. We got into the maelstrom while still a cable length off shore. We got out of it! *America* was motoring against it for a long while, but having insufficient power to overcome the adverse current, she finally gave up. We shaped a course for Rarotonga, the main island of the Cook Islands.

The wind so unsteady over the past ten days showed remarkable improvement by nightfall. Clouds made up and the wind freshened to force six, which put *America* over the horizon in a short time. Bob's message over the radio said,

"Well, folks, it looks like the real thing. We'll be seeing you in Rarotonga. Good luck, good speed - over and out!"

Bob must have been the most frustrated man on that passage, when in the morning he saw tiny *Thlaloca* wiggle away merrily on his port bow. The deep grin on his face revealed the fine sportsman he was. If he was frustrated with this crazy weather pattern, so were we. But not for much longer. Towards noon, threatening cumulus clouds moved up from the southeast and at once gave us all the wind we ever hoped for. Very turbulent at that, with a huge amount of rain. The *America*, with all sails drawing soon disappeared into a downpour, and that was the last we saw of her until Rarotonga. We were alone again. And no message from Bob either!

In general it may be said, it was like entering a new weather zone. The excellent weather we experienced on the whole since we had left Panama was over for good. From then on the wind blew much more forceful and unsteady. We had to wait for the South Atlantic to give us back what we had lost.

It blew, it rained, it thundered throughout that night, and only by morning did it clear briefly with a settled wind from the southeast. We promptly set our dark-red kite, which sped

Island Hopping

Thlaloca through the water up to seven knots. By degrees the wind crept forward of the beam, so down came the balloon, and the mainsail to its first reef. Occasionally it blew great guns, with rain so thick it felt like being submerged. The sails had to come down many times during the following days.

When Rarotonga Island peeked over the horizon it was bearing southeast. Not exactly the approach we hoped for, as it kept us hard on the wind which was gusting fresh over the mountainous island. By late afternoon however, every trace of wind had vanished and left us wallowing in a crazy sea. *Thlaloca's* mast was swinging wildly, and the motion caused havoc in our digestive tracts. The pint of fuel still left in the tank of the outboard motor gained us yards, and the only resource left was the paddles. It exhausted us rather quickly.

We counted the empty fuel bottles, sure enough, a quart was missing. That the missing one had to be a full one was a foregone conclusion. While Siggi was steering to gain an inch or two, I searched through the lazaret. Nothing found, we concluded that it had slipped under the cockpit - supported by a similar experience we had once before.

We had to find this bottle under the cockpit, as we could not leave it there for safety reasons alone. But to get under the cockpit was an exercise that would do credit to an acrobat. Besides, the approach was barred by numerous items that had to be removed first. All of it I piled in heaps in the bunks. The final obstacle was a five gallon water container that had to be lifted out of the restricted side compartment to free the manhole. The temperature inside the boat was probably ninety degrees and contributed much to my discomfort, I cursed to make it bearable. To lift a fifty-pound container in a most awkward position is a job for a he-man. The physical as well as the mental strength this demanded can only be mustered when a person is desperate. Somehow the container got out of the hole. At that instant *Thlaloca* gave one of her violent jerks, for which she was famous, and sent all the nicely staked heaps helter-skelter. I left it and instead wiggled myself underneath the cockpit to search for a lousy quart of petrol; knowing darn well it would be a quart I almost busted my guts for.

Only faintly I heard Siggi's jubilant outcry, "I found it!" Where else but the lazaret! It was enough to make me cry!

I dumped the fuel into the tank, started the motor, and let Siggi steer for the pass, while I went below to bring things

145

back to normal. An hour or so later we moored alongside the *America*, which surprisingly had arrived only two hours ahead of us. Immediately, Nancy rushed to the nearest public phone and notified the authorities of our arrival. The result was disappointing. We were told that we had entered after office hours. Not true! Should we wish to be cleared that afternoon it would cost us ten pounds sterling plus taxi fare. If not, we were ordered to anchor out for the night. This we did, but not before Nancy had handed us two loaves of bread and a dish with butter.

The customs official came an hour later in his private car and asked if we wanted to be cleared for the requested fee. We declined. This behavior was strange. It was obvious the official was being nasty. As we heard later he was even despised by the local people. True is the fact, that there are rotten apples even in paradise. We personally could not complain - the case just quoted was more in the category of small-mindedness. Not so in the case of the yacht *Sarabande* two weeks earlier - same place, same officer. The yacht had come in to tie up. One of the crew jumped ashore to belay the lines, and he was charged with violation of customs law. The officer's colleagues made him realize how ridiculous the charge was, accordingly he withdrew.

The following morning we were cleared without ill feelings. In fact, in any dealings we had with him later we found him most cordial.

Lovely Nancy, who would never suppress a good story, entertained us with the following: The *America* had arrived two hours ahead of us. Because of the bad weather on the passage, Bob had told the customs official of a small boat that should be arriving in a couple of days time. When Bob noticed us entering the harbor, he told Nancy, "If these guys beat us to New Zealand, I will never live it down!"

The Griffiths had many friends in Rarotonga. All we had to do was step in and they became our friends as well. The beauty of it, we didn't have to present our life story as was normal, because Nancy had already done it for us, and so much more eloquently.

Bob was alarmed by a severe leak along the garboard of the *America*. So before we had a chance to do sightseeing I helped Bob correct the problem. And a real problem it was! We discovered that the mast step had rotted out. Instead of replacing the rot with sound timbers at the time, it was repaired by dumping a quarter of a ton of concrete under the mast step. This left the heel of the mast sitting directly on the keelson. When sailing hard, the compression of the mast transferred onto the keelson and opened up the garboard. To correct the fault we raised the mast as much we could and placed cribbing around the heel, spreading the cribbing for and aft over a wide area, and then through bolted the lot horizontally. We were confident it would do until New Zealand, where something proper would replace the jury-rig.

It was common knowledge amongst cruising folks at that time, that the Griffiths had successfully weathered some crushing misfortunes in their sailing career. Where the ordinary bloke would be worried stiff to go on a difficult passage, like down to New Zealand in the middle of winter with such a deficiency, we are sure that Bob and Nancy thought of it only as a minor inconvenience.

In the process of cutting timbers with my rusty and dull handsaw I slipped and contracted a nasty cut diagonally across the thumb through to the bone. Bob put on his glasses and pasted the cut with some of his own mysterious concoction of an ointment, only Bob would know the ingredients. Siggi was convinced it was a leftover from when he practiced as a veterinary surgeon. Covered with a bandage we let it go at that.

This cut became septic on the next passage. So bad we feared blood poisoning. With no doctor in sight for a fortnight it was a frightening experience. In addition I was plagued by a cyst on my instep, plus a score of coral cuts which refused to heal. In short, I was not in the best of shape. Siggi's begging to stay in harbor and be treated, I had refused, much to my regret. Wounds in the tropics take ages to heal - another rotten apple in an otherwise perfect world - are unfortunate by-products. One is well advised to take along as much medicine as possible that would treat all "the rotten apples" under suspicion.

But the climate in Rarotonga wasn't exactly tropical, for we remember that for the first time in months we wore sweaters. The reputation of the island is that it enjoys the healthiest climate in the tropical Pacific, with uniform temperatures between 75 and 85 degrees.

Bob hired a car to sight-see in style, but mainly to make up for lost time working on his boat. Partly up a steep mountain trail the car stopped in front of a native dwelling, to visit a family the Griffiths knew well. Mama Tiare, the head of a sizable family, was a most charming native lady, who made us feel at home instantly. The meeting lasted only minutes, and we parted with an invitation to a native feast that evening.

When we arrived, we joined a party of half a dozen native men sitting tailor-fashion around a huge wooden bowl sampling kava-brew, a liquid that is derived from dried kava roots. Next to me sat the oldest man of the lot, I judged him to be "very-very-old". His face suggested a collision with a hard object back in time, because it was much deformed and scarred. He only had one eye, the blind eye a dark-blue indentation. His gaping mouth revealed two yellowish-brown cuspids he conveniently folded over the lower lip when he wasn't drinking, and this made him look like a walrus.

The drinking out of a coconut shell was conducted in the usual one-bowl-making-the-round manner. The old man sat to windward of me and I had to drink after him. He used to hand me the bowl with his mouth in an open position, and there was a strange gleam in his healthy eye that sent shivers up and down my spine. Never a doubt that my perspiring white skin was evaluated highly. Natives believe in plenty of food - and not only natives! There was an abundance of it heaped on a long table - chicken, mutton, lamb, pork, corned beef, etc., taro in coconut cream for salad, and every fruit the tropics are famous for. Before we were allowed to dig in, a basin with soap and water was handed around, as our fingers were destined to be the cutlery. That I enjoyed the meal enormously I take Siggi's words for: "You were the best example of native eating habits, at least what quantity concerns!"

Next day we inspected a large fishing vessel a New Zealander was building. There we met an elderly gentleman who introduced himself as Colonel Forbes. He was most interested in our voyage, as he had heard of us around town. After a few spoken words it dawned on him we must be German. That it had taken that long surprised me because I once met a Frenchmen who instantly said, "You must be German," before I had even opened my mouth.

"What gives you the idea?" I countered.

"Because you have such a big neck!"

Now, I do know people who observe me closely whether my head shows any "squares," but unaware that a big neck reveals national identity. Well, one is never too old to learn!

Island Hopping

Back to Colonel Forbes. He had been aide-de-camp to an English Duke in Germany after World War One. His recollection of names and addresses was astonishing. For instance, he still remembered the full names and addresses of every *Fräulein* he ever dated.

He must have enjoyed his time in Germany because he emphatically pressed upon us the use of his cottage on Kawau Island in New Zealand for as long we wanted, once we got there. Also he presented us with a list of his close relatives, "And don't forget to look up all the influential people I have on the list. They will help you a lot!"

He was on Rarotonga only for a visit with his son and daughter-in-law. At their home we met her but not his son, who was on business somewhere. We remember her as a stunningly beautiful native woman. A lively two hour conversation, with tea and cake to boot, ended an enjoyable afternoon.

Back aboard we did odd things to prepare the boat for the upcoming passage to New Zealand, when we were startled by an explosive clatter approaching from the village. In view came a very battered 1928 Chevy car that stopped alongside the *America*. Out stepped an attractive young lady, Beverly White. With her husband, Brian, who worked as a salesclerk at the local Trading Post, she had sailed a small yacht from New Zealand to Tahiti. On the return passage in a pitch-black night they had collided with one of the Cook Islands. Their yacht a total loss! In Rarotonga they had found a job. Henceforth they were planning to build a trimaran. Later, Brian showed us the building site where he had just finished a dinghy - "As good a beginning as any," he remarked.

That same afternoon, the girls decided to collect oranges from a deserted grove on the south side of the island. With Beverly behind the wheel screaming encouragement to Nancy and Siggi who were pushing to get the car started, it was an act fit for a comic movie. Once the engine had started there evolved a huge oily cloud from the rear of the car that blackened the scene. Accelerating mercilessly, the deafening sound from the faulty exhaust was audible for a long while. Bob and I shaking our heads, none too sure whether they would return with the same vehicle; or with any, for that matter!

Mr. and Mrs. Rose's invitation was the last we followed. Their house was just across the street from where we were moored. This location was convenient to meet every yacht that

149

had visited the island over the past fourteen years. They kept a log, and it was interesting to read the register. Many stories were told, some excruciatingly funny, others very sad. The one thing all sailors had in common, that all had left eventually in search for more adventures on the ocean highways of our wonderful world - as we would tomorrow.

Starting early next morning, we made the all familiar round saying good-bye to all our newly found friends. With the harbor office we cleared for New Zealand. Even, though, the passage from Rarotonga to "Down-Under" was considered a downhill slide, the Pilot Chart also indicated the possibility of nasty gales.

On leaving Avarua Harbor, the wind stood fresh from the southeast. A long swell was breaking furiously on the reefs skirting the coast. Breaking seas on the reefs to leeward gave us an uncomfortable feeling, and we were anxious to gain an offing quickly.

The island is without a doubt a charming place to visit, but the two harbors of the island are not really ports but merely indentations in a reef that are open to the north. Any vessel caught there in a blow has very little chance to escape unscathed. One of the victims was the Brigantine *Yankee*, shortly after our departure; the same ship that had the tragic experience in the Galápagos Islands, which I mentioned earlier

The weather remained unsettled, and it blew hard day and night, and the sails stood stiff as wooden boards under the mighty press of wind. *Thlaloca's* performance was our only joy. In addition to the gusty wind, it was the cold that bothered us even more, and it seemed that it was getting colder with every minute of latitude we gained south. We were doing vigorous exercises for lack of warm clothing. Great was the joy when Siggi found a pair of long-Johns that were hidden away somewhere since we had left California. Siggi had no warm garments and huddled around a roaring Primus, while I sat in the cockpit cursing the misery of cold weather sailing. My sores bugged me and it looked like as if I would get blood poisoning in my left arm, due to the nasty cut in my thumb. Siggi was deeply worried, and so was I!

All considered we found it foolish to sail into the middle of a winter with our meager resources in winter clothing and money, when several hundred miles to the north we could bake our hides in a warm sun. Finally, it was imperative to see

150

a doctor as quickly as possible.

Two days after leaving Rarotonga we made a drastic course-change for the island of Nui. It did not improve the weather one bit. If anything it got more uncomfortable because the change of course brought the wind abeam. If *Thlaloca* takes the seas from that angle quite well, it was us who complained bitterly, being drenched constantly by the water shooting over the side and falling into the cockpit. The bright side of it all, it got warmer, and the swelling in my arm lessened. Surely due to Siggi's excellent care in wrapping my arm in vinegar-soaked cloth quite often.

We never did see Nui Island because the cloud cover was so dense it hid all the heavenly bodies we needed to plot our position. The only indication that an island was near was a dark blotch to our south and the many birds out hunting for food. We did not feel bad as the pilot book gave little encouragement of finding a decent anchorage in inclement weather. We shaped a course for the Tonga Islands. Those islands are divided in three principal groups: The Tongatabu Group in the south, the Hapai Group in the middle, and the one we had chosen, the Vava'u Group, in the north. The lot stretches over three latitudes in a solid wall of reefs on its eastern approaches. The reason for deciding on the Vava'u Group was that they were considered off the beaten track, and therefore so much more appealing.

With that much reef-line in front of us we did some careful navigating. Even hand-steered between fixes to retain control of our DR.. Still, in weather so lousy it could upset the best steering and calculations. Luckily, though, the sun was available for a few seconds at a time, and being quick about it I was able to snatch a line of position eleven miles east of the reef. Unable to obtain a latitude observation that day, we hoped that our careful steering over the past twenty-four hours since our last fix was not upset by some treacherous current.

With daylight fading fast, our worries increased proportionally as no land was sighted anywhere. Shortly it would be dark, and then what? The wind and the current would surely drive us into danger. The prospect of tacking against a twenty knot wind all night made us shudder. I went below and settled into what had became already routine - rechecking my sights. Suddenly, Siggi shouted, "Land-ho!" I popped up to see it, but it had already been taken away by low hanging clouds. But the Admiral had taken a bearing, and this freed us of all worries.

Half an hour later, the island stood picturesque in the fiery red of the dying sun, about two miles away. It was our trickiest landfall so far, and my confidence in navigation had received a tremendous boost.

We soon worked ourselves into the lee of the island where we hove-to for the night. Around midnight, though, the wind came up strong, gusting gale force over the top of the island.

Two hours later we had to admit to ourselves that the island so near only that long ago was getting awfully small - and a lot smaller as the night dragged on. On the chart I measured off the distance to the next group of islands - the Fiji Islands, 600 miles to the west. This was ridiculous. If this was to become the norm we would be in trouble.

Up went the sails, and we tacked towards where we had last seen the island. It was a wet drive for the rest of the night, to get back in the lee of the land where the seas got smaller. Once inside a mass of islands we were well protected for the long beat to Neiafu, the settlement. Much of the surrounding area reminded us of home, the Georgian Bay with its thousands of islands. Most of them stood out of the sea, as pretty as mushrooms, the lower portion nibbled away to a stump by the wash of the sea.

Past noon we tied up to the government pier to await the officials. In the meantime a crowd of natives had gathered to check us out. None of the folks spoke a word, and we thought desperately of means to break the silence. All of our questions were answered only by shy giggles. When Siggi handed me a pan of water out in the cockpit to wash the salt off my face, the crowd roared out in laughter. The ice was broken.

The officials marched on in spotless white zulus, the traditional wrap-around skirt worn only by men. The paperwork was quickly taken care of and we were welcomed to the island in a very friendly manner. Captain Cook must have been right when he named these islands, The Friendly Islands.

Captain Bligh, of course, judged them quite differently. And so does history! It tells us that the Tongans were a savage and warlike people and never too friendly to any foreigners. As fierce warriors, the Tongans quarreled much amongst themselves and they lived mostly off the spoils of war and victory. We all remember the classic story of The Mutiny on the Bounty. Once Captain Bligh with his faithful was cast adrift in a longboat, their first attempt to land to fetch water was on one of the Tonga islands. The party was ambushed and one man was killed. Subsequently, they never tried again, for fear of a repeat, until, finally, on Timor Island in the Indian Ocean.

The Fijians, 600 miles to the west, were their traditional enemies. When their yearning for booty became paramount, the peaceful Fijians were their logical prey. There the Tongan warriors found in abundance what they themselves lacked completely, namely suitable timber to build boats with, and the Fijians themselves who were expert craftsmen in boatbuilding; whom they simply kidnapped. It is said, that some of the captured boats were of a size that could carry a hundred men and provisions for weeks, to cross long stretches of ocean.

Modern Tonga was a Kingdom, a self governed community with Queen Salote as head of State, and her very able son, Prince Tungi as roving ambassador (1964). The seat of government is located in Nukualofa on the island of Tongatabu.

Once cleared, we shifted *Thlaloca* to a small jetty off the Copra Board building. With us had shifted the native crowd, and it became obvious that we would have to anchor out to secure privacy. On the other hand we didn't want to be rude to those simple people, especially the little children who stared at us with their big round eyes as if we were people from another planet. Siggi prepared a pitcher of chocolate milk and motioned the mothers to bring their children aboard. In no time at all *Thlaloca* was doing her best to stay afloat under the weight of a dozen people. Now, everyone spoke, either a sort of Pidgin English or the native tongue. Soon girls appeared with baskets full of fruit and vegetables. Men came with written recommendations they had received from previous visitors, which stated, "The best painter . . . " The best laundry man . . . " it was like reading TV commercials. Highly amusing was this one, "Mr. . . . is guaranteed the best electronic mechanic on the island. He repaired our radio and toilet." It either was a rude joke by some careless individual, or most likely he had composed it himself. In that case, he did well in covering all possible avenues. I asked him, "Are you a mechanic or a technician?" "A mechanic, sir! What is a technician, sir?" Subsequently, we found the men fairly cunning. At that moment a large and dignified man approached us from across the street, this caused the natives to disperse.

And thus we met Mr. Kaho, the manager of the Copra

Board. He invited us for tea. It was the first time that we experienced the full meaning of "teatime." What we expected literally turned out to be a full course meal, prepared by the kindest person in the world - Katrin, his wife. The food was served on a long table. I had always considered myself a hearty eater, but Siggi and I sure had a surprise coming, because with us was a skinny young native, and the volume of food he consumed was unbelievable; from mouth to foot he must have been all stomach. Our host did even better, only it made sense. Weighing in at over a sixth of a short-ton, he was entitled to.

While the teatime dragged on, the Kahos encouraged us to hang around for at least a month, and to make it convenient for us, we should make our home in the big house. With their children in New Zealand attending school, there was plenty of room. "What about our boat?" we inquired." "I will have a twenty-four hour guard to watch her out at anchor!" Mr. Kaho promised.

The population was largely engaged in producing copra; some farmed; some made a living by fishing. Despite a devastating cyclone in 1952, the town was very neat and clean. A paved road is not often found in a small island-village, but Neiafu sported one, thanks to the Americans who had a base there during World War II.

It was no secret that Tongan men were generally lazy, and a woman's lot wasn't easy. But this was traditional from way back when men were warriors and women servants. No one seemed to mind, and we hadn't noticed an unhappy woman.

In the large copra shed, near a wooden wharf, we watched the women doing all kinds of jobs. The more fascinating was the making of tapa cloth from the treated inner bark of a kind of mulberry tree. As we understood it, the bark has to be soaked and then beaten with sticks to a thin layer. The sheets are then laminated, and by staggering the joints, almost any size of cloth can be made. After that, each cloth is hand painted in different patterns. Anything that is needed to fabricate the cloth such as glue and pigment is extracted from trees.

In another corner of the warehouse sat women crosslegged. In a happy squabbling mood they were stringing sea shells to leis. It was obvious that only women would have the patience required to do such a tedious job. One of the women had just put the finishing touches to a *lei* of delicate shells. To our surprise she put it around Siggi's neck with a timid smile.

154

Knowing how rude it would be to reject it or offer payment, we were desperate in finding adequate words of thanks. Later we counted more than two hundred shells in this beautiful necklace.

One weekend the Kahos suggested we should spend a day at their plantation. It involved a boat trip through a maze of islets and reefs, we accepted eagerly. The longboat was launched and seven of us boarded it. Down the harbor we sped following the curving shoreline for miles over jewel colored reefs, until we slid ashore in a tiny, shallow cove. The Kahos were very disturbed when Siggi and I pitched in to clear the campsite of rubbish, to be burned. Mr. Kaho, being of noble birth and directly related to the kings house (a cousin to Prince Tungi) figured rightly that work wasn't for him. For this reason exactly he brought along three workers. At any rate, we convinced him of our need of vigorous exercise, he finally conceded.

In the meantime, one of the boys went out fishing while another made preparation for cooking a meal. Being a plantation, there was no shortage of fruits and vegetables. With the arrival of freshly caught fish, all was there for a real feast. The cooking process was labor intensive but simple - the way it was done over past centuries - in a hole in the ground; which was already there. The bottom of the hole was covered with dry coconut husks and set ablaze. With a good fire going, rocks were placed on top of it. By that time, Mrs. Kaho had extracted the milk from scraped coconuts. The fish, taro leaves and milk were placed on banana leaves, rolled up and tied securely with fibers from the stem of banana leaves. Several bundles with different foods were made up in identical fashion, and the lot placed on the heated rocks in the hole. On top of this were placed more banana leaves to provide a tight cover, weighed down with rocks, followed by more leaves, burlap sacks, and last a layer of dirt. The result of all this was a delicious meal in about one hour.

By evening we sat around a camp fire contentedly, very relaxed and listened to native songs, accompanied by a guitar, while to the west we observed a fiercely burning sky where the sun buried itself into the ocean.

☆

Every morning we were awakened by the high pitched sound of a bell that announced the return of the launch with freshly caught fish. People with baskets would come to inspect the catch lying on the ground and then buy the amount needed. After unloading the fish, the launch would head out to the eastern reef to take the water temperature around a pearl culture, which the Japanese had established some months back under the charter of their foreign aid program. We took part in one of the trips; a passage where we dodged around a huge number of shallow coral heads, and where no sailboat could possibly venture. In fact, it was the crew that used long sticks that got us around tight curves. That none of the spiky coral pierced the hull, was to the credit of the natives' keen sense in reading the water. Siggi and I would tense up when a shallow head was dead ahead, expecting a crash. Missing it by the depth of our goose pimples, we looked at each other dumbfounded.

The occasion of a ship's arrival in an island is the equal to any of our holidays, only more colorful and vastly more exciting. The inter-island ship, the *Hifofua*, with Prince Tungi aboard, was expected. At daybreak already a long line of people had formed, loaded with every merchandise imaginable; among it every domestic animal known to man; all items to sell ore trade. The people sat around in groups, and a hundred voices spoke at the same time. One could only marvel at the exuberant mood of those simple people who had so little in material things; but so much more to enjoy life because of what they didn't have!

The Prince had "tea" with the Kahos, and we were also invited. His easy going manner was the secret of his huge popularity with his people, and there was no doubt that he would in time make a king as fascinating as his mother - Queen Salote. This brings us to a story told to us by one of Mr. Kaho's friends: When American Samoa received its self-government, the Queen, at the time engaged otherwise, sent as representative the Prince and Mr. Kaho. Status was measured by body weight in many islands, and so in Samoa. It so happened that Mr. Kaho brought considerable more weight to bear than his cousin the Prince. When the plane landed and the two of them walked down the gangway, there was confusion within the reception committee as to who was the Prince? Easy, the larger man, of course! So it was Mr. Kaho who received the respect of the committee, and the adulation of the crowd. Evidently, the Prince dismissed it all as being funny; as much as we did when he jokingly suggested that he would like to spend the night sleeping aboard *Thlaloca*. That would have required removing the entire cabin structure to get him inside!

We did not stay in Vava'u for a month, as Mr. Kaho had suggested, but already much longer than we thought we would. We still wanted to visit the southern groups of islands - Ha'pai and Tongatabu. When we received the clearance paper, it was heavily sealed in wax.

Our boat had shrunk another foot, so it seemed after the spacious living quarters we enjoyed ashore. We were loading cases of taro on board, when a messenger from the port office arrived with a telegram from Nukualofa, the capital. It refused us permission to land on any other of the Tonga Islands, "to prevent the spread of rhinoceros beetles." It meant that *Thlaloca* was declared "a dirty ship."

We had heard of this evil before. The way those bugs behave is as follows: They fly only at night between sunset and before sunrise, and then only over a distance of four hundred yards at the most. So, for a ship to remain clean, it must leave the pier one hour before sunset and anchor at least five hundred yards off any land, and not come back until one hour after sunrise. Like it or not, we had to obey the law, despite Mr. Kaho's willingness to intervene. We did not want that! That the law was somewhat ridiculous is born out by the fact that inter-island trade is going on constantly without observance of time limits. Plus, that the islands were already heavily infested.

☆

On July the third, after sixteen memorable days, we said our last *malo e lelei*. With only a feeble wind we drifted down the ship channel. Hard in our wake followed one of those peculiar native sailing crafts. Cat-rigged it boasted an enormous sail on a short mast, but a very long boom that extended well past the stern. It soon became apparent that it was closing the distance rather quickly. So as not to be out-sailed by such a clumsy craft we set every stitch of canvas. It was one occasion when even the Admiral agreed without much undue palaver. With every square foot of sail up and drawing, we had only seconds to dodge below to escape the terrible grins on the people's faces as they sped by - Jack Giles would hear about that!

Once we were clear of the maze of islands, we had the high peak of Late Island before us as a perfect landmark for the helmsman to steer by. The wind blew force four from the south and piled up a nasty chop that had *Thlaloca* dancing a jitterbug, which in turn squeezed our last meal up our throats and out over the side. The bitter taste it left behind we cleared with several cups of strong coffee. Normally, this is routine commencing a passage, after that we feel fine.

With the wind from the south, we thought it best to pass Late Island on its windward side - going north about we might lose the wind. The breeze gradually freshened throughout the day, it also had veered some degrees that put us on a close reach. It was interesting to read the Sailing Directions, to realize we were cruising among a chain of active and dormant volcanoes. There was Falcon Island, a submerged volcano, it had risen and disappeared three times in the last seventy-five years; the last in 1959. The mark on the chart of a "not examined" reef we treated with utmost respect (ever since off the coast of Corinto, Nicaragua).

The very height of the island had us fooled. It loomed ahead close enough to touch, but it deceived our judgement. It was still a long way off at that stage. When the sun dipped below the distant horizon, darkness followed quickly, as it does in the tropics. For us it was far too soon, with the wind rising another octave, and the blasted island to leeward a menacing wall. Oh, how we hated it! "Breakers to starboard ahead, oh God!" Siggi screamed with fear in her voice. It meant trouble, and I felt my knees turning soft. I hauled *Thlaloca* close onto the wind. It made her stagger into the seas with awful groans, and cutting her forward motion to a crawl. We now saw a line of breakers close to starboard, the spume illuminating a rocky shore. It sure didn't look right. And how did we ever get this close?

Every time the boat peaked a wave we saw the ugly boulders, whitewashed momentarily by a foaming olive-green sea. Each sea that rolled underneath the boat's bottom exploded ashore about ten seconds later. We were close and we were terrified. Worse, it appeared as if we were not moving at all. We tacked, but realized the mistake almost at once. Back she went on the port tack.

While Siggi kept the boat sailing tight on the wind, I feverishly dug out the outboard motor from underneath miscellaneous stores in the lazaret. Exhausted by fear and work, I mustered my last ounce of strength and heaved the motor over the stern onto the bracket, when the rubber sleeve over the handle, on which I was holding the motor, slipped off, and the motor took a permanent dive to the depth of the ocean! From then on

Island Hopping

it was up to our *Thlaloca* to get us out of that mess! One will never know fully the inherent ability of a good ship until she shows her ability to sail off a dangerous lee-shore. That awful night she saved us from becoming one more casualty in the long register of vessels lost in the Pacific. Once clear of the danger, we patted her fat belly in appreciation. It also brought to mind Tom Steel's casual remark, back in Panama, "Never pass an Island on its windward side."

On the third day out, the horizon to the south tinted a dark gray, grotesquely interwoven by huge blotches of ugly black. A sure sign of bad weather in the offing. The increasing wind made us shorten sail. Eventually there was only the tiny storm jib and a closely reefed mains'l left to drive the boat into the onrushing seas. Crawling ahead at a snail's pace we saw little sense in that. We hove-to under a backed jib and a reefed mains'l.

Away from the screaming wind, inside a battened down cabin, it was remarkably peaceful. And would have been more so, had the leach of the mains'l not surrendered to the wind. We recovered the sail and dragged the wet cloth inside, where we took turns stitching it up. It was the first tear in any of our sails, and it hurt! To see the lighter side of it we thought back twenty-four hours, off Late Island. Had it happened then, it would have saved us stitching it ever, and that would have been worse!

The night was uncomfortable. The wind shrieked fiercely at times, and we felt very uneasy to say the least. In turns we pounded the barometer to make it go up.

By daybreak the wind had eased but the seas were still up and wild. We got a move on by resetting the patched-up mainsail, and let *Thlaloca* renew her fetch to windward.

A latitude sight confirmed our fear that it wasn't possible to get around the southern end of the Lau Group of islands without tacking. Oh, well, perhaps the wind will change. We squeezed another few degrees to windward. *Thlaloca* took this as an insult and in revenge drenched us with tons of water over her bows. Siggi was quick to lend solidarity to the "other she" and in protest retired below to escape the salty exposure.

The Lau group of island we sighted on July 6, and had we had a decent chart we could surely have found a pass through it. But we didn't have a detailed chart, and that forced us to tack around the southern end of the group of islands.

WEST! SAIL WEST, MAN!

Once clear of the last island, we executed a dogleg to starboard which brought the wind over the hind quarter, and once again sailing became the sort we enjoy.

Not only had we changed course from sailing to windward to running before it, it also changed our behavior without being conscious of the gradual transition. For one, it had wiped the sullen looks off our faces, and before we knew it, we were laughing and happy again. Sure enough, Siggi was back in the cockpit exuberant, now that her "baby" was treated in a civilized manner.

Totoya Island, 1,200 feet high, stood to our port, and we gave its extensive reefs a wide berth. Then the wind dropped and the wrinkled sea flattened to a glassy surface, undulated only by a soft swell from the south. Darkness descended quickly and we progressed into a pleasantly warm night, lit up by our heavenly bodies. With the radio tuned to BBC, we relished in the soft music that flavored the exceptional moment in time, when we drifted across the International Date Line. From then on we had to plot our positions "east" instead of "west" of Greenwich. It raised mild confusion in our navigation department, until our brains were tuned to the conversion. Proof that all was in order presented itself when the island of Viti Levu, the principal Fijian Island, showed itself where it should be.

In the morning, the island stood close before us; yet so far, because the wind that had gone to sleep the night before had not awakened, and it was already late in the afternoon. The reason we had advanced this far was mainly due to a favorable current. The silent world was only disturbed by the motor-noise and wake of a passing yacht that was headed for the pass into Suva Harbor, two miles away.

This peaceful atmosphere lasted until about two hours short of midnight. Clouds moved in and blanketed the heavenly lights, and with it came wind - and a lot of it!

The leading lights through the pass - our position check - soon became visible only intermittently between rain squalls. We had wind all right, but we were in no mood to enter a treacherous pass in the middle of a dark and stormy night.

The thunder of breaking seas on the reefs became audible as soon the tormented sails lay lashed on deck and on the boom. How much distance lay between us and the deadly reefs was impossible to guess, but a rumbling noise to leeward told us we were close. Our margin of safety was the leading lights into the lagoon. But a sharp lookout was poor compensation for our deep worries, when the leading lights had disappeared in protracted rain squalls.

When we saw the spume thrashing the reefs, we had an idea how close we were, and it propelled us into action. Up went the shortened sails. We laid *Thlaloca* hard on the wind and let her pound against the southeast gale.

We tacked against the wind for many hours in an effort to compensate for the drift. It was strangely cold, therefore miserable, and it was wet. There was no doubt, that to heave-to would have lost us the distance in minutes what we had gained in hours tacking. What shall we do?

My suggestion to enter the pass met the Admiral's veto - and rightly so! Suva Radio reported gusts to forty knots, with no encouragement in future developments. We weighed the pros and cons, and finally decided to enter the pass as the lesser evil.

With a huge sea and all that wind behind her, *Thlaloca* raced towards safety or total destruction innocently, directed by two frightened characters, worse the world had not seen. Imagine the sensational feeling racing towards a sound-source that grew louder with every yard of advance. It was shredding our nerves.

"Is it the right thing we are doing?"

"Do we still have time to turn around?"

The breaking seas glistened as they exploded on the jagged reefs to either side, we hoped to be on a save course.

"Are we still in line?" I screamed from my attentive position on the compass to Siggi watching the leading lights.

"I can't see the lights!"

" Now I do, more to the right!"

"Too much!" "Can't see!" "We are right on!" So it went until we noticed the first indication of safety, when the large seas flattened gradually in the lee of the coral bulwark. Aware of reefs within the lagoon, we anchored in five fathoms. Elated beyond belief, sleep came easy that very early morning.

We had a rather rude awakening by a voice coming from a motor launch, "Hey! You are on the reef!" Jumping into the cockpit, we hadn't noticed anything unusual, but looking over the stern, the brownish looking reef loomed close astern. With so much wind blowing, we didn't want to gamble and sail off the hook, instead we accepted the launch's offer of a tow.

WEST! SAIL WEST, MAN!

We were lucky that we had anchored when we did!

We got towed to the quarantine anchorage, where we dropped the hook abeam the Kiwi yacht *Kathrine*. The very yacht that had rocked our peaceful world of the day before. Once cleared with the authorities we re-anchored facing the Royal Suva Yacht Club, where we were granted honorary membership. Our first trip was for the showers. After a bath, a shave, and clad in salt-free clothing, it is astonishing how terrific a person feels. No more thoughts of gales, a treacherous pass, only a desire to head for the big city, "to celebrate!"

☆

Suva is a very pleasant city, and the bustling life is quite colorful. Being a free-port, the shops were stocked with an abundance of merchandise from around the world. The prices were very reasonable, and one definitely had the choice between cheap and quality products - not that it mattered to us one way or another. Our interest was only in one expensive item, a 2 hp. Seagull outboard motor.

The yacht club is a long distance from the city. There was bus service, however, as a walk in the hot humid climate was exhausting - an occasionally regretful experience when we had missed the bus! To shorten the distance to town, we asked Mr. Colin White, the manager of Miller's Shipyard, for permission to lay at one of their piers. Besides a shorter walk, or drive, I had the advantage to do some work inside their workshop.

As this was winter in the Southern Hemisphere, we had two months respite before we intended to sail to New Zealand. The wonderful sunny days we experienced the first ten days suddenly changed to unpleasant weather. It drizzled almost continuously for the remainder of our stay. When the sun visited us one day, and the weather people had promised more of it, we painted the deck. It started to drizzle before we had finished. And what was already painted was still tacky when we sailed off weeks later.

Suva has an annual precipitation of 200 inches. To escape from some of them we boarded a bus for a tour around the island. This got us in the lee of the mountain range that crosses the island. There the people were praying for rain!

☆

The bus was loaded with predominantly Fijian people. Both, men and women come in large sizes. They are the friendliest and most kindhearted folks one could wish for. In

162

total contrast to the industrious East Indians who were in the majority, and effectively controlled the economic and political life - much to the detriment of race relation. Should they have had the same positive attributes as the native Fijians, we were not given the opportunity to notice. Our hearts went out to those gentle giants who were never shy to show that they liked you. We could have followed any number of invitations we received from the people on the bus and elsewhere, but "the baby at home" was crying, to do work on her. As it turned out, the only work we did was fabricating and welding up a new bow fitting.

Ahead of us lay a magnificent aluminum yacht, the *Ford III*. Her skipper had lost his life in a diving accident a month earlier. Her new owner was expected to sail her back to the U.S. shortly. Mrs. Sutherland, the proprietress of the Oceanic Hotel, had been closely acquainted with the deceased, and came to the yacht for a last look, before it would be taken away. She emerged from a chauffeur driven Rolls Royce, a most impressive lady. Very much favoring seafaring people, we instantly received an invitation to be her guests at the hotel. It was a long and perspiring walk up to the top of a high ridge to the east of the city. The location was perfectly located to give a guest instant rapport with the exceptional panorama of Suva and the surrounding mountains, reefs and bays. The establishment was rather like a guest house, catering to a clientele considerably more endowed than us. Sufficient reason for Siggi to check me out critically; that my shirt had no unsightly spots, and that my fingernails were filed and clean!

Barnabassi was the shipyard's watchman, a truly wonderful man. We made his acquaintance when he brought a huge bowl of kava aboard *Thlaloca*; the traditional offering of friendship. Just as in Rarotonga, we didn't fancy a drink that gave us nothing but a numb mouth, similar to the aftereffect of Novocain. Siggi despised the liquid, whereas I grew fond of it and hardly ever walked through the workshop, where it was offered to the employees in a large basin, without taking a dollop.

Suva was a large base for the Japanese fishing fleet. One of the vessels was lying alongside the pier for repairs. The wireless operator spoke English poorly, but it did not hinder us from becoming well acquainted with him and the entire crew. One evening we were invited aboard for a party. Several empty banana crates were stacked up on the poop deck like a throne for us to sit on, surrounded by the whole crew sitting tailor-fashion on the deck. Some played guitar, others sang American western songs in Japanese. Wine, fruits and chocolate bars were handed around freely.

Barnabassi, on his tour of duty was walking past, and was invited to join. When he finally showed up it was with the, us so familiar, large bowl of kava. His deep-brown face, in which splendidly large white teeth glistened like jewels, was all in smiles. It was shocking to watch that his offerings were either spit on the deck or over the side. It devastated the good man's cultural integrity. Deeply hurt he had lost his smile and refused stoically any handouts. It brought home to us how important it is not to take lightly the delicate balance that exists between different cultures, and avoid by all means what is disrespectful - not just superficially, but treat it as a duty!

The *St. Briac*, our neighbor from Tahiti, had sailed in, and we lost no time to scramble aboard her to exchange experiences of the past months. As always, Bernadette succumbed to our begging and played Chopin on the full size piano. What a wonderful life cruising is, being entertained by a master pianist in the cozy great cabin of a super-yacht. Their future course was New Caledonia and Australia. If lucky we might meet again.

We decided to clean and paint *Thlaloca*'s bottom, by beaching her off Mosquito Island, a small *motu* within the lagoon. With the tidal action only minimal, we did one side at a time. We could have postponed the painting, but a good policy is to grab the chance when presented.

It is a lovely island despite its ugly name. We hung around for several days, doing work on the boat, but mainly swimming and diving among spectacular coral reefs. On weekends, launches brought loads of tourists to the island, mostly from visiting Union Steamship liners. All were Kiwis, and all were exuberantly happy. Supported by loads of food and drinks, they danced to music from gramophones. Attracted by the mouthwatering fragrance of barbecued steaks we moved in ostentatiously close, and soon were invited to join. We had a marvelous time and parted with half a dozen invitations from our Kiwi aquaintances, once we had arrived in New Zealand.

Again the dreaded time had come to part with all the people we had grown to love. Monte and Colin White invited us to another of their sumptuous dinners, and showed us an expertly edited 16mm movie film of their recent vacation through the Pacific Islands and the U.S.. Mrs. Sutherland came in her chauffeur-driven Rolls Royce to hand us a fried chicken.

"Let's hear from you once in a while!" were her parting words. We did!

☆

On September 4th, the forecast was for fresh southeasterly winds. We did not like the "fresh" in the forecast as our course would be dead to windward. But we never liked to postpone sailing once our good-byes had been said. So off we went.

Once clear of the pass we reduced sails and let *Thlaloca* slug to windward. The going was slow and wet, and by sundown we had covered only twenty miles. All was under control, until a spinnaker pole got adrift. To retrieve it we made several passes, tacking back and forth. When opening the hatch to get the boathook from inside, it happened that a sea charged through the opening, wetting the entire inside. With the pole back aboard and back to thrashing to windward, it was the foresail that exploded next. We realized it wasn't our day. We went back! Four hours later we tied up to the *Paisano*, another acquaintance from Tahiti.

XIV

FIJI TO NEW ZEALAND

We waited three days for the prediction of light winds and slight seas - three days that were needed to dry out the boat and mend the damaged sail.

It was calm the morning we left. We had to mount the motor to propel us safely through the pass. Three hours later we were still motoring. Two hours after that we carried a double reefed mains'l and the jib. For the x-time we wondered how educated people - meteorologists - could be so wrong in their predictions. If our first attempt was bad, it was worse now with a fundamental difference, we could not return without making fools of ourselves. Instead we bravely slugged on to windward. By the time Fiji Radio adjusted the forecast, " - - - - - - - gale force southeasterly winds - - - - - -warning to shipping!" we hoped to slip into the lee of Kandavu Island. But first we had to clear Mbengga Island to leeward, and that required tacking. But once this inconvenience was cleared, we had no more worries - only misery!

Our *Thlaloca* was never a boat that would go to windward lightly - none of them is. Basically she was much too small and light to develop any drive. With no dodger to protect us we got soaked to the skin, and opening the hatch to get in and out of the cabin required precise timing, because should we miss only once would mean a drenched cabin for the rest of a passage.

WEST! SAIL WEST, MAN!

With the wind gusting force six from the east, add to this a west flowing current, we had to compensate for the expected drift. It put us hard on the wind. The sun showed only intermittently between low racing clouds, and that made taking a sight on the sun for a line of position very difficult. It was the dangerous Conway Reef that had all our concern, and made fixing our position imperative, in order to have peace of mind throughout a dark and stormy night.

The cockpit was much too small to spread the legs sufficiently to balance the wild motion of the boat. Therefore I tied myself from the waist belt to places around the cockpit, while Siggi placed herself in a position to observe the bulkhead-mounted clock to take the exact time. This position wedged her into a space of about eighteen by thirty inches; and only inches away from where Siggi was boiling eggs in seawater on the gimbaled stove.

The normal movements of the boat were violently interrupted when a big sea crashed aboard and laid her way over. The force of the blow was severe enough to send me sprawling to the cockpit floor, desperately holding on to the sextant, and to prevent it from being smashed against some hard object. I could have remained there for a time to collect my senses, but it was Siggi's shocking screams that had me freeing the lashings in a hurry. I stuffed the sextant into the lazaret, amongst ropes and sails to be secure.

Opening the hatch and peering inside was a sight that sickened me, and I shrink even yet from visualizing it too sharply. The force of the blow had ripped the entire gimbals off its foundation. The heat-glowing stove and the pot lay in Siggi's lap. Mercifully, the flame was extinguished, but with the tank still under pressure, the stove was spewing hot kerosene gases in a belching cloud.

Siggi, then in shock, did not make a sound. The smallness of the area she was wedged in, and the restriction of the boat itself made it impossible to help her in any civilized manner. Instead I had to work from the cockpit in an upside-down position, to free her first from the stove and pot, and then manhandle her into a position to get a handle on her from inside the boat, to place her into a bunk. What made the situation even more ghastly that during the operation the hatch had to be left open. That had let a huge amount of seawater into the boat - and into Siggi's awful wounds!

168

I reasoned with myself that it could only be right to free her of all the water and kerosene soaked garments while she was still unconscious, as otherwise it would be a most painful operation. Peeling off her clothes, the skin came with it in large patches. It was enough to drive me insane. Of interest was to observe how dozens of blisters formed, like rain splashing on a puddle of water, and then merged to become large ones.

From the waist down to her toes, her body was a sea of blisters, the flesh exposed in several places, The back of her legs was one huge blister. Shocking to see was the area around her abdomen and thighs, where all the boiling water and the kerosene had collected without escape.

How could I save a most precious being from an environment that was so hostile in every respect? One thousand miles to reach New Zealand, three hundred miles back to Suva; the wind, the current, the weather all intertwined to make the going rough in any direction. New Caledonia would have been the best bet, but the reef-infested water around it, without a chart, made it the least attractive choice of any.

First, I had to suppress my terror that something terrible would happen to her in a very short time. To that end I started bailing the massive amount of water that was rolling and splashing into every corner of the boat, and, of course, was falling on Siggi's body. Next I grabbed the "doctor book," which advised," . . . make the patient comfy and call a doctor" - bull! (How fortunate are we today to have medical advice written by experts for the inexperienced).

Siggi had come back to life, and her first words were: "I'm all right, don't worry!" Those words of a very brave lady brought tears to my eyes. She wasn't even aware how severely she was wounded.

Of medical supplies we had very little. And the little we had was thanks to our friends, the Heyers, we had met in Tahiti. As they were going home, they had given us all the medicine they normally carried on extended trips abroad. The two important ones, Codine and Sulfadiazine, proved real life-savers. Vaseline and aspirin we had plenty ourselves. I gave her some of the first two. Vaseline I spooned onto her seething body and spread it with a soft cloth.

Back in the cockpit I thought about the action that had to be taken to get Siggi into a doctor's care as quickly as possibly. I reasoned that Kandavu Island, (one of the Fiji Islands) being the closest, was our best bet. It was a good choice for one other reason, the Conway Reef was still somewhere close, and on the new heading, northeast, we would be sailing away from it.

The new course was basically the reciprocal of the previous one. But again compensating for the expected drift towards the west, it still was a beat to windward. The only benefit we derived from sailing to windward, that the boat steered herself perfectly, even without lashing the tiller. It gave me time to attend to Siggi's needs.

A rudimentary fix the following noon confirmed, that for every three miles gained, we lost one to leeward. It was obvious that Kandavu Island had become a hopeless goal. I consulted with Siggi about the dilemma we were up against, especially about the pros and cons of New Caledonia - reefs and no chart - she was all for New Zealand. "I'll be O.K.," she whispered. A marvel of a gal! The main lesson we learned at that time, to always have charts for places downwind.

What Siggi went through in the following weeks can only be described as heroic. Confined to her bunk with only minimal movements, inside a battened down cabin that ran with condensation, and salt water from a leaking mast collar that wetted her bunk and wounds. The agony using the head (bucket). Foul-smelling bandages I could only wash in seawater and sparingly rinse in precious drinking water. The constant pounding of the boat working to windward. The salt in her wounds that caused such excruciating pain. It was hell!

Gradually Siggi's condition improved, and so did the weather. Once in the horse-latitudes (the southern belt of variables, similar to the doldrums near the equator) there were days with light winds and a warm sun. A welcome break to air the cabin and bedding. Unwelcome only, because I had to hand-steer day and night as much as possible to gain miles.

The light weather was replaced by a hard blow from the southwest. We thought it best to lay ahull. What followed was a spooky incident that would worry us for the rest of the passage.

Even though the wind was screaming furiously in the rigging, the boat did nobly, and I was exhausted enough to fall into a deep sleep. I was awakened brutally by the strangest impact on the starboard aft quarter. Before I could raise myself out of the cramped position - the storm-seat as we called it - (the same seat in which Siggi got trapped previously) another blow followed, and a lot more severe. It also brought the boom down, as the topping lift had parted.

All the compartments I checked were dry and that eased our minds, but never erased our worries about the horrible incident throughout that night.

By morning the wind had lessened, and the first positive move I made, I climbed the mast as high as the spreaders to fasten a temporary topping lift. I raised the sails and brought the boat on course - south! *Ooh, lá-lá!* What happened? I was able to move the tiller only little to either side of midship. It would have been foolish to force it without inspecting it first. And this meant I had to dive. I informed Siggi about it, but she pleaded with me not to do it - a very understandable request in her condition. Later, in Auckland, we found the steel skeg three quarters of it's length ripped off the hull, and the ¼-inch steel rudder blade split six inches horizontally at the pintle. The whole assembly was bent to one side. Only God knows what had hit us that night. And we had reason to thank the lord for saving us from another blow during the remainder of the passage.

Sixteen days from the day of the scalding we sailed into the Bay of Islands in New Zealand. From the cockpit I described to Siggi the fascinating scenery; the neat houses, the green meadows speckled with countless grazing sheep. She could not resist seeing it for herself. So, for the first time in as many days she forced her wounded legs over the partial bulkhead to see for herself the wonderland I had described. She found the new skin already formed much too inflexible to move freely, and she was happy to crawl back into her bunk.

I moored the boat to the government pier, and asked a man to notify Immigration and Customs of our arrival. In the meantime a doctor from the Health Department had arrived - as was common practice. After examining Siggi he expressed surprise that no infection had occurred. He called her recovery, "a case for the Medical Journal."

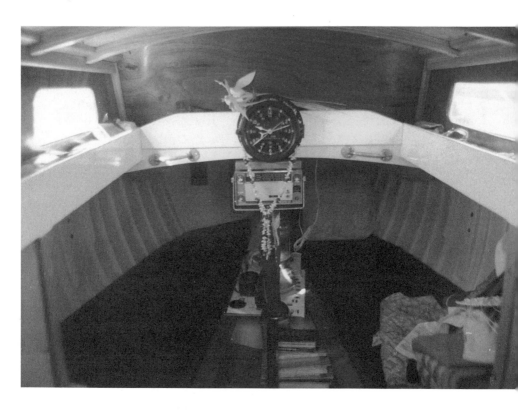

At Siggi's feet is the place where the accident happend

XV

NEW ZEALAND

Back in Suva we had been given the name of a Canadian couple, the Gradys, who had sailed their yacht, the *Seeadler*, from Vancouver to New Zealand, and there had built a larger yacht, the *Joshua S.*. She was moored in one of the delightful bays. We sailed over and bumped alongside her. Gordon emerged from below and greeted us, "Oh, hallo Canada."

Gordon's wife was in the hospital, expecting their first child. The three of us were pleased to have found company. Us in particular because we had instantly gained additional living space. What made the meeting so valuable to us, was Gordon's generosity in presenting us with the new Canadian flag. He told us of his patriotic sensibility that prohibited sailing with any flag with the emblem of Great Britain. When the Canadian legislature had decided on a new flag, he had entered the design-contest. It so happened that his design was like the one adopted. We are pleased and honored to have sailed the new Canadian ensign the rest the way around the world. The first Maple Leaf to make a circumnavigation.

Dick MacIlvride, New Zealand's well known yachtsman, came by to invite us to the club, and to his house for a meal. He had come with an inflatable, and he went out of the way to point out some of the delightful anchorages available within the exceptionally fine Bay of Islands. What never failed to impress us, was the incredibly pronounced green of the pastures, one felt like biting into, where the fluffy white of the sheep moved about like cotton balls in a light wind. The thought we expressed earlier, when we met our first coral island - paradise, that would haunt us for the rest of our lives - New Zealand has a quality all its own, and every bit as impressive. We felt at home perhaps because we were living in a cultural setting not unlike the one we grew up with, yet in a way vastly different. Besides the easy going lifestyle, it is the people that make New Zealand so incredibly appealing - very generous, always open, forever proud.

At the MacIlvride's home we met Pat, Dicks wife, already preparing a meal. For the first time I ate lamb, very delicious. Had I known that it was lamb, some sort of excuse would have prevented me from eating it, but it had me fooled. My aversion to anything not related to beef and pork is notorious, I can't get it down. Unknowingly, I have no problem. A perfect example of how screwed up I am!

Pat, a nurse, was helpful to Siggi in providing medicine and bandages. Later we visited the building site where their new 48-foot ketch was shaping up nicely. Building in traditional wood, I envied the beautiful kauri timber he was using; some of the best available woods to builders. It grows huge, in size similar to our Sitka spruce in British Columbia or redwood in California. Once prolific it was ravaged to near extinction within a century. To prevent further decline it was protected under the law.

What stood out obviously when traveling about the country, that it was primarily a sheep and dairy country, with no large industry evident. One reason, perhaps, why the land was so clean. We visited Waitangi, the site of the first European landing. And more significant, where the Treaty of Waitangi was signed in 1840, which joined all tribes under the Queen's sovereignty.

One day we parted with the *Joshua S* and went daysailing within the spacious bay. This delightful experience made us realize to do more of it before leaving New Zealand for good. The next day saw us sailing down the coast toward Auckland.

Tutukaka Bay lay handily on the way to break the passage. It had one flaw, however, as much we tried to set the Danforth anchor, it wouldn't. At last we let it go at that and we hoped for a calm night. The sun's gorgeous setting over the western ridges of high land excited our taste buds, longing for a good cup of coffee. Unfortunately, the only coffee aboard was the unroasted beans Mateta had given us a long time back, in Tahaa. Siggi browned the lot in a pan over the Primus. Placed in a cloth I pounded the beans to powder with the winch handle, on top the winch. It wasn't exactly powder. Neither was it exactly our taste! We left early the following morning.

The wind blowing fresh and cold against us we selected Urquhart Bay as our next stop, only a few miles farther south. We rounded Bream Head and anchored among small fishing craft. The chilly wind compelled us to seek warmth in our sleeping bags. But a knock on the hull put an end to that.

Thus we met Archie and Joyce West, who welcomed us to New Zealand. They had come loaded with bread, butter, coffee and a dozen eggs. The four of us huddled inside *Thlaloca's* cramped cabin. None of us seemed to mind considering the alternative, the chilly wind outside! Our lively talk was well lubricated with real coffee, straight from the horse's mouth - the store! At the end of that short meeting we sensed that we had met some of the most kindhearted people in the world.

The following morning we made slow miles against a fiercely gusting southwest wind. We had decided on Kavau Island as a desirable break of the windward-slug. But as much we tried to get close, we did not succeed; the wind blew too strong, the seas too steep and too short, impossible for *Thlaloca* to overcome. We changed course for Auckland.

Off Tiritiri Matangi Island, the wind went to sleep. A very beautiful night followed, lit up by the city lights to the west, a welcome guide to the harbor. Sailing only to a zephyr of wind, we had made it as far as Rangitoto Island by morning. Then the darn wind from the west started to blow again. Had we thought we could make harbor with dry skins, we were mistaken. A pilot boat came close and inquired if we were all right. We asked for direction to an anchorage, this we were given in detail. We parted with their promise of a visit soon.

We tied up to a derelict ferry, close to where the Griffiths were building their new *Awahnee*. We celebrated a very happy reunion. Next day, Siggi and I had a job, helping to build their new boat, with Siggi doing the cooking for all of us on *America*. We were home - at least for the next six months.

☆

Our *Thlaloca* had been afloat for a year and a half at that point and had sailed nearly 14,000 miles. She needed a thorough refit. The manager of the ferry company allowed us to have the boat stored in their yard. During a low tide, we removed the bent rudder assembly and unbolted the fin keel. At high tide the hull floated off the keel, and a truck pulled the boat ashore. We blocked her up securely for the many months she was to remain there. Empty oil drums, tied to the keel for floatation at low tide, raised the keel and floated it ashore.

The new *Awahnee* was to be build in concrete; a material very popular with potential builders, and there must have been dozens of boats in various stages of construction around Auckland alone. This unique type of construction was claimed to be fast, cheap and strong. No skilled labor was necessary. Thus it was advertised in many publications. The subsequent history of concrete yachts has received staggering blows to its reputation from virtually thousands of abandoned structures around the world, which in too many cases had no resemblance to what even a boat should look like. In contrast, and to be fair, there are examples of "The Proper Yacht" that are equal to those built in conventional material.

Our prime goal while in New Zealand, was to earn money we needed to continue our voyage. For the most part we worked ten hours a day, seven days a week. This doesn't seem much fun, but who could expect a four year vacation without the inconvenience of work?

Not all opportunities were missed, though, and we took advantage of anything that promised fun. There were all sorts of parties at the Akarana Yacht Club. Private parties, sailing trips to the outer islands, automobile trips. Invitations came in unique ways, like messages tagged to the boat, "We must see you, please call!" or "Want to build same boat, must talk to you!" It was impossible to take advantage of all the offerings. Some of our newly made friends reached out far, like Geofrey and Betty Decker. Between us we had a special bond because we were sailing the same class boats. Geofrey came with a pickup truck to collect all our sails for washing and repair, the navigational instruments for cleaning. The sextant mirrors were finally re-silvered - after removing the alu-foil I had placed there in the Gulf of Panama! He fabricated all new mast fittings. Betty, his German wife, was an expert cook and pastry maker. We spent Christmas Day at their lovely home and thoroughly enjoyed the company of people with whom we had so much in common. The Sayers, Everett and Josephine, was another couple who went out of their way to make our visit memorable. Everett, a general contractor, together with his crew did the plastering on *Awahnee*.

Also, there was the company of yachties, Bill Nance and his *Cardinal Vertue*, who later rounded stormy Cape Horn. His brother, Bob, was there, who in the future would entertain the sailing world with similar exploits. Our old friends from across the Pacific sailed in as well, the *Kochab, Elsie* and the *Gannet*. Meeting old friends, sharing with them the fun and tribulations of the past are the moments we treasure most in cruising life.

By the middle of February, we had to leave our jobs with the Griffiths, and concentrate solely on *Thlaloca*; we had to if we wanted to do all the things we had to do. As much as Jack Forsyth, a leading hand with the Harbor Board, helped the Griffiths, he still found time to assist us. On his inspection tours, he came by for a chat nearly every day. Anything he could do for us he did with enthusiasm.

Alongside one of the decommissioned ferries lay a Tongan schooner. Her skipper, David Fifita, with other islanders had sailed her down from Tonga, and were preparing her for the return trip. David had made news several years before, when he and a dozen other men had sailed a boat out from Tonga to New Zealand. With some error in navigation, the boat ran onto Minerva Reef - a total wreck. They found refuge on a Japanese fishing craft, which had foundered there months before, but was still in good enough shape to provide shelter. After a month, with no help in sight, they started to construct an out-rigger craft out of the timbers from the wreck of the fishing vessel. This was done without tools, except a hammer and a couple of spikes which they had pounded to chisels. David, his son, and one more man sailed this flimsy craft 600 miles to Kandavu Island for help. Only half a mile from safety the craft was lost on a reef. It forced the men to swim to shore. All made it except David's son who unfortunately had drowned. After 103 days on Minerva Reef the remaining men were taken off by a seaplane. These exploits were documented in a book, which we had read while in Tonga. We were so pleased to have met David, a fine and brave man indeed.

Very slowly, our boat was getting back in shape. Our main concern was the skeg and rudder. This time I chose wood over steel, mainly because it is a material I'm familiar with. To give it all super strength I laminated the parts of excellent Kauri wood and reinforced it heavily with fiberglass. The skeg was through-bolted to the keelson with three ½-inch Everdure bronze bolts. It was very strong and gave us the needed confidence for the future. For the first time we noticed vane-steering devices on boats. I copied the one I liked best, and installed it on *Thlaloca*. We were anxious to find out how it would perform.

With the help of our good Aussi buddy, Len Black, 6'3, 250 lbs., and as strong as an ox, we manhandled the 1,000-lbs. keel as far into the water as we could at low tide. For setting the boat onto the keel, I selected a dozen heavyweights from around the yard. To our surprise we found the boat heavier than we thought. We had no other choice but to built a slide and a cradle for the boat to get her far enough into the water, where the rising tide would do the rest. A Kiwi friend, John Jarvis, gave us a hand getting the keel fastened to the boat. It was a chilly night and I hated the thought of getting into that cold water. With a swell in the harbor, we had an exasperating job matching the holes of the finkeel to the angle irons of the boat below water. We nearly froze to death. At low tide we installed the rest of the bolts and torqued them. After antifouling all the bare spots, the job was complete. And no one was more pleased than good sport Siggi, who, ankle deep in mud and shivering uncontrollably, gave me light with a pressure lamp. Once we had re-stepped the mast, the boat was ready for the ocean.

Quite unexpectedly, our good friends Hardy and Billy Wright from *Barlovento*, our neighbor in Tahiti, popped up. We could hardly believe it because they were reported missing during a cyclone between Tonga and Samoa. It was a relief to see them, and knowing that their yacht was safely moored in Suva Harbor. Billy was in need of medical attention, and they had flown in. In their rented car we took a day to explore the west coast of the island. It gave us a glimpse of the Tasman Sea, a place of ill repute, we expected to be sailing on soon. For several days, these two fine people made themselves available to drive us around to do the multi-chores that pop up before a passage. After seven months in that lovely country it was depressing to think of leaving; the fun we had, the sights we've seen, the truly wonderful people we met - people we then called friends but soon would mingle with others along our path around the world.

XVI

FAILED PASSAGE TO AUSTRALIA

On April 10th, 1965, we departed from Auckland. A few friends were at hand to bid us farewell. Drifting off slowly, Billy and Hardy came rushing up the jetty waving a bottle. We tacked back to receive it, "medicine against snake bites," Hardy remarked. With many thanks and good-byes we parted.

Having chosen the wrong tide, we tacked to clear the river but without much success. Jack Forsyth who was watching us from shore, came over with a launch to tow us clear of the river. Off Hauraki Island we broke our last human contact with anyone in Auckland.

We sailed up the coast to a very light westerly. After sundown, the wind picked up and got us flying towards Whangarei, where we intended to visit before finally jumping off from the Bay of Islands for Australia. During the night we had ample opportunity to test our newly installed vane-steering. It was directly coupled to the main rudder via the tiller. As it was, we needed more vane power, or the leverage was too little. In later stages we kept improving it, and by the time we had reached the Indian Ocean it was working very well, even better than the best helmsman. By "better" we mean, it never got tired!

Next day we entered Urquhart Bay to visit our good friends, the Wests. Normally they were out fishing. We were pleased when we found them at home. Both were hard working people but who never missed a chance to give the overseas yachtsman an introduction to generosity the New Zealanders abound. Archie volunteered to pilot us up river to Whangarei, and Joyce and their son wanted to come for a sail as well.

Although the river is well marked, it was still an intricate channel through swamp land. The fair wind we had at the outset had petered out as we got closer to town. Archie, very vocal about his piloting skill, was still bragging when *Thlaloca* showed definite signs that all his boasting wouldn't get us off the sandbank we were sitting on. To this very day, Siggi and I have the greatest fun commenting on Archie's expression at that moment; we distinctly remember his unbelieving eyes becoming the size of saucers, showing total astonishment. It was the only time we ever enjoyed running aground! By rocking the boat and using the spinnaker poles to push, we got off easily. We finally made Whangarei without tearing more chunks out of Archie's pride as a pilot.

Whangarei has a most convenient yacht basin, located smack in the middle of town. It was a small place therefore not very suitable for outfitting a yacht, as most manufacturing establishments were concentrated around Auckland. We had a few nice days and then sailed back to Urquhart Bay. The following day, April 14th, we said so-long to two of the kindest people we know. As a farewell gift, the Wests presented Siggi with a valuable "tiki" as a good luck charm, plus a five pound fruit cake. "Do not open until Australia," was clearly marked on the box.

☆

Once again back in the Bay of Islands we waited for favorable weather to get us on our way. The night before the intended departure, the wind blew fiercely from the west. With the boat's stern hanging dangerously close to a rocky shore, prudence demanded the setting of another anchor. By dawn the wind had abated. Up went the anchors and sails, and we were off. Barely had we gained a safe offing, when the wind increased suddenly to gale force, with gusts so violent it forced us to lower all sails. We lay ahull. Perhaps just a short blast, no problem! We turned on the radio for a weather forecast, but missed it as we had the one before leaving. In the afternoon, however, the wind had decreased to give us a splendid reach, the land to port only a faint smudge. The following morning showed signs that the weather was shaping up to what looked like a ghastly development. The tumbling barometer indicated bad things to come. It is true we had already sailed many thousands of ocean miles and had gained experiences in many ways, but nothing in terms of a full gale that was about to strike.

Careless with our DR., we were uncertain of our position; which didn't matter much, with well over a thousand miles between us and Australia. We guessed to be some twenty miles northeast of Cape Reinga, the north end of New Zealand.

Hindsight told us we should have hove-to to await developments, but we sailed on towards the north, and thereby exposed ourselves more and more to the westerly winds. Also we failed to consider the relatively shallow water in that area, that could make things very unpleasant.

With low speeding clouds under the umbrella of a murky sky, and towering seas racing towards us, the likes we had not seen before, caused serious thinking of what should be done. The deteriorating weather screamed out for a decision. The sensible one, running before wind and sea, we were reluctant to follow as it meant a course 180 degrees away from our goal. With our smallest sails we stuck to a northerly course. Perhaps it would blow itself out soon, so we hoped.

Frantically we searched the frequency band for a weather bulletin. When we finally succeeded, it was discouraging news. It spoke of a severe gale, and warnings to shipping. The gusts reported were up to 69 knots at Cape Reinga.

Suddenly, out of the low scudding clouds appeared a ship, perhaps a mile to windward. We agreed, that Siggi should go below and brew up something hot, while I remain on deck and observe the ships course. When the ship had vanished from my view and didn't reappear after a long while, I thought it safe to join Siggi below for a hot chocolate drink.

Shaking from the cold, and no doubt inner tension, we huddled in the cramped cabin and sipped hot chocolate. This relatively pleasant occupation was at once shattered by the blast of a siren as close as our masthead. Both of us bolted for the hatch at the same time. Ripping open the hatch cover, what we saw was the steel wall of a huge ship lying across our stern, almost close enough to touch - a Russian whaling factory ship.

The meeting with this ship was an experience never to be forgotten. For one thing, it was reassuring to know we were not alone in that mess. But what really impressed us, that it gave us an idea of how high the seas were running. For seemingly endless seconds found us in a deep valley and we looked up the towering ship to the bridge where a dozen people gazed at us, some with binoculars. Next we were even with the bridge - an elavator-like motion that was repeated at precise intervals. We brought out the Canadian flag and held it spread to be recognized, which was not easy in those days, because the flag had been in existence only a short time.

The ship's command and crew waved enthusiastically and surely wondered how a boat that small could survive the raging seas. By degrees, the ship had moved away, and half an hour later was out of sight - buried in a wall of grey seas and dark clouds.

Hardly could the emotional impact on us have been greater as it was then in weather so dreadful, when all seemed so vulnerable, and there that huge ship massively built of steel, radiating security, confidence and warmth. Once the ship had gone, we were silent for a long time, each of us reflecting on the wisdom of our chosen path. Those were moments of self- doubt and we could only hope that "the good man upstairs" would look kindly upon our endeavor and bless us with a helping hand.

The screaming wind had increased another octave, and the seas piled up larger. We lay ahull - still refusing the proper course, running before wind and seas. We lay in our bunks, alert to the frantic motion of the boat. Sound through the water is very acute, and every time we heard a rumbling noise, reminiscent to a Wagnerian crescendo, we jumped out of our bunks and almost fought over the windward cabin-port. Whoever succeeded first would shout "Hold on!" when it looked like a breaking sea would lay us flat.

Then it happened. A monster of a sea overwhelmed the boat. We experienced the sensation as if riding a carousel, and there was water everywhere. We are goners, was my first thought. When we regained our senses we found ourselves in water up to our knees. The hatch was wrenched open and left a gaping hole, into which the seas fell unhindered. The mast was still standing, thank God, but the topping lift had parted, the loose boom ratching across the cockpit coamings violently. The vane-steering I had built only a short while back was only a bundle of twisted bronze and stainless steel. To this day we can't say with certainty how far the boat had been heeled, perhaps even rolled. The confusion below was suggestive of the latter. Now, survival lay in running before it. Siggi did a magnificent job bailing with the bucket. With the water she dumped into the self-draining cockpit came rice, sugar, flour, in short everything that was stored in containers and had opened, or bags that had dissolved.

My job was to steer the boat before the breaking seas. Dragging the sea-anchor over the stern, it did it's assigned job, slowing the speed of the boat. Very fortunate we were, that the hatch cover was still held by one slide and had not gone adrift. With half a ton of seawater sloshing through the boat, her behavior was sluggish and unpredictable, especially so when the stern lifted to one of the monster seas and the water shot forward. It could have caused the bow to cut under and not recover before the next onslaught. To stop the rush of water over the stern and straight into the cabin (the hatch had to be left open for bailing) I tied the storm jib across the backstays. It was a sail on the wrong end of the boat and made steering even more difficult, but it helped decisively in bailing the boat dry - as much that was possible!

Our aim, Australia, was out of the question, even with the storm abating, for we had lost nearly all our staple food. The two five gallon plastic water containers had collided with the deck beams and had burst, the surviving water contaminated with seawater. The smaller cans luckily had weathered the ordeal. Of the three navigational instruments aboard - sextant, clock and radio, the latter important for time-tick, looked a complete loss, as it got soaked. A hard object had shattered the glass on the clock, and possibly hurt the movement as well. Without the help of these important instruments it would have been folly to approach the dangers of the Great Barrier Reef.

Not a stitch of clothing had escaped the soaking - and the wind felt so terribly cold! What we needed were calm seas and a warm sun. Better than that, a total refit in a protected anchorage.

Between dreading seas we edged towards the southeast. When the wind allowed us to carry sail again, we sailed in a direction where we thought New Zealand must be.

Two days after the mishap, the spilled food, rice in particular, hiding in every crevice started to ferment, causing a repulsive sewage-like odor. We much preferred hanging out in the cockpit, wrapped in a sail, the only fabric that at least felt dry. As of food, we remembered the fruit cake Joyce had given us (luckily it was stored in a sealed tin can). We conveniently destroyed the note, "Do not open until Australia," and we had a ball eating the energy-rich cake. It was the only ready-made food aboard, and certainly the best we could wish for.

Seven days after our departure from the Bay of Islands we made landfall near Urquhart Bay, to be reunited with our splendid friends, the Wests, who would help us tirelessly to get our ship back into shape.

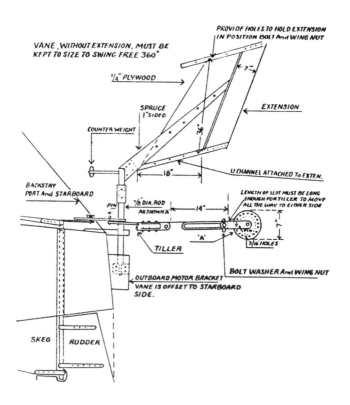

Self-steering vane gear

XVII

NEW ZEALAND TO AUSTRALIA

(Second Attempt)

A lot of work and money put the boat back in the running. And this was only possible with the vigorous assistance of the Wests. Numerous trips to Whangarei were necessary to have the clock repaired, and had the sextant professionally adjusted. How lucky we were with the radio. Once it dried out it started to function again - even though the inside wiring looked like a greenhouse. It was not lost time in any case because the wind blew strong day after day and the cold had us huddled around an electric space heater in our temporary sleeping quarters in West's house. When the barometer started to rise, we moved the "hundred and one things" we had cleaned, repaired, and stored in the house back aboard. One item that was beyond repair, and one that hurt us immeasurably, was our inflatable dinghy. Lashed to the cabin top, the knockdown had ripped it so badly that repairing it was impossible. Our "kitty" could not afford a new one, so we bought the largest tractor inner-tube available. Squeezed into a canoe-like shape, we sewed it up in canvas to hold that shape, and *ooh-lá-lá*, the result was a flotation device that got the two of us ashore and back without getting wet - if no-one coughed and thereby upset the contraption!

WEST! SAIL WEST, MAN!

The Wests towed us around Bream Head. There we bade our last good-byes. Through the binoculars we watched our dear friends disappear beyond the horizon. We were alone again with our thoughts and our hopes for a more pleasant passage.

With a deep depression just passed, we hoped to be well clear of Cape Reinga before encountering another one. There was no doubt, that the severe blow we experienced had ingrained in us a deep respect of the power of the ocean. Again, it was another lesson we had learned, to be stored in our memory for a more intelligent approach should it become necessary. Off the Three Kings, a few rocky islands just north of Cape Reinga, we had one last look back to an exceptional country, we trust that with God's help we may visit again someday.

In variable winds we banged our way to within fifty miles of Norfolk Island. Then the barometer took a tumble, and a storm soon followed. We lay ahull to winds from the southwest. With the last gale still fresh in our minds, we were not taking any chances and had our eyes peeled to windward for waves that broke dangerously; that would have made us run before it!

A noon fix the next day confirmed that we had been blown off our last position by thirty miles. Such a large drift really surprised us. It was during one of my watches that I observed a sunset so foreboding it brought to mind the making of a cyclone. I had a quick dive below, and sure enough the barometer was "diving" also. The entire sky was the dirtiest red imaginable, solid with cirrus clouds and mare's tails. I was glad that Siggi was asleep and didn't see it, otherwise she would have worried as much as I did. In my mind I had rehearsed all the things that should be done in case of real bad weather. Let's not be kidding, I'm scared stiff as perhaps most of us in this game, of any sign that could spell potential disaster. I often asked myself the reason why. In this context I envy single-handers, who's only concern is their boat and themselves. With a precious partner aboard one carries an awesome responsibility. My primary job was to protect her and the boat and to bring the voyage to a safe conclusion, (with her active help, of course) which, when the voyage is over, would be our only success. That this success could be jeopardized by something that could happen to her, was my constant worry.

186

Expecting disaster, instead we got becalmed on a lumpy sea! To pass the time, we watched the flight of the albatross.

We distinctly noticed that for one reason or another *Thlaloca* was acting unusual. The seconds she occasionally lay still, there was a peculiar flip under the boat that had us puzzled. I checked the keelson area for leaks that would indicate possible loose keelbolts. As none was found, I put on the diving goggles and dove. I was shocked when I saw three bolts out of the dozen holding the fin between the angle irons missing, and the rest were all loose. The fin was actually flapping about between the two angle irons

This was serious business, that needed immediate attention. We searched the boat for approximate size bolts. With a couple of wrenches on a string around my neck and a safety rope around my waist, I went over the side. Siggi had precise instructions to watch for any fish larger than one foot in length! She was nervous enough and signaled danger via the safety-line when sighting imaginary shadows!

For at least one hour I worked with mounting exasperation a job that by any standard required four hands and a tank full of compressed air. The constant movement of the boat did not allow new bolts into the holes. Instead I had to be satisfied with tightening the loose ones as much as possible, and that only when the bolts were momentarily jammed, otherwise they were "wheelers." Some had damaged threads and could not be tightened at all. Of tremendous help would have been a tool that today is on the market under the name of "Vise-Grip". Relieved of a nagging worry, we felt a lot better, and only hoped that the repair would suffice until it could be taken care of properly.

The cause of it we blamed on New Zealand. Unable to locate stainless steel lock-washers, we had to use electroplated ones instead, which obviously had shed the plating very quickly, and the rust had robbed it's effectiveness.

Once we had passed Lady Elliot Island close to port, we entered the southern end of the Great Barrier Reef; a reef that stretches for a thousand miles along the east coast of Australia. In fitful winds, and by using the motor only sparingly, we worked ourselves towards the coast. Out of wind, and almost out of fuel we let the boat drift for the night. We regretted not having detailed charts, perhaps we could have found an anchorage. The charts we did have for the Great Barrier

WEST! SAIL WEST, MAN!

Reef, were issued to the *Kaiserliche Deutsche Marine* (Imperial German Navy) in 1914 and were given to us by a man in New Zealand; a friend of a German fellow who had sailed there in 1936 and who had died since. The charts were beautifully constructed of the best of paper and linen-backed.

The town of Gladstone, was still a long way off, and with the calm prevailing and hardly any propellant juice left in the tank, we aimlessly drifted on a glassy sea. We asked a passing fishing vessel for an anchorage. They handed us a chart and pointed out an anchorage about two miles to the northwest. When they returned two hours later and offered us a tow we gladly accepted.

Pancake Bay is a fine anchorage, where we expected to remain until a fair wind would come up. A while later came the three men from the fishing boat, Roy and Cliff Perry and an older man by the name of Joe, over for a chat. They were surprised when we told them from where we had come, as they were unable to read our flag. They had thought we were locals out for a sail, and the flag a pennant of a yacht club! We all boarded their workboat and went ashore.

Ashore lived an old bachelor with his dog in a large untidy shack, where the cockroaches were having a ball. He was a very likable chap, the fishermen seemed to be fond of him. His impaired hearing resulted in a throaty conversation. He offered us tea in rather filthy cups, he had already placed on the table. There was no chance to talk ourselves out of it. "No one leaves my place without having a good cuppa," he said.

The moment he went to fetch firewood to boil the water, Siggi took the cups to the beach and scrubbed them with sand and water. "You didn't have to bring your own cups," he scolded us on his return. When Siggi told what she did, his expression suggested that it would spoil the taste of tea for months. Anyway, we thoroughly enjoyed the taste as it was.

Finally, he gave us two gallons of fuel in his own container and refused any payment. Although we tried to convince him to accept by refusing the fuel, he didn't budge. Later we gave the fishermen a couple of bucks, to purchase items he might need and deliver it the next time they visit.

On the way back to the boats, Mr. Perry, the skipper, offered us a tow to Gladstone. We upped the anchor, and with only a nylon line to connect us we were off. It got dark on the way, but no worry, we had the best of pilots to guide us. By

7:30 p.m. we were in Gladstone Harbor and securely tied-up to an excursion boat for the night.

In the morning, as every morning, we hoisted the Canadian flag; it seemed that the Maple Leaf puzzled nearly everyone. People would ask, "What flag is that?" "Canadian!" We would reply. "Darned if I ever seen it!" Was their response. Most amusing were the comments of a couple ashore we overheard listening from inside, "Some new state in Africa, I suppose!"

Roy Perry had notified the officials, and one of them made us fill out a stack of different forms. These were handed to us in a sealed envelope the day of our departure. The papers had to be presented at every customs station along the coast. A drag and time consuming procedure to be sure, but time was free and plentiful!

The first things we did, we beached the boat and corrected the fin to hull fastenings, and for good measure antifouled the bottom. Roy came by and suggested tying *Thlaloca* alongside his boat in the river and use his workboat to ferry us to and from shore. A splendid arrangement.

Fishing vessels are generally smelly and infested with cockroaches, and whenever possible we kept away from them. But not Perry's boat. It was like most yachts, scrupulously clean - it even stood the test of Siggi's keen sense of smell - a keenness that will drive the average guy up the wall!

Nearly every day the Perrys insisted we should have a meal at their comfortable home. Siggi in particular looked forward to it with delight, because of the wonderful company Mrs. Perry was. Every minute of their spare time was reserved to drive us around the country to get a fair appreciation of a continent that encompasses so many variations in culture and landscape; the jungle-like vegetation of the coastal regions to the desert within the span of a half-day excursion. One remarkable attribute of the hardy Australian people - a conclusion we reached later - there wasn't that immediate outpouring of friendship we had experienced so far. It was much more subtle. We were scrutinized more thoroughly, we suppose, but once you fitted a particular niche, you won the lottery of everlasting friendship. As the saying goes: "A fast friendship, never lasting. One that is slow, is forever!" We find this statement substantially true and appealing, perhaps because it fits more closely our German characteristics.

We remember Gladstone as a very pleasant and clean town.

WEST! SAIL WEST, MAN!

From the vantage point of a hill, one has a good view of the surrounding country, especially the extensive bay; very shallow for the most part, but underwent a huge dredging operation to accommodate large vessels for the transport of bauxite, Kaiser Aluminum was mining in the area.

Cautiously, Roy asked us whether we would like to consider going to church? "Well, yes!" We haven't been to a sermon for a long time and thought it only fair to thank our *Herrgott* for his guidance on our travels so far and through our prayers remind Him that we needed more of the same in the future!

In the Baptist church we were introduced as the "two people from a faraway land!" The sermon was given by a young minister in a strong voice. The words chosen were dead on course into our hearts. He spoke of perils at sea . . . men and women struggling to survive . . . the light at the end of a dark tunnel . . . the haven of God . . . ! It caused a surge in emotional feelings the likes I never experienced in any church. Siggi's lovely face was bathed in tears, and she had to use every bit of willpower not to blare out. We were impressed! So much, that we eagerly awaited the day to follow their dinner invitation.

He was a master in presenting a sermon, and equally proficient in telling of life in the "outbacks" where he with his family had spent two years. His tales were blended harmoniously with those of his wife and children. It remains a memorable meeting to this day. We parted with a standing invitation, and to speak up should we like to be driven around.

Heading for town one day, we spotted a pair of familiar looking masts among the local yachts. Sure enough, it was the *St. Briac*, we last met in Suva, the Fiji Islands. We immediately changed directions and went aboard her for a surprise reunion. They had spent the last few months in Brisbane. By ship they had visited Japan and many other places along the way. (It beats being broke!) From there on both parties had the same objective - sailing up the Great Barrier Reef. And in company, as much that was possible.

XVIII

THE GREAT BARRIER
REEF

The Great Barrier Reef stretches a thousand miles to the north, and the first miles we were about to make were on June 11th, 1965, the day we departed from Gladstone. The channel for larger craft gaining the shipping channel is long. We had chosen the North Channel, between Facing Island and Curtis Island, being a short-cut. The passage is intricate, and with a blustering southeast wind pushing us fast, we experienced some unpleasant moments among the rocks. Once clear we had a quick run to Hammocky Island. Expecting a safe anchorage, the protection was only marginal. We anchored close under the lee, but the surge was such it had the boat constantly dancing around the anchor, impossible to find a minute of peace, for fear it might trip the anchor. The *St. Briac* arrived a short time later because due to her draft she had to take the long way around Facing Island. She came in under full sail; a sight of grandeur that made our hearts leap with admiration. She was no racing type vessel - how could she be, looking so stunningly beautiful! Nor was she young. Quite the contrary. With the combination of a substantial bowsprit and bulwarks, she resembled a square-rigger of former days. Ketch-rigged, she was equipped with the best of gear money could buy. Below she was spacious and luxurious. A dependable Mercedes-Benz diesel gave her ample power. Equally spacious was the refriger-

191

ation plant, that could accommodate enough steaks and lobsters and beer and . . . to last months. She also carried a full size piano, on which Bernadette was a master. It was the ultimate vessel in which to enjoy the world; in Siggi's evaluation the perfect size and equipment! With them were three Australians as crew members - Peter Bouch, Bernhard and Don Cameron. Don, being the youngest, was the more colorful. In the words of Didier, the skipper, "He turns a delicate green every time the word 'work' is mentioned!"

The anchorage was lousy, and sleep impossible. It was a relief to raise anchor in the morning for a run to Kepple Island. Being a much larger island, the protection was superb. It held us for several days until a furious gale blew itself to moderation. Past Percy Island we sailed for Mackay Harbor. A wonderful sail in moderate winds, feasting our eyes on the many islands around us, and watching *Thlaloca*'s bow slicing the apple-green water, the trademark for much of the Great Barrier Reef. Clouds stole by the sun's disk and darkened the water in patches. We didn't like it because we thought of them as an intrusion in an otherwise perfect world. Here and there we sailed through large patches of dust. Coral-ash in the local jargon!

As soon we had the anchor down inside the breakwater, I boarded the dinghy and went ashore. Siggi came in *St. Briac*'s inflatable, and as I wanted to act the gentleman, I intended to help the girls out of the dinghy, an effort that nearly broke my neck. It was low tide and the landing thirty feet down wooden steps. The receding water had left the steps very slimy, I had failed to consider, and the moment I stepped on them, I got into a slide. To check my tumble, I embraced several barnacle encrusted pilings, which scratched me deeply. Messed up in slime and blood, it spoiled my day.

In a restroom, Siggi and I washed the dirt and blood out of my clothing and body. In the meantime, Didier had called for a taxi, to drive us the three miles to town. We did not fail to notice the beautiful flower arrangements all along the main street. It is normal to think of Australia as an arid country. This may be true for much of the interior but not along the coast. It was a pleasant surprise to see all the towns putting great emphasis on that mode of ornamentation.

Having cleared with customs and shopped for needed supplies, we got into a taxi that took us back to the landing.

The next haul brought us to Brampton Island, just then

emerging as a major tourist attraction. A motorboat, belonging to the resort, met us and guided us to an anchorage, but shallow water kept us a long way from shore. But not to worry, minutes later the man came back with an invitation from the management, to be their guests at the "Island Night", commencing after sundown. Siggi spruced herself up with grass skirt and headdress, stunningly beautiful as the best of *vahines*. How she does it all inside our "doghouse" is always amazing to me - as it is to others!

Mr. Fiz Mclean, the manager, welcomed us sincerely and offered free use of all facilities and festivities during the length of our stay. He handed us over into the care of Steve Steen, the skipper of the *M.V. Batja*, a Fairmile the resort was using for taking guests on excursion. Steve offered us a trip to Dent Island in the morning; as it turned out, the highlight of our stay.

But first the Island Night, a night made to have fun. All the guests, women in particular, were dressed in island costumes; only that Siggi's dress and ornaments came straight from "the horse's mouth!" *Lampions* of all shades and colors illuminated dimly the tepid star-studded night, and island music amplified that intoned its flavor into eternal memory. One other flavor that really excites my senses, is that of a barbecue. There was enough grilling space to cook thirty steaks at a time - very much needed to feed the crowd, and me!

In the morning we boarded the *M.V. Batja* for the run to Dent Island. The day was just glorious, and the sea as smooth as glass. We sat in easy-chairs under an awning sipping cold Beck's beer while absorbing the beauty of the many islands, bays and reefs en route. The cruise followed the Whitsunday Passage, perhaps the most beautiful area of the Great Barrier Reef. We believe that a lighthouse never fails to enhance the looks of a scene, and this is certainly true of Dent Island, in itself home to one of the world's most elaborate coral collection. It is tended to by two families, who extract a living by selling beautiful, some exquisite, coral sculptures to tourists.

On the return trip we got acquainted with an Aussie couple who had their home inland. They confirmed to us what the news media was talking about for weeks, that the country was in the grip of the severest drought in history. The couple told us in gruesome detail the meaning of it; of tens of thousands of sheep and cattle that succumbed to an agonizing death, that forced the government to mercy-killing the unfortunate ani-

The Kahos, Vavau Group, Tonga Islands

Dent Island, the Great Barrier Reef

Sailing the Great Barrier Reef

mals. To a lesser extent, it is what the country experiences almost every year.

The following day we walked the island to digest the sinful act of overeating; the result of yet another steak-night. We were surprised to see so many wild goats. Only fleeting glimpses mind you, because the animals were very shy. In former days, the British Government had stocked all major islands with goats,as food supply for shipwrecked sailors. It was puzzling to us, how starving sailors were supposed to catch one of those shy and speedy critters without any kind of a weapon!

During the night the wind had come up fresh from the west, making the anchorage exposed and bumpy. We set a second anchor and hoped we wouldn't be forced to leave in the middle of a dark night. With no moderation in sight we left with the first light at dawn. A fast run got us to Lindeman Island. And the following day to South Molle. It was a sail that would turn any diehard critic of sailing into a true believer. Propelled by a blustering southeaster and a good current, a flat sea under a brilliant blue sky and with many islands around to gaze at in wonderment we averaged eight knots. One word describes it all - *wunderbar!*

Taking walks over the island, and refreshing drinks at the club, we enjoyed it enormously. The National Film Board was preparing a film to promote tourism. *Thlaloca* the only sailboat, and a foreign boat at that, and us came just handy for stand-ins. What looked like fun, turned out to be a tiring operation as we were pushed around like dummies!

Townsville is one of the principal towns along the way, and there we found rest alongside a Fairmile boat, operated by three men who offered us their more spacious quarters to do whatever we liked. The men had families and homes ashore, so we had their boat as additional living space. It was a welcome break for Siggi, preparing meals on a stove that accommodated more than one pot. The local paper emphasized that *Thlaloca* was the first vessel in the harbor that exhibited the new Canadian flag. This in itself caused an avalanche of curious people. What irked us, that so little was known about Canada, one of the largest countries in the world, and some people, obviously extremely stupid or ignorant, had not even heard of it. Small wonder, though, we saw the only other Canadian flag a year later in the West Indies. Some boats we met were Canadian, but their skippers, for reason only known to them, refused to carry the new flag!

One afternoon, we received an invitation for dinner from the captain of the Swedish ship *M.V. Cervia*. Making sure we wouldn't forget, he sent his chief to fetch us. A lively conversation - in German for a change - detained us well past dinner. We then walked back to the boat with the assurance that we had experienced Swedish hospitality at its best. The captain's standing invitation to dinner, we reciprocated with our own - very formal in writing: " . . . compliments of The Canadian Sailing Yacht *Thlaloca*." The captain and the chief were with us aboard our boat the following day. Siggi had prepared a three-course meal on the stove of the Fairmile, that had the Swedes totally baffled. Would there be a Guinness Book of unusual sights, one strange sight would have gone down as that on July 13. 1965 in the form of two distinguished looking officers in spotless white and gold-braided cuffs among two insignificant characters in shorts and T-shirts displaying Tim Horten and the Maple Leaf, sitting cramped around a two-by-three-foot cockpit, each balancing a plate in hand, desperately trying to catch the ever escaping potato salad and hamburger. Their admiration for what we were doing, and for our lifestyle in general, didn't bring to light the amusing picture we must have presented.

Only a dollop of wind pushed us past Magnetic Island and on to Palm Island, where we anchored off the mission station for Aborigines. We went ashore but failed to make contact. The Aborigines are the natives of Australia, as the Indians are of America. Some are the blackest black, and are considered inherently friendly. A young fellow circled around the boat in a skiff. As Siggi was baking pancakes, I invited him aboard. He turned out to be a very smart and well mannered boy but, my lord, could that guy eat! He actually ate the whole lot that was meant for the two of us, and he would have eaten more, had there been more!

More anchorages followed over the next days that provided security and rest for the nights. What was missing was the company of other yachts and people. People were scarce, other yachts none! Occasionally we met up with the *St. Briac*; rare episodes that brought us joy and happiness. With five people aboard her and with a lot of equipment to enjoy the water, such as a fast dinghy and scuba-gear, we thought it best to plot our own course rather than hang around and become a burden of consideration.

At Dunk Island we anchored close to the beach within a crescent-shaped bay. A motorboat came out to greet us, it was Peter, a Rhodesian, who had settled in Australia a few years back, and was then helping boats with mechanical problems. Outside of the Seagull motor, which showed tenacious resistance to starting occasionally, mechanical problems were alien to us. So his help was more in the nature of pointing out places of interest.

Most, if not all, principal islands in the Great Barrier Reef are National Parks, therefore free domain to all people. Dunk Island came close to what we would look for in an ideal island. Beginning with the sandy beach and an anchorage that is well protected, the land has magnificent trails to meander. The one we took was completely enclosed like a tunnel, with lush vegetation, the sun's rays penetrating the tight cover of nature, piercing the darkness like torches. In all a fantastic display of glittering lights and color. The earth so moist, it gave the sensation as of walking on velvet carpet. Toward the top of the island, the vegetation gave way to larger openings which revealed a splendid view of distant islands dotting the reef-colored water. Way below in the bay we detected a tiny speck - our *Thlaloca*, the magnificent vessel that provided the means by which we explored the wonders of our planet.

The town of Cairns was our next destination. It was a long beat up the ship channel. Once clear of it, we anchored beside the *Paisano*, an old acquaintance.

Our giant Australian friend in New Zealand, Len Black, who had helped us so much in getting our boat back into the water, had given us the names, address and phone numbers of his and Joyce's (Len's wife) families in Cairns. We had promised to look them up - and so we did! Thus we met the Storers and the Savages. A meeting that had the benefit of real adventure.

Over the next couple of days we were driven hundreds of miles around the country, visiting places of interest of our choosing, selected from tourist brochures supplied by the tourist office. One thing what really intrigued us was the huge ant-hills that lined the roads like stumps of giant trees. The amount of food Mrs. Savage had packed in the boot of the car, gave the impression of going on safari for a week. Still, she judged it right. With me around, plenty was just enough! Parked for picnic at one of the scenic spots, Mrs. Savage remarked, "You Hein, please fetch the cake out of the trunk, because if my husband does it he dumps it on the ground every time!" Well, Hein dumped it on the ground as well, much to my embarrassment and Siggi's scorn, drowned out quickly by the hilarious laughter of our magnificent hosts.

Last we visited an automated sugar-mill, where the entire process, from the field to the finished product, was fully demonstrated.

Again, it was people, total strangers at the beginning, with whom we would form a deep bond of friendship on the premise of understanding and consideration. Two simple principles that could help the world. But why become philosophical!

With Cairn the last significant town, we engaged in major shopping. It had to last us a long way, possibly as far as Mauritius Island in the Indian Ocean. Another well known "watering hole".

It was suggested that the port captain knew every square inch of water within the Great Barrier Reef. With our charts we went to see him, to mark for us suitable anchorages. We were told that navigation north of Cairns becomes tricky, and in the captain's words, "The most difficult stretch of water in the world!" (How many times shall we hear this in our years of cruising!) He scared us into buying another ten dollars-worth of charts.

Later we came to realize there was no reason to be alarmed. If ships drawing forty feet of water were able to find a safe passage, a boat drawing a tenth of that should find a greater margin of safety. But being prepared is superior to not at all! Better than that, should one survive despite all warning, we had every reason to credit our magnificent intelligence!

Along the way to Cooktown, there were several anchorages that harbored us overnight. But since the town has historical significance, the *St. Briac* and we wanted to pause for a time. It was there that Captain Cook in 1770 repaired his *Endeavor* after striking a reef nearby. How easy that could happen was obvious by the presence of large patches of shallow reefs all over the place. We had to watch closely. With the sun in the wrong position we experienced mental murder before we found the can buoy marking the entrance into Endeavor River. We were elated when *Thlaloca* was safely tied alongside a small supply boat.

197

WEST! SAIL WEST, MAN!

Cooktown was once a thriving community during gold-mining days, but since had become a ghost town. Derelict stone structures were the only reminders of a once prosperous era. A monument to Captain Cook stood loftily above the desolation.

Equipped with shears and clippers, Siggi and I walked through the town in search of a suitable structure, to give each other a needed haircut. When we walked back to the boat half an hour later, it was amazing what a person could do with a dull pair of clippers within minutes, when my scalp was transformed from one like Rasputin's to that of a Mohawk Indian; and the person who did the damage angry because of my refusal to say, "Thank you!" Siggi was fortunate (I as well) in so far that civilization, as a possible witness to the slaughter, was a long way off.

☆

On July 17th, we left Cooktown for Lizard Island. It was blowing great guns. The *St. Briac* reported gusts to forty knots. We had panicky moments in recovering the spinnaker. After clearing Cape Belford, the course was due north. Close-reefed *Thlaloca* was virtually flying. That impressed Bernhard on *St. Briac*, and he snapped some excellent photos. The anchorage in the lee of the island was secure; and it better was because it was gusting great guns over top of the island. That particular area of the Great Barrier Reef seemed notorious for strong winds, as many reports indicated. All night it blew, and it made *Thlaloca* stagger under the onslaught. Yawing great half-circles and tugging hard on her mooring made sleep impossible. The same condition prevailed in the morning. Warnings of a severe storm were in the forecast. We were undecided whether we should proceed or not - finally we did.

Once clear of the island, Didier in passing - speaking through a loud-hailer - reported a wind-force of 33 knots, gusting 48 knots. The day's course was dead west, thus bringing the wind and seas abeam. It gave the *St. Briac* all the advantage of a ketch and her thirty-ton displacement. It gave us a horrible ride! The seas inside the reef may be smaller than out on the ocean, but they can still be big. And more to our detriment, short and vicious!

The conditions being much in *St. Briac*'s favor, she was escaping us fast. Puny *Thlaloca* with reefed mains'l and #2 genoa was doing her best not to be beaten too badly. Strong gusts which forced the boat to roundup many times should have been warnings enough (emphasized by the Admiral to the point of hitting me over the head) that more sail had to be reefed. Not heeding, we stumbled on.

Through the tiller we sensed the tremendous pressure on the steering gear. But sure of the excellent repair I had made in New Zealand, I was confident of its everlasting quality. One of the gusts hit us more severely than any before. We rounded up terribly, almost throwing us on the other tack. With force on the tiller, I tried to prevent it. When the boat had recovered I knew that something was wrong with the rudder - for God's sake not in a place like this! We reduced sail. Siggi took the tiller and confirmed my suspicion. The rudder became more and more restricted and finally jammed.

We shot off red flares to attract the attention of the *St. Briac*. When she didn't respond, we had to think of something effective to steer the boat with quickly. A full gale blowing; twenty miles to the nearest anchorage; reefs all around us, how could we possibly survive a night? To make me feel better I blamed it all on the Frenchmen, for sailing too fast! That's when the Admiral checked my tirade with a quote out of Slocum's book, *Sailing Alone Around The World*, she was just reading: "Every fool knows how to carry full sail, but only a real sailor knows when to reef!" Obviously, I still had a lot to learn! We fastened the paddle to one of the two 8-foot long 2x4-inch timbers we carried as permanent fixtures on the foredeck for exactly these or similar mishaps, and tied it to the starboard backstay chainplate. With only the smallest sails, sweat and a lot of work, we made it into the lee of Brewick Island, where the *St. Briac* lay at anchor.

After notifying our neighbors of what had happened, I went over the side to check on the damage. The entire assembly was bent in an angle. The skeg with a 2½-inch base had simply collapsed under compression. The result was a useless skeg, a bent rudder stock and trunk pipe. Very serious damage indeed!

Our previous rudder problems were in no way related to this one. We came to realize it was a failure of design rather than a structural fault of ours - there was no way I could have built it stronger! The boat was overburdened, all right, I agree, but a rudder assembly should be designed and built in a way that nothing could harm it, short of a collision with something hard.

WEST! SAIL WEST, MAN!

Subsequently we notified Laurent Giles, the designer of the boat, about the problem. Back came the answer: *"Trekka,* (the prototype) has sailed around the world with no problems. We can't understand why you should have any!" It is like saying: Someone drives an identical car without a problem, it is impossible that you can have any! A very disappointing statement, for which the office later apologized after I had corrected the problem without their help.

A steak dinner on *St. Briac* did much to ease our low spirits. When Didier offered every assistance, we felt very relieved. Looking at the chart we selected the Flinders Islands as best suited to find shelter, and a spot to beach the boat. While Siggi stayed with the *St. Briac,* (I hated the thought of "my lucky star" on another boat) I had Don with me for the 40-mile sail. With the advantage of *St. Briac's* long oar to steer with and in steadily decreasing winds, it was fairly easy. In fact, we had to finally set the spinnaker to make us move at all.

Don, who always expressed a desire to sail on our boat, keenly evaluated the pros and cons between the two vessels. In particular the work involved in upkeep and sailing. While *Thlaloca* may have come out on top in terms of "work," it was "comfort" he finally opted for; he demonstrated so well on arrival, when he swam for the *St. Briac* the minute our anchor hit bottom.

The anchorage between two islands was secure, no problem there. Disappointing was our failure to find a suitable spot to beach the boat. "Forget it!" Didier said, "We'll do it in the water." With Didier the Scuba-gear agent for all of North America, one could expect all necessary gear available to do a proper job. And with Peter a professional diver, things got moving fast. With the assembly removed, it was the bent rudder-stock that posed the real problem. How are we going to straighten out a one-inch shaft without a hard place in sight ashore.

Didier suggested using his boat's steel bollard as an anvil, and the 75-lbs Fisherman anchor as a hammer to pound with. It was against all my grain to expose any ship to such hellish abuse. Still, Didier insisted. After the first hit, shaking the vessel from trunk to keel I paused waiting for his signal to stop.

"What are you waiting for?" Didier asked.
The pounding continued. It chased the crew into the dinghy and

off they went. I had every reason to admire Didier enormously for his stoic insistence on hammering away when I thought we were pounding the bollard right through the deck.

As for the skeg, I increased the base area by fitting a piece of 2x4-inch timber on each side, well glued and through-bolted. Unable to find any suitable bolts from Didier's well stocked "spare parts department" we straightened the old ones. Not perfect, but it had to suffice as far as Thursday Island, 350 miles away, to replace them with new ones.

While Peter and I put the skeg and rudder back on, Didier with the rest of the crew went pig hunting. Before nightfall they returned with the evening meal. Bernadette, very French, very beautiful and an excellent cook, marinated the meat with all kinds of exotic spices and cognac. Still, the meat didn't fancy our taste buds.

Two-and-one-half days of intensive labor got the boat back in the running, thanks to the active help of all our friends. Not a complete job, but much better than we could have hoped for at the beginning.

In very light winds we made Hannah Island. It was stifling hot, which made us jump into the water as soon the anchor had grabbed hold. Don, wading in two or three feet of water along the shore, was thrashing about like a kid, when our peaceful world was pierced with the scream, "Shark, shark!" from the deck of the *St. Briac*. Siggi and I were back aboard in seconds, from where we observed a shark that was going for Don, who was hopping toward shore like a kangaroo. In his eagerness, the shark had grounded itself and was fighting madly to get back into deeper water. The experience left Don stunned for quite some time, and for a change had turned his facial color to a ghostly white rather than the "delicate green" when the word "work" was mentioned! To Siggi and me it brought home the dictum of our Aussie friend, Len, back in New Zealand. Apparently, the people who live near the water have a mutual agreement with the sharks: "We stay out of their water, they stay out of our bathtubs!" From there on we followed this sensible advice more intently.

North of Cooktown, sailing became rather dull. Settlements were scarce, and so were people. The coastline as barren as that of Mexico. The many islands presented only a passing interest. Some were endowed with green shrubbery, others only sand hills. With the barrier reef five to ten miles offshore, there was an abundance of reefs inside; parts of which were visible only at low tide, or indicated by broken water. A constant reminder to caution.

The run to Night Island progressed in glorious weather. The *St. Briac* was way behind us, doing her best in the light conditions. The chart indicated a widespread reef extending north from the island. The setting sun in our eyes made it impossible to see the outline of the reef, which we had to round in order to gain the good anchorage behind Night Island.

Groping in cautiously, we turned west when we thought it safe to do so. But it wasn't! A panic-tack prevented us running onto the reef. Back on a northerly heading, the next attempt ended with the same result - damn it!

We finally took a bearing on Waterwitch Island Light, and when it bore sixty degrees, we headed in. This worked fine and we dropped the hook in the lee of Night Island.

Looking back, with the sun behind us, we could clearly see the whole of the reef. Just then came the *St. Briac* moving fast under power. Cutting west short, she was headed for the reef. Frantically we motioned with the paddle. They guessed rightly that something had to be wrong, she slowed to a crawl, and then she hit the reef! She backed off without much effort and continued north. More tries followed, we waved her off. Eventually she came to rest besides us. Their appreciation of our help pleased us very much, because we saw in our warnings a modest repayment of all the good things they had done for us.

We decided on Cairn Cross Island as our last anchorage in the Great Barrier Reef. We arrived there during low tide, and were surprised at the size of the island. Lying well protected in the lee of it, assured a restful night. Like hell it was!

The lively motion of the boat woke us in the middle of the moonlit night. Looking out of the hatch there was no more island, just a speck of dead coral with the lighthouse on it. We spent an awful night, and yearned for dawn to push on.

Adolphus Island, just outside the reef, was our next break. It has a large sheltered bay on its west side, where we anchored for the night. Looking back we concluded that the last one thousand miles had been wonderful, mainly because they produced some of the finest and fastest sailing we would ever experience. What made it so much more rewarding, was the pleasant company of another boat for much of the way.

Our intention was to give the boat a thorough refit once we

got to Thursday Island, we already started with stripping her varnish. But with the previous night's sleep to catch up on, we didn't get far and turned in early. Next day we had our final run in the greatest of all oceans, the Pacific, to Thursday Island. There, on July 28th, we anchored *Thlaloca* among numerous pearl luggers.

In meeting Jim and Bernice Hall, our problems were solved in many ways. Jim let us use his steel cradle, in which we beached the boat right in front of their house. There we also found a home ashore. Over the following seven days we brought our little ship back to showroom standard. The skeg and rudder received our special attention, mainly replacing the bronze through-bolts and fitting the cheek-blocks to skeg and hull more precisely. It was all we were able to do, short of redesigning and building an entirely new skeg and rudder assembly.

The town itself was not very attractive. Water was scarce and not recommended for drinking without boiling it first. It seemed though, that one could easily be fascinated with this rather frontier life, as it was demonstrated by a sailing couple we got to know very well, Len and Carol Fox, who repeatedly postponed leaving for the past five years!

Diving for oysters (pearl-fishing) was the major industry, and at one time had a large fleet of eighty luggers. The introduction of plastic ornaments and buttons destroyed the enterprise, and most luggers were up for sale, although some of them had converted to Scuba diving and became competitive.

Because the drinking water on Thursday Island was of bad quality, Siggi's last job before leaving was boiling every drop of thirty gallons for the voyage. It was only possible with the help of the Halls who let us use their kitchen.

A broken rudder in the Great Barrier Reef

On the beach in Thursday Island

XIX

ANOTHER OCEAN TO THE WEST

On August 15th, we left for the 2,300-mile passage to the Cocos Keeling Islands. During the time of our stay in Thursday Island, the wind had been blowing fresh to strong every day. So severely at times it was impossible to get ashore with our dinghy. Now that we needed some, there was hardly any. Only a favorable tidal current propelled us past Booby Island, where a breeze finally blew of sufficient force to activate the self-steering. With the twin staysails drawing nicely, we let *Thlaloca* waltz her way gradually into the Indian Ocean. The wind held crossing part of the Gulf of Carpentaria, with daily runs around 130 miles. We were ecstatic!

Five days after leaving, the propellant force and excellent runs were only a memory as we lay becalmed on a glassy ocean. Plotting our daily noon positions was an easy matter of placing a circle on top of the one before - or nearly so! No wind, no current, no move!

The heat became unbearable, and to prevent our brains from drying out we rigged some cloth to give us shade. Rationing water became a necessity. We drenched ourselves with buckets of saltwater, which helped to make life tolerable.

We intended calling on Port Essington, a place that had been pointed out to us as being worth a visit, and where there was water, although limited but perhaps enough to help us out.

It also had the reputation of being hospitable. But how to get there was another matter that could only be solved with the help of wind.

With the occasional cat's-paw of wind from the south we worked ourselves toward the west. We dropped Port Essington as a "watering hole" and chose Christmas Island as a better solution. The new course was more northerly, closer to Indonesia as a possible source of water, should it become necessary. It was unfortunate that Indonesia had such a bad reputation on political grounds, that it was recommended to stay away from it. But in a pinch any place must do!

There were plenty of fish around the boat, but very small. We lay on our bellies looking over the stern and tried to catch their wagging tails extending out from under the transom. Not one did we catch, but it gave us something to do. We played games with them by flipping pieces of paper into the water, which attracted the fish instantly. They would dash for it, but just as quickly retracted, back under the boat - seeking shade as we did!

A family of hammerhead sharks - mama, papa and baby, judging by their size - frustrated our desire for a dip over the side. When we thought they had left, we stuck the paddle in the water and made swirling motions, it brought them back every time. Even more sinister creatures were the sea-snakes. Most were about three feet long and had yellowish-brown under-bodies. Some clung to the hull and tried to crawl up, but the boat's slippery sides prevented an invasion. Still, and it may read funny, we had legitimate concern that one of the slimy beasts might indeed succeed getting aboard and demand a place in our bunks. The Admiral's rich imagination went a lot further, to a point that she ordered night watches!

August 29th dawned to become a memorable day. Sailing along nicely to a flicker of wind that had ruffled the water, I noticed a disturbance ahead on the starboard bow. I called for Siggi and the binoculars. We judged the disturbance as being a school of fish. A slight course-change brought the object of our curiosity dead on the bow. As we drew close we recognized the impressive outline of a giant sperm whale. This monster lay motionless, its barnacles encrusted back exposed on which a flock of birds were picking. One could think the animal as being dead had it not been for short spouts of steam emanating from its blowhole. The body was marked with deep scars, a sign that he was an old warrior who must have had more than one battle with giant squids. The fellow had also a bad case of halitosis, that brought home the fact we were too damn close to a potentially dangerous animal. We knew personally the *Easterly* and the *Valkyrie*, two yachts that were severely damaged by whales.

I kicked the helm over at precisely the second this monster raised its blunt head sufficiently to expose a relatively tiny eye to look for the "nuts" who so rudely invaded his sphere of privacy. A tremendous flip of his giant tail set this immense mass of blubber in motion, dead for minute *Thlaloca*. At that instant Siggi's eyes became the size of saucers and for once she lost her speech, while I put on a careless indifference to say for me, "Heck, that's nothing!" In reality I braced myself tightly in the cockpit and fighting a heart attack. In a last gesture of defiance I kicked the helm over to change course, hoping that it would confuse the fellow. The beast broke water twenty feet astern and showered us with a geyser of foul smelling water that must have come straight out of his bowels. Down he went - for another try?

Siggi observed the water to port, I to starboard, perhaps we could outwit his intentions. Again we changed course, and again we prayed for survival. Next we heard and saw a geyser of water a mile away. We exhaled deeply, relieved to be still afloat. Only gradually did the pudding in our knees solidify; and Siggi's rich imagination took command of our conversation for days on end, about all the things that could have happened.

After ten exasperating days of almost total calm, the wind finally gathered force from the south, filling our limp sails, and giving us assurance that there was still something in our world, called "wind".

One morning we noticed our logline gone, and with it the whole back end of the register. We reasoned that only a shark would be mean enough to do this and hoped that whatever had done such a thing would choke on it. We mourned the loss of this important navigational instrument for days; made worse by the thought that along the way we must purchase a new one. Later, in Durban, South Africa, we contacted the firm of Walker in England, and got it replaced without any fuss. Three cheers for a honorable firm!

We passed Roti Island about ten miles to our starboard. From then on the trades blew mighty strong and boisterous at times, and piled up a sea out of any proportion to the wind-force. It was the first occasion I remembered the words of Bob Griffith: "Until you experience the Indian Ocean, you haven't seen a thing!"

At the time we were assured of one thing, that *Thlaloca* was pacing extremely fast! Soon we were down to one boomed-out jib, without reduction of speed. Many times in the past and future we admired the performance of our little craft amidst big oceans. Thrashed about, chased by menacing seas, overburdened many times, she came out of it in true fashion of a magnificent sea-boat. There was no hiding the fact that among the three of us was a love affair; a bond that was invested foremost in a bundle of wood, fiberglass, glue, nuts and bolts, welded together to a common denominator - *Thlaloca*. And there was the pride in ourselves who exposed this "bundle" to the test in the mightiest oceans of the world. Pass the bottle!

The morning of September 7th, showed a large rain squall where Christmas Island was supposed to be. With our change of direction to Christmas Island instead of Cocos Keeling, we had no chart of the place. And the one chance to find a harbor was by closing in and look for what might be one.

We were passing the eastern end of the island quite close, when without any previous warnings the sea stood behind us in a steep wall, what looked to us the height of our mast. Before we had a chance to reduce or strike sails, we were surfing at breakneck speed down collapsing walls of cascading water. When one wall had collapsed there was another close behind. Running before it, Siggi had difficulty getting the mains'l down. Before the next onslaught tumbled over the boat I screamed out, "Hold on!" I tried to hold the boat in line as much as possible, but to no avail. I let go the tiller and held on to the mainsheet with all my strength, while a seemingly endless volume of foaming water washed over the boat. I had the sensation as if floating somewhere in orbit without orientation. I grabbed the nearest thing floating by, the steering vane. When we broke surface my first look was for Siggi. What a relief, she was lying flat on her belly, with her feet dangling between the shrouds and her arms embracing the mast, choking and coughing intensely to get the ocean out of her lungs.

After convincing myself that we still had a mast and a rudder, I noticed the familiar rattle of my dentures (come to think of it, they have to be tightened before they get lost) and that made me realize that I was as frightened as Siggi - if not more so!

With a lot more struggle, Siggi got the main down all the way. Still scudding before it, we managed to edge towards the lee of the island. Another mile and the sea was as flat as a pond. We had come very close to being buried by a savage ground-sea. Those were scary moments we will never forget. In today's world, with all kinds of electronic gadgets available, a depth-sounder at least, venturing into shallow water without a warning is hardly possible; short of coral reefs where the water may shallow within yards, from infinity to zero. To have a decent chart of a place may even be more helpful. No excuse there!

Off the settlement, in the Flying Fish Cove, we tied the bow of the boat to a mooring buoy and the stern to a steel jetty. The port captain arrived to inspect our passports. Also the doctor, who declared us healthy enough to go ashore. When we mentioned our experience of a short while ago, he informed us that the spot is known locally as "hell-hole," that acts up when the wind, current and tide engage in a battle for supremacy. It seemed to us that we have a knack of being somewhere at the wrong blooming time! We received an invitation to a party that night. All seemed so unreal, to think that an hour or so past we were fighting for our lives, and already Siggi was brushing the mildew out of her shore going dress, and I was torturing my face to get rid of a month-growth of beard. Well, take advantage of the present, to hell with the past. Such is life!

The party was given in honor of a returning colleague. We were surprised to see that all the men wore beards - something unusual in those days. Bill Houston, the club's commodore, pointed out that all the men had sworn to grow a beard until Christmas, and any violation was punishable by paying the price of the most expensive bottle of Scotch whiskey. Later he mentioned that he had given me all kinds of signs from the jetty not to shave my beard. Given our special status, we were punished to taste every brand of liquor the well stocked bar had to offer.

The white population, mostly Scottish, was engaged in operating the phosphate mining industry. They were a happy and extremely generous group, who forever changed our ingrained belief of Scottish characteristics to the contrary. After sampling a good segment of the available brands, and well nourished with barbecued steaks, we only managed a crawling retreat. Whatever brands of liquor Siggi was subjected to gave her a case of the giggles, that caused excessive rocking of the dinghy, which in turn affected its delicate balance. We ended up swimming for the boat, accompanied by hilarious laughter from our gracious hosts on the jetty.

Christmas Island was administered by the Australian Government. A large deposit of phosphate resulted in a sizable mining operation. At the time of our visit, about three hundred whites and 3,000 Malays and Chinese lived there, all employed in one way or another by the mining operation. It was a fine example of people of different races and cultures living and working together in harmony and peace without the ugly byproduct of discrimination.

Our many Scottish friends did their best to make this island unforgettable. Bill and his wife Helen offered their home as our haven ashore. Every day we were driven around by different people, or invited to their homes. It was a continuous party. One only had to mention in passing, say for example that we missed something, or something on the boat wasn't working properly, etc., it was presented as soon it was located, or repaired or made in the large machine shop. We were careful in avoiding any remarks that could precipitate favors. Still, Christmas Island lived up to it's name, in a way we could not have imagined.

The mining was an open-pit operation, and very interesting to witness. As the deposits were concentrated in small pockets, care was taken to avoid too much byproduct - common earth - which required skillful hydraulic shovel operators. Before the introduction of modern equipment, it was done manually with pick and shovel by the durable Asians. The mined-out area, with thousands of pinnacles closely spaced, resembled a stalagmite cavern.

Mr. Stoke, the administrator of the island, came by for a visit and presented us with a large box of fruit. During the conversation he mentioned the cockroach problem in all the houses. This made us remember our own misfortune with these pests back in Costa Rica. It was an effective treatment for a short time only, because some of the eggs had survived, and that put us back to square one. He promised immediate help - without side effects, guaranteed!

The same day a truck pulled up the jetty, and the attendant handed us a long hose. The man sprayed the boat within half an hour, and we haven't seen a cockroach in all the years after!

During the regular monsoon season there was a steady traffic of ships, loading and transporting the phosphate to Singapore and Australia. Due to the great depth of the cove, a complicated mooring system was provided for, and ships were loaded from specially designed lighters. Having read reports about the Island, we were under the impression that the anchorage for boats was equally deep. But not so. Right at the pier there was seven feet of the clearest water, and ample anchorage west of the pier. Swimming and diving was a delight, of which we had daily exercise with our Scottish friends.

Not only was the island an oasis for lonely travelers, it was an inexpensive place to provision, we took advantage of by loading the boat to maximum capacity.

A Ham-operator on the island was in contact with his counterpart on Cocos Keeling, who conveyed a message to us, that the *St. Briac* was in Cocos Keeling and wanted us to bring a case of whiskey. Apparently it was well known that Christmas Island was inexpensive in any commodity.

As much we hated the thought of leaving, we could not afford to postpone it any longer. With the sailing date set (it was posted in the shipping office) we were approached by the postal service to carry a bag of mail for the Cocos islanders. Next came the Asians who begged us to take all kinds of produce to their relatives there. With the case of booze already blocking fifty percent of our floor space; it wasn't just to place a large box of twelve bottles on the floor, each bottle had to be wrapped and stored securely. The bag of mail covered the other fifty percent. It was hard to imagine how on earth we were able to take on more. To show our goodwill we accepted two bags of some sort of grain, about a hundred pounds. To convince the people of our good intentions, we invited some aboard to have a glimpse of our cramped quarters.

With emotional good-byes to all our precious friends who had congregated on the pier, ended our "holiday season." The wide open ocean was beckoning for new adventures. The ships' sirens that saluted us were the last sounds of civilization we heard for the next four days.

A huge beam sea made for rough sailing. The wind thirty knots or so reduced us to a reefed mains'l and small genoa.

Thlaloca, as ever, did nobly. By the end of the third day we had 170 miles remaining of the 540 miles total. It was a time to decide, either go as fast as possible and take a chance making harbor before nightfall the following day, or slow down and hang on another day. Against the Admiral's mild protest I decided on going fast!

Determined not to waste an inch of progress, I disconnected the self-steering, and we hand-steered for a more precise course. To prevent the boat from clawing into the wind, we set a boomed-out jib to windward.

As *Thlaloca* sliced through the water far exceeding her designed hull speed, it made the fin-keel quiver. The pounding and the rush of water along the hull was amplified through the ½-inch cedar planking in nerve-wracking crescendos. The noise made it unbearable for a person to remain below. It glued both of us to the cockpit, feeding each other warm drinks and goodies - parting gifts from our Scottish friends. Siggi protested bitterly, "You will drive her to her grave," and similar portentous predictions were common over the next twenty-four hours.

With sunrise we upped the spinnaker - after silencing Siggi's opposition - and what a sail we had! A pale-blue sky above deep-blue glittering water and a twenty-knot wind - hallelujah! The boat spurted as never before, a sensation that stirred spontaneous delight even in the opposition. Great was the suspense when we plotted our position at noon; great however my disappointment, for we had sailed only 152 miles in twenty-four hours. Four miles short of our record so far. It was obvious we had no helpful current which would have boosted the total. In any case, it was still an exceptional run for a boat with a waterline of eighteen feet.

Booby birds and gulls were out in numbers, which confirmed that land was near. Five miles off we sighted the antenna towers on Direction Island. One hour later we were anchored in the tranquil beauty of transparent water, facing golden beaches and swaying palm trees. We were elated, happy, and once again "home" for many days.

Cocos Keeling consists of many large and smaller islands, all within a lagoon. The most important one is Home Island where Clunis Ross, (supposedly of English heritage) as "King of the islands," had his residence, complete with a police force. It was forbidden to land there without prior permission. This group of islands was deeded to the Ross's family in a 99-year lease by Queen Victoria. As we carried mail and two bags of grain for his people, we probably would have received permission, but why force it? If a man with his Malays wishes to be alone, he must have good reasons which should be respected.

West Island with its airstrip was of vital importance to Qantas Air, the Australian carrier, in maintaining air travel between Mauritius, Africa and the Near East. The introduction of jet aircraft might soon make it less important.

Direction Island was the location of a powerful cable station, linking airwaves from around the world. One can imagine that in a war such a communication link has tremendous importance, as was recognized by the captain of the German light cruiser *Emden* in World War I. It sent out a raiding party to destroy it. While engaged, the Australian heavy cruiser *Sidney* showed up. A battle ensued in which the out gunned *Emden* suffered terrible. To save the crew, the captain run her aground at North Keeling, a few miles north of Direction Island. Later, the *Sidney* sank as well from mortal wounds received during that battle.

Lieutenant Miller, the leader of the raiding party watched the battle from atop a building. As the outcome became clear, the party shanghaied the old unseaworthy schooner *Ayesha* that was moored in the bay, and with it sailed to Batavia, which then was under the jurisdiction of neutral Netherlands. There they abandoned the vessel and by various means got back to Germany a year later. It is one of the epic stories that had fascinated me in my youth.

Of the thirty men who operated the cable station only four had their family with them. Under contract for a period of nine months on a lonely outpost in the vast Indian Ocean, one can easily imagine that life was boring most of the time. No doubt, the pay was good, and at the end of the contract one could walk off with a lot of money. For recreation there was the whole lagoon for sailing, swimming, diving and snorkeling on some of the world's most exquisite reefs; a separate world of unbelievable beauty.

A day late, John the Doctor, a huge Australian chap, came aboard to stamp us fit. We handed him the mail and grain for Home Island. He was most interested in our lifestyle, and we promised him a sail on *Thlaloca*.

With him came four men from the station, loaded with food and beer. It lowered the waterline of the boat to a point she couldn't perform. This didn't seem to bother anyone, as we all indulged rather excessively in the goodies they had brought; with beer being the more attractive item in demand. When it was over there was general regret, except our little ship, which rejoiced at having shed such heavy burden.

The "headman" took us to the residence of the manager and his wife, Mr. and Mrs. Hart, to be formally introduced. We found them very attractive, and who made us stay for a long time, eager to hear about the highlights of our voyage. Two days later, we received a written dinner invitation. The formality of it all gave cause to panic aboard *Thlaloca*. It meant that the mildewed garments had to be washed and ironed (as expected, Siggi had a miniature iron aboard). The canvas shoes were a real problem, they attracted mold like a swamp does mosquitoes.

The party was high class. With dishes so dainty I feared I might crush them in my clumsy hands. The fine china wasn't displayed to be ostentatious, we were certain of that, but simply a desire to entertain once in a while in a manner they were used to back in Australia. There they have without a doubt a fine home, and friends who own more than a couple of washed-out shirts, and shorts, and tormented canvas shoes; men who had no trouble tying knots in their ties, which I had almost forgotten!

The Harts were perfect hosts, and we suspect that they more than appreciated an outside visitor as a welcome break in an otherwise lonely life.

The cook was away on vacation in Australia, and we were offered his room as our home ashore. An offer we did not refuse. Our normal breakfast aboard ship was pancakes and instant coffee. It underwent a drastic change to toast and Tia Maria!

In the meantime two other yachts had arrived, the *Trekka* and the *Karen Margaret*. The occasion called for a night of hectic partying and dancing. The *St. Briac* left the next day in the direction of the Suez Canal. It was the last we saw of them. Much later we received the shocking news that Didier had been electrocuted by an electric drill while working on the boat. Very sad, he was truly a fine friend.

With *Trekka* (the prototype of our design) close at hand, I had a quick dive on her bottom to see if there were any differences to ours. I discovered there were indeed fundamental changes made on ours that explained the rudder problems we had in the past, and before long would happen again. I found, that the two angle irons, to which the fin-keel was bolted to, were carried aft to accommodate the skeg as well. In our case the angle irons were only the length of the fin-keel; the skeg attached to the keelson separately. Our rudder was also much larger. We questioned the reason that made it necessary to tamper with a proven design? Apparently, the design was modified to compete as a Midget Ocean Racer. By cutting short the angle irons saved a few pounds, and by enlarging the rudder area the boat would be quicker around buoys. Those were important changes we were not aware of.

It dawned on us we had to get a move on. Again we realized how much more fun sailing would be if it weren't for the ever present "windows," a time-span in which a passage should be completed on account of weather cycles. It was already the third of October, and a lot of sailing ahead to beat the cyclone season west of Mauritius Island.

In beautiful weather we cleared the edge of the reef. A last look back; a last cheer to the boys of the cable station in the escort-boat. We were alone again!

In the Cocos Keeling Islands with the *Saint Briac*

XX

A GHASTLY PASSAGE

Our next goal, the island of Rodriguez, lay two thousand miles to the southwest. On leaving the Cocos Keeling Islands, the wind blew fair for a fast offing. By sundown, however, storm clouds were moving in from the southeast, and with them came accelerating wind that soon whistled a high tune in the rigging. It was the prelude to a ghastly passage.

Bad weather was definitely in the offing, and why it couldn't be predicted hours earlier by the boys of the cable station, who were in contact with appropriate channels, we did not understand.

The night saw us sailing under one boomed-out jib only. Our efficient helmsman, the vane-steering, was doing as well as any of us. Again we noticed the unusual correlation between wind and sea. The wind force only about twenty knots, which normaly is close to perfect; and would have been perfect had it not been for the seas that piled up to some awful height and broke dangerously. "You haven't seen a thing until you experience the Indian Ocean!" Isn't this what Bob Griffith had warned us about?

It was impossible to let all this good wind go to waste with only one jib drawing. Up went the other "wing", with the immediate effect that the higher speed seemed to draw the monstrous breaking seas very close astern, with the inherent danger of getting pooped a real threat. There was no way the self-steering was able to compensate the necessary corrections in time to prevent broaching. It forced us to hand-steering.

The seas came marching on in an ever more threatening manner. When one of them stood behind us and broke close astern, it carried the boat forward at breakneck speed, bathed in a welter of foam. This was repeated again and again. It was exhilarating sailing, but tiring on the helmsman, and dangerous!

One wave in particular I noticed in the buildup, still a long way off. A real beauty. Coming closer and ever larger, I raced forward, unhitched the halyards and let the sails drop to the deck to reduce speed. Back in the cockpit I braced myself, to prevent being dumped over the side, and shouted a warning to Siggi inside the cabin, "Hold on!" The mountain collapsed astern with tons of water avalanching down the slope. I clutched the tiller tightly, and through it felt the terrific pressure on the rudder as *Thlaloca* was surfing into the valley. There, the water slammed over her stern filling the cockpit and for seconds buried the entire boat. This was really interesting to observe, because with the boat submerged it was my head and the mast the only objects sticking out of the water. Unfortunately, Siggi was thrown out of her seat and flung against the mast. The pain of her injured arm she was to feel for years to come.

Three days later we were still in the same mess, and when the barometer had dropped more notches, it scared us half to death because it could only mean that worse was to come.

Would it not be for the sheer horror of it, one could become philosophical about it and be thankful for being granted the privilege in witnessing the infinite power of nature that was on display one terrifying night, when low clouds scudded across the sky, driven by high winds from the southeast. Intermittently a large moon broke through the clouds and lit up a panorama of uncommon beauty. Shadows danced across the seascape like outstretched tentacles of a monster squid and showed every detail of the heaving mass of ocean around us. One illuminated moment found us on the bottom of a giant valley, surrounded by a chain of fluid mountains and cliffs that collapsed in a glittering display of fireworks. Next we were sitting atop a pinnacle, as if hoisted by a gigantic crane, peering into a hole of endless dimensions.

It brought home rather dramatically the insignificance of us

A Ghastly Passage

mortal beings, as only some microscopic flotsam in an alien world in which we have no intrinsic part, rather only a tenuous existence, to be rejected at will by an infinitely worldly power - the majesty of nature! It is a farce to think that we could ever claim survival on the strength of intelligence and physical power alone. Whoever survives this irresistible force has every reason to thank providence. Of course there are essentials that give survival a better chance, namely: a good ship, preparations and . . . yes, intelligence and physical strength, whatever value we are prepared to give it. As for us we claim two: A good ship, and that indispensable ingredient called "luck"; that one must have in any endeavor to succeed.

Scudding before big seas with the tiny boomed-out stormsail, a big sea grabbed the boat and planted it across the onrushing seas. Submerged in foaming water I had lost my grip on the winch and was washed overboard. This caused a moment of panic until I felt the tightening pressure of the safety line around my waist. Puffing and coughing up seawater, I hoisted my shaking hulk back aboard. Dazed I grabbed the tiller to get the boat back before the wind again. Both of us prayed and hoped for this nightmare to end soon.

Another big sea clutched the boat the very next day, two hours before noon. Rigid as a wall it came charging, the upper ten feet curled in a light green color. We didn't like it one bit. This mountain fell apart perhaps twenty yards off our stern. For about five seconds I had the boat under control as it raced into the abyss with a bow-wave standing way above deck level. It was a fantastic sight. Then I lost my bearings, let go the tiller and we scrambled and embraced the winches for safety as not to be flipped over the side. When the deluge had subsided, the boat emerged and shook herself like a wet dog.

Placing myself back behind the tiller to resume steering, I realized *Thlaloca* did not respond. Her skeg and rudder had collapsed again! The disturbing racket underneath her stern made that perfectly clear. I lowered the jib. Siggi checked the lazaret and found water seeping in around the through-bolts. With a safety line around my waist I jumped into the water to check on the damage. Again, the whole assembly was bent to one side; the skeg had given way under compression - below the cheek-blocks!

With the boat dancing and bouncing about uncontrollably, it was a frustrating job in getting a line around the damaged

219

parts, to be hoisted on deck once the nuts inside the lazaret were removed; the motion of the boat sufficed to shake the skeg free of the hull. The holes in the keelson we plugged up with wooden dowels.

What next? We started with kicked the sea-anchor over the stern to meet the steamrollers end on, or nearly so. This at least gave us pause to reflect on what had happened to us. Once we considered that it was still 1,600 miles to the nearest harbor, we were facing a bleak prospect indeed.

We both sat in the cockpit in deep thought to digest the calamity and find a way to overcome it. I stole glances at Siggi sitting across from me, her hands clutching the coaming tightly to prevent being bounced over the side. Her normally so orderly hair baked in streaks to her salt encrusted face. She was a sorry picture, but calm and collected. It gave me reason to admire her enormously. As a couple of times in the past, despite her pitiful appearance she radiated that "certain something" that assured me that together we'll overcome. And I knew only too well, she was our lucky star that would always shine upon us.

It wasn't that the wind and sea had moderated in an act of mercy, the fact that the boat was stationary, the wind was piping even a higher tune, and the seas as vicious as before.

As permanent fixtures we always carried two 2×4-inch by eight feet long timbers, lashed to forestay and shrouds along the foredeck, for the purpose of any repairs needed. Stored in the lazaret was a two-foot square piece of ¾-inch plywood. Screws, nails, bolts, etc., we had plenty. We bolted the piece of plywood between the timbers and lashed it to the chainplate of the starboard backstay. It didn't work! For one: We were unable to hold ourselves on the slippery aft deck. Two: The inboard end of the steering oar had to be held excessively high to get sufficient wetted surface on the blade. It had us exhausted quickly.

The following night became a nightmare. True, the sea-anchor did an acceptable job in keeping the stern to the onslaught, but only when everything was perfectly lined up. As soon as the boat got in the trough, the pull on the sea-anchor relaxed and the boat immediately turned broadside to the seas. With the rudder and skeg gone, the hull's lateral stability was nil. Lying in the trough she rolled and turned and twisted mercilessly. It was quite obvious that in this manner we wouldn't get anywhere. We tied the sea-anchor to the port aft cleat, raised a jib, and this seemed the best solution until something more effective would be found.

In the morning I put our thoughts into something constructive. Oh, brother, what a job it turned out to be! After unbolting the piece of plywood, I got it inside the boat. The rusty and dull handsaw that had given me the nasty cut in Rarotonga I had chucked overboard a long time ago. The only tool suitable to cut the piece of plywood diagonally, was a hacksaw blade. A piece of cloth wrapped around one end of the blade served as a handle. With the wood and myself being constantly yanked off position, I was convinced that all the gods were out to break me apart. Hot and sweaty as it was inside, I asked Siggi to open the hatch when it was safe to do so. When she missed I was drenched by the water charging through the opening. It was sheer hell. I tried to relieve my frustration with cursing, that prompted Siggi to remind me of the consequences this may force on "our Maker" who is surely watching us with great concern.

"You keep on like this and we will never see land again!" With Siggi balancing on my legs, I hung over the stern and bolted one diagonal - large end down - to the side of the outboard motor bracket, to act as a mini skeg. To the other diagonal I bolted cheeks of plywood, to a total length of about three feet. Into the leading edge of the cheeks I drilled two ¾-inch diameter holes and wrapped them tightly with stainless steel wire, to prevent chafe. To the top of the blade I bolted one of the 2×4 timbers to act as a tiller. The blade, with the holes towards the outboard motor bracket, I fastened to the bracket with yards of nylon cord. This contraption was a bit on the shaky side but seemed strong. Above all, it worked!

With the sea-anchor recovered, we knotted together all our ropes, taking care that the knots were big to create additional drag, these we paid out over the stern in a bight. It effectively supported the steering. Once again we forged ahead. And with everything holding together well, we realized the first glimmer of hope that all will be fine in the end. The next two days gave us ninety and ninety-two miles. But then came October 11th, which started with the most ominous looking bank of clouds to the east. The onslaught blew the tops of the waves in solid sheets across the boiling seascape. Survival lay in running before it under bare poles. We spent a frightful night. A position line the following day confirmed that we had been driven forty-two miles to the west of our rhumb line. We had not taken a sight the previous day, so it was possible that part of the large drift occurred the day before. The drift worried us in so far, that the small rudder did not permit us carrying the mains'l as it made the boat roundup into the wind. With every mile lost towards the west made sailing to a beam wind with foresails only increasingly more difficult. Any sea that bounced against the hull aft of midship yanked the stern to leeward and put us on the wind, leaving us dead in the water. The tiny rudder was then unable to get us out of irons quickly, and the resulting clatter of the sails gnawed on our nerves. If this tendency of losing easting continues, we must adjust our course to an island more to the west.

Something had to be done to make the boat sail better. As only foresails could be considered for reasons just mentioned, we cut off the bottom of an old canvas jib that Ron on *Gannet* had given us in Panama. I heavily re-enforced the tack and clew of the top part, and ended up with a sail of about fifteen square feet. Our stormsail was twenty-nine!

Boomed out, the new sail sheeted flat some twenty degrees to windward. It effectively prevented the boat from rounding up, and it certainly added drive. This was really a decisive moment, because from then on the boat sailed well.

Continually exposed to saltwater eventually peeled the skin around our seats, and the salt in the wounds bothered us a lot. Not able to sit, we knelt on the cockpit floor, but soon had the same problem on our knees. It became an agonizing struggle to find an acceptable position.

On October 15th we sailed through a series of rainstorms. The undulating sea ran in huge mountains still, but no white-caps. It indicated a change in the weather. Yearning for a longer period of rest other than the usual two hours on and off over the past fortnight, we called it quits. We dismounted the rudder to save it from wear. Removing the rudder was a good half an hour of strenuous work; exactly the reason we declined doing it before. The weather, of course, was a deciding factor as well.

As one bunk was loaded with the broken rudder and skeg, for which there was no room on deck, we both squeezed into the port bunk and spent a rough night. But still better than the two-hourly watches over the past fortnight. A large dose of Vaseline smeared on our tormented bottoms and knees did wonders. The morning blessed us with the first rays of sunshine that lasted for more than a fleeting moment. A substantial breakfast supercharged our energies to an unprecedented high, and with a harbor almost in sight, had erased all our worries. We remounted the rudder, and back we were on the dreaded watches.

October 20th, was the first day the sun shone all day, the wind a consistent force four. We even hoisted the masthead genoa, with the drag-line doing a fine job in supporting the steering. Two days later, a star-fix placed us within a day of a landfall.

The following morning surrounded us with at least six benign rain squalls, and any one of these to the south of us could hide the island. Siggi had her keen-smelling nose circling like a radar antenna. When she announced the island towards the west, I flipped. On many occasions in the past, her keen smell had me agitated to the point of hitting the roof. But every time so far she had been right. This time, no way! After all, what she had sniffed was to leeward, crazy! When the horizon had cleared, Siggi screamed, "Land ho!" she was right again. The island was there where she knew it to be all along. I never doubted her nose again!

We hauled in the drag-line. The wind decreasing, we chanced hoisting the closely reefed mains'l. It worked, and slowly made our way towards the island. Still a fair distance off, we hove-to for the night. A wonderful night under the umbrella of myriads of stars and a gentle wind blowing. Content in the knowledge that the ordeal was almost over, we slumbered into a restful sleep.

We raised sails very early in the morning, and ever so slowly closed in on a reef that stretched as far we could see. We were unaware that the reef, marked on the general ocean chart as only a small dotted outline, was so large, and then so far offshore. Had we known, our sleep would hardly have been what it was! We had reason to be thankful to our friends at the Cocos Keeling cable station, who had notified their colleagues in Rodriguez of our impending arrival. A motor launch came out and towed us through an intricate channel into a small but safe harbor.

Broken rudder in the Indian Ocean

Arrival in Rodriguez Island (Note jury-rudder and skeg)

XXI

RODRIGUEZ
AND ISLANDS BEYOND

A lot of people were present when we entered the harbor; as any arrival of a vessel is a special occasion for the islanders. Monsieur Vallet, the magistrate of Rodriguez, and his wife welcomed us. That we had trouble was obvious by the pile of lines staked all over the boat and the jury rig we had for steering. We answered his inquiry by giving a short account of the past two weeks. He promised every assistance. To prove it, he called for Mr. Nicolai, the head engineer of the island. To him we explained our problems. He recommended that the boat should be hauled the following morning. Another VIP we were introduced to was Mr. Remy, the Chief of Police, and his wife who immediately took us to their house for a well appreciated shower and a meal.

We lightened the boat as much as possible and stored the items in a warehouse close by. The portable crane arrived, and with it a large crowd of people, who never missed a chance to see something different, as a welcome break in an otherwise quite boring island life.

On a solid stretch of asphalt, the crane took position alongside *Thlaloca*. On nicely cushioned rope slings around the hull, the boat began to rise slowly. When the hull had cleared the water by about six inches, the boat suddenly plunged back. The wheels and the outriggers on the side of the load had bro-

225

ken through the blacktop, down to the axles. No one could have possibly imagined that seepage over the years had undermined what should have been terra firma. With the crane leaning at a dangerous angle towards the boat, I jumped aboard her and freed the load, while Siggi very smartly pulled her from under the "leaning tower."

What aggravated an already precarious balance was, that the crane operator in a moment of panic had swung the boom to the opposite side, meaning to lessen the burden on the leaning side, but inadvertently had brought the counterweight - the heavier weight - to bear where it was wanted least! Now it really looked as if the whole rig was going to tumble into the water, as the ground crumbled away more and more.

To this day we admire the people of Rodriguez who exhibited exceptional acts of courage, by rushing to the counterweight and using puny manual strength to prevent the rig from tumbling into the water. Equally brave was the crane operator, who instinctively, I suppose, should have deserted, but instead stood by his rig and swung the boom onto the lubber-line, thereby neutralizing the weights.

A large lorry pulled the crane out of the hole. Shifting to another location, *Thlaloca* was out of the water without further mishap. Mr. Nicolai put two men on the job who were absolute experts. Knowing exactly what was called for, the work in making the fittings progressed smoothly. In an attempt to locate a suitable piece of material to replace the bent rudder shaft, Mr. Remy had spread the word around town. Sure enough, a local business man came forward and donated a stainless steel shaft. Bless his heart! It measured two inches in diameter to the one inch we needed, but Mr. Nicolai said, "No problem, we'll whittle it down!"

Very frustrated about our constant rudder problems despite all our effort in improving its strength after every mishap, I finally reduced the rudder area to a size I had measured on *Trekka* in Cocos Keeling. That the move was in the right direction is proven by the fact that *Thlaloca* sailed a further 30,000 miles while she was ours without any troubles, and with no change in performance.

It was recommended not to live aboard the boat while she was on the hard. We were offered quarters in the Red Cross Building nearby. The building was almost new and had all the amenities to support comfortable living. The largest room,

Siggi immediately converted to a living room, and it was astonishing to see how quickly she had found furniture, mostly dressed-up cardboard boxes she had snatched from somewhere. It made for camping in high style. A welcome change from "doghouse-living" - paradise or not!

Mr. Nicolai and his crew had the steering and skeg assembly ready in three days of careful work. Siggi and I put it back on. We cannot say that it was done better and stronger than before; better and stronger wasn't possible, only smaller!

With the boat back in the water, and all the gear back aboard as well, we retained our shore quarters - Siggi wasn't about to exchange comfort for a "doghouse" until imminent departure!

Sailing off was put on hold until a nasty gale had blown itself to moderation. The delay provided opportunities to explore the island, which despite its small size supported 24,000 people; a conglomeration of many races, but mostly Chinese. Before it became British, the island had been French; and French was still spoken extensively.

While attending a party, a doctor among the guests received an emergency call from the hospital; a woman had to have a Cesarean delivery, *pronto!* He asked us to attend. I was ambivalent about it, not sure of myself when seeing blood. Siggi was the opposite and dragged me along. When we arrived there, it was discovered that no oxygen was left in the bottles. A new supply was on a ship out at anchor but unable to unload on account of the bad weather. I checked the dozen or so empty bottles that stood around and put aside the ones still partially loaded. It was interesting, while I hammered on the bottles trying to loosen worn out fittings with tools just as bad, in the same room lay the young mother to be in pain, and the operating personnel, doctors and nurses, sat around in devoted prayers!

During the operation, the doctor gave a running commentary, explaining every detail of the procedure. Suddenly there was a "thump" where Siggi had passed out on the floor. I carried her to an adjoining room, where she came back to life. Fascinated by what was taking place I rejoined the operation, and was surprised that I hadn't passed out myself. That we couldn't afford because of the botlles, which had to be changed often - a job I had perfected to a science!

The arrival of a ship in the islands may be compared to a

national holiday in our country. It causes feverish activities days before, when all kinds of locally produced merchandise was carted to the harbor and stored in piles. Evidently, Rodriguez was raising a lot of livestock, judging by the numerous cages in which the animals were penned. We thought that the pigs got an exceptionally rotten deal because each pig was confined in a round wire cage, stacked five or more rows high, like a pyramid. After a day of intestinal discharge from the top rows, the pigs on the bottom were not recognizable as pigs anymore, and this must surely hurt even a pig's self-esteem!

By daybreak, gaily dressed people had gathered to occupy a favorable spot around the harbor. Most had come out of curiosity, others expected relatives, friends or mail.

The transport of cattle to the big ship offshore was handled efficiently, but we thought rather cruel. A rope connected one fore and one hind leg on one side of the cattle. A man would work from the opposite side under the cattle's belly, grab the rope and jerk very hard, causing the animal to crash onto the hard tarmac. Never a miss! Quickly, while the animal was still stunned, all four legs were lashed together, hooked to the crane (thank God it was saved, because it was the only crane on the island) and on their backs were placed into a longboat stacked against each other. Thus, a relatively small boat was able to carry as many as eight critters. Transferring them onto the ship was simply a matter of hooking onto the ropes. The whole lot in one shot!

The head of the Agricultural Department, Philip Hutchins, came by in his Land Rover, to take us for a drive into the mountains. The highest point gave us a wonderful view of the island and the ocean beyond. In particular we noticed the huge reef that extended north from the island. To think that we were hove-to and slept through the night without being aware of close-by danger, gave us a belated case of the shivers.

Farther on we visited a convent, where we were invited into the presence of three Catholic priests. They opened their hearts and their liquor storage, which we thought was more than amply stocked with the choicest brands from around the world. One of the fathers had resided for years on La Réunion, a French island 400 miles to the west of Rodriguez. We were given a slide-presentation that emphasized the exceptional beauty of the place. How nice it would be to visit the island but, like all French possessions around the world, they were expensive - places like that we preferred to bypass! The fertile land on Rodriguez was worked by the industrious Chinese, who had cultivated every morsel of it, and as a reward grew an abundance of vegetables. The island being hilly for the most part, the slopes were all worked in terraces; an effort that must have taken generations to accomplish. On top of a plateau we visited a large dairy farm. The proprietor was a skinny man who spoke only limited English. I know very little of cows and their genetic make-up, but I do know there are different breeds; and what breed they were I wanted to find out - more, perhaps, in an effort to show up the little I know about cattle in general in the face of Philip's overwhelming expertise. So I asked the skinny man, "What sort of breed is it?" The way the good man looked at me there was no doubt in his mind that he thought of me as a complete idiot. "Tees is cow, Monsieur!" he retorted.

One day we received a dinner invitation from the magistrate, Monsieur Vallet and his wife, to a Chinese restaurant. The place appeared like a mole-house; we entered through a dark tunnel that led to the sparsely lit kitchen, where the most prominent implement was a massive iron stove on which simmered mysterious food in monster iron pots. In an almost ceremonial manner we were encouraged to sample the contents of each pan; observed by three Chinese men wearing long pigtails, bowing constantly in a submissive manner.

My lord, what am I getting into here? were my thoughts, having fleeting imaginations of all the strange things the Chinese fancy to eat. Adjoining the kitchen was an equally dark room, lit dimly by *lampions* in different colors, which gave the room a festive character. We were seated at a table that could have easily accommodated a dozen people.

The unusual food we were served was delicious. Monsieur and Madame Vallet being French, therefore the dinner was enhanced with exquisite French wines and cheeses, and a lively conversation that lasted for hours. We must admit that the French style of dining has *das gewisse Etwas*!

☆

Our magnificent mechanics were definite in refusing any payments for their generous work. As a token of appreciation we made them accept two cases of Becks beer, and a bottle of Scotch for each.

Again we had reason to believe that it takes more than

fortitude to sail the world. Above it all one must be lucky and have the support of generous people.

November 5th, was our date for leaving. The wind had been blowing strong for the past week, and still was with no moderation in sight. In view of the cyclone season already established, we had to get moving. The launch, with the Chief of Police, Mr. Remy, aboard, with whom we had spent so many pleasant hours, towed us clear of the winding channel. A last farewell, then we were alone again.

Closely reefed, *Thlaloca* reeled off the miles in grand style. The "little hop" of 320 miles to the island of Mauritius we made in three days. The island is very high, rising to 2,000 feet in the center. With its abundance of lush greenery it looked inviting. After rounding the north end, we beat our way to Port Louis, the main harbor.

With darkness closing in quickly, and not much of a chart to go by, we pulled off the channel to anchor, but ran aground. This forced me into the water, and with a fairly hard footing under me, I managed to push the boat off. For the night we anchored under the stern of the 12,000 ton cargo carrier, the *Sycamore Hill*. In the morning we found an excellent berth owned by the Blythe Brothers, an import/export firm.

Mauritius Island was considered the most densely populated country in the world; almost a thousand people to the square mile. Yet, touring the island we were surprised seeing so much agriculture land compared to housing. The population consisted of a mixture of races, but with a pronounced East Indian influence. We often asked ourselves, do these people have a distinct breeding technique, or is it indeed only by way of the natural process that produces such profuse numbers we witnessed in so many places. The majority of people are disgustingly poor. School buildings especially where mostly ramshackle huts.

Port Louis, the principal town gave an untidy impression on the whole despite some highly modern buildings, such as banks! The shopping however was excellent for those with a flair for haggling, of which Siggi classified herself superior. I'm afraid that her belief in her excellence was a poor match to the crafty vendors.

Mr. Bouchet, the leading hand with the Blythe Brothers, drove us around the country, where nature's beauty is bountiful, and could well become the base for mass tourism at some time in the future. Whatever direction we turned we faced a dazzling panorama of nature, and gorgeous beaches everywhere. One attraction that was said to be unique in the word was "colored earth", which changes kaleidoscopically. Geologists from many lands studied this peculiar phenomenon, without ever finding an answer.

We met Jeff Mathews when he with his 53-foot ketch *Dida* pulled alongside the same pier we were lying to. He had sailed singlehanded from Indonesia. The reason we remember *Dida* so well, is on account of her enormous self-steering paraphernalia. The vane was literally the size of a barn door. Being all steel, the entire assembly must have weighed a ton. Yet, he claimed that it worked just perfect.

Jeff, who had made a small fortune as a crocodile-hunter in Australia, was well endowed to hire a car for a run to Grand Bay, considered to be the most attractive part of the island. We were invited to come along. There we were introduced to the Smith brothers and their wives and friends, who were at their cottage for the weekend. The brothers were the owners of a large shipyard in Port Louis. There was immediate rapport among us, and we spent the afternoon frolicking on the beach, swimming and diving on coral reefs; well supplied with cocktails and yummy food. The Port Captain, Mr. Bouker, was there, with whom we spent enjoyable times later. Also present was a television personality whom we will always remember as the funniest man we ever met. By any standard, it was a super afternoon.

Shopping at Appavou's Market, we met Mr. Bouker again, who introduced us to the skipper of the *Sycamore Hill*, Captain Gock Campbell. He invited us for lunch at the Merchant Marine Club. We had no idea that such a club existed. It had all desirable facilities one could wish for, such as a swimming pool, showers, library and a loaded bar!

Aboard his ship we sampled the vodka he had brought from Russia. During the conversation he named all the "bloody" mistakes we Germans had made, which contributed to losing the "bloody" war. What he failed to mention, but certainly hinted, that the decisive weapon in the Allied arsenal was the Scottish soldier. We drank to that! It made him very happy to a point when he exuberantly exclaimed, "I have a 'bloody' ton of corn flakes aboard, my 'bloody' crew is sick and tired of. Do you want the 'bloody' lot?"

WEST! SAIL WEST, MAN!

Well, we didn't want the whole "bloody" ton, but some;
much to the annoyance of the Port Captain, who was present,
because he was delegated to smuggle the corn flakes, packed in
a large suitcase, through customs, and in case of getting caught
it would wreck his distinguished career. Needled by the captain
mercilessly, the guardian of law and order, with a sour look on
his face finally committed himself to perform the unlawful act.
On parting he extracted from us the promise we would not
trade, sell nor do anything unlawful. Our promise of compli-
ance lightened his conscience a marked degree!

Jeff wanted to take *Dida* around to Grand Bay, before departing for South Africa. He asked us to come along for the
short sail. It was a thrill sailing on something larger than
Thlaloca. The wind only moderate, gave us a most enjoyable
sail. The boat clawing ahead with minimal motion, we compared with *Thlaloca*'s popping-about performance in similar
conditions. And what comfort! If one spot wasn't just right, we
moved to another . . . bring up the cushions . . . make some
drinks . . . While you down there . . .!

But not all was "cushion" and "drinks" and . . .! Looking
around, at the massive gear, the huge vessel in itself and considering the upkeep, brought home a significant fact: That in
sailing - as it is with most things in life - there is a "golden
middle" that needs careful evaluation. That a 20-foot boat is far
too small to enjoy cruising is true without argument. It is indeed what Siggi repeated so often, only an oversized doghouse.
In inclement weather, whether at sea or in harbor, it could be
very uncomfortable. Still, it gave us the only chance to see the
world on a low - very low - budget. Think of it! We had left
Panama with eighty-five dollars and some change in the kitty.
Two years later (Mauritius) we had three hundred. Like a dog
that buries a bone for bad times, Siggi had this awesome treasure hidden away deep in the bowels of our ship, and guarded it
with the alertness of a pit-bull!

Back to "careful evaluation": we concluded that for a couple in love a thirty-foot boat well equipped would be ample. If
"love" is on the shaky side, chances are that even the largest
vessel would not suffice.

☆

Again the pressure of leaving was mounting. Postponing
the inevitable from one day to the next is great, but it doesn't
get us anywhere. November 19th found us drifting slowly away

from the berth, where Gock and Mr. Bouchet gave us a last farewell. We had just cleared the channel when we spotted a launch following us. We wondered what it meant. Had we forgotten something? We rounded up into the wind and let the launch approach. It was the Smith brothers, wanting to give us a final farewell. We were so happy and thankful for such a noble gesture. Once clear of the island we set the tradewind-rig to a northeasterly wind and let *Thlaloca* steer herself towards the southwest, where at the end of the passage was to be South Africa.

Perhaps the most unforgiving navigational error I had made so far, was allowing our ship to run aground back in Mexico - and almost losing her. On leaving Mauritius Island I made a boo-boo even worse. With a decided difference though, that the latest error would give us the highlight of our voyage around the world. The error: I had computed the magnetic variation the wrong way - 20 east for what should have been 20 west - putting us forty degrees south of our course!

Unaware of the mistake, we had a wonderful sleep throughout the night, and even missed the occasional glimpse outside. First light in the morning had us gazing to the south, where La Reunion Island was supposed to be! Nothing sighted, we concentrated our attention to the north, where an enormous black cloud topped a dense haze. The thought of an approaching squall was dismissed by Siggi's sober remark, " Darned, that is land!" "Land, my foot!" I retorted defensively. When it dawned on me that she was right - it really irked me that she was - I lectured her to be a bit more gentle in presenting statements of that sort. Nothing, however, could soothe the fact that we were looking at the top of Vulcan des Furnaise, towering 8,000 and some feet into the sky! Facing truth we realized, had the island extended two miles further south, we would have experienced a D-day landing on hard rock. Not a pleasant thought, and a reminder to be more careful in the future.

In the lee of this colossal mountain we lay becalmed, and with sails flapping in nerve-deadening bangs we made every effort to escape it. But all that day and the following night *Thlaloca* rolled mercilessly, and the damn mountain as close as ever. Listening in on the Mauritius weather report, we learned of a large high pressure cell, with little hope of a change soon.

The report forced the "Seagull" over the transom, and we motored towards the island. As we had no intention of calling on this island, we had no detailed chart to go by. We therefore skirted the coast to find water shallow enough to anchor. When the color of the water suggested suitable depth, along came an old man in a canoe-like craft, motoring. When we waved, he came close. In our best French - we hoped we wouldn't scare him off with that - we repeated "-'arbor, '-arbor," (silencing the "h" to make it sound perfect). We followed the direction he had indicated, but failed to detect anything that would resemble a harbor. When we sighted a rocky bottom under us, we headed off. The good man must have had an eye on us all the while because he returned and led us into a most perfect small basin where we anchored, well shielded by a massive concrete break-water. Thus we had arrived at a place called St. Pierre,

Our arrival appeared to be something extraordinary, because of the many people that had gathered. In Monsieur Ramoux we found a person with whom we were able to converse in English. He wanted us to come ashore. But not sure how the French officials would react to such liberty, we said "no" and in pantomime demonstrated the action of the guillotine. This caused hilarious laughter among the crowd. The Port Captain was notified, who eventually appeared in a sparkling white uniform and richly gold-embroidered epaulets; the cause for renewed laughter and hand-clapping. Later we were told that *Thlaloca* was the first foreign yacht that was cleared in this harbor. Apparently, the captain didn't even have authority to do so, as the only Port of Entry was Saint Denis, in the north of the island. But one can always count on the French officials to be fair and courteous. (This we found substantially true considering the many years of our future sailing in the Mediterranean Sea). Monsieur Ramoux loaded us into his car and drove us to see the sous-prefect, Monsieur Rousseau, who occupied a highly modern office building. In a mixture of English and German he made us understand, that we were to be his guests for the length of our stay, and immediately outlined a program for a week. Not one word was mentioned about us leaving with the first sign of wind. When we did mention it, Monsieur Rousseau called up the airport weather office, "No wind for a week," he announced!

We were offered quarters in a brand new guest house with all facilities imaginable. It was decorated with natural timbers and had a stone-built fireplace. A very posh place indeed. "What about our boat, is it safe?" We inquired. "Don't worry, I

Rodriguez and Islands Beyond

will appoint a permanent guard!" He replied.

What followed remains in our memory as the most exceptional and wonderful days in our travels. His office and residence was well staffed and exquisitely furnished. Monsieur
Rousseau, a former officer in the French Army and a gentleman; Madame Rousseau, very French, very petite, beautiful
and a perfect lady. Their daughter, Françoise, had the manners
and beauty of her mother. (Very unfortunately, Françoise died
of cancer a few years ago. Very tragic, very sad).

To facilitate a smooth conversation, a college professor of
English, from the capital, was invited for the evening, with
other guests. It was obvious that I could not appear in shorts
and sandals for such an occasion we sensed would be rather
formal. We submitted to the same ritual we went through in
Cocos Keeling. Siggi got to work to rid our clothing of mildew. My job was to get my canvas shoes in presentable condition. The shoes, excessively abused already back then, did
react rather restrained to my brazen attack of scrubbing, which
resulted in ever larger patches of discoloration. What now!

There are times when even I come up with a splendid idea
without Siggi's coaching, bathe the shoes in a strong solution
of instant coffee. The result was twofold: One, it did a marvelous job enhancing the rather spotty fabric to a coherent chocolate color. Two: It took care of the repulsive odor of mildew.
For good measure, I siphoned off some of the coffee-syrup into
a tiny jar (plastic film container) and with a shortened tooth-
brush as a spreading tool, joined the party with confidence.

The party was wonderful. Nudged occasionally by Siggi, to
remind me that the shoes needed another pasting. The trouble
was that the body-heat caused the canvas to dry in patches! My
frequent runs to the toilet must have puzzled our gracious
hosts, who surely suspected a bladder problem!

For the next two days we were allotted a car and chauffeur,
and were free to go anywhere. The island being very mountainous, there followed one spectacular sight after the other. The
roads were excellent. And so was the driver! Anything less than
that would have landed us in one of the deep gorges, as he was
driving like any self-respecting Frenchman would - too damn
fast! We asked him if the island has anything like a Highway
Patrol, expecting that it would scare him to reduce speed.
"Yes," he said, "No problem, Monsieur Rousseau is the Chief
of Police!" This, obviously, took care of any of our ex-

235

pectations.

"Our chauffeur" stopped at a charming pavilion 3,000 feet above sea-level for a picnic. In the boot of the car was everything a sensible picnic requires: fried pork chops, chicken-nuggets, half a dozen French sticks, brie cheese, wine and cognac.

This was repeated the following day along a different route. In addition we had a sumptuous dinner at a most exclusive hotel in Saint Denis, the capital. On returning to St. Pierre we received an invitation to the riding club. Again one of those elaborate French dinners that stretches for hours. It was all so unbelievable gorgeous. It was living in high style, still so casually. Always a conversation, always plenty of time; it seems that only the French people are relaxed enough to do so. We came to admire their lifestyle enormously, as it hinted the secret to longevity.

On our return, driving along the seashore we noticed wind, and we were anxious to leave. Talking to Monsieur Rousseau about it, he regretted our decision since he had already made plans for more than a week ahead.

Right there one could have easily thrown in the towel and let developments decide destiny. Strictly sailing it is fairly easy to get around the world, but there are those wonderful people along the way who exert such powerful brakes. But leave we must, because the cyclone season was already far advanced.

But the devil was in the weather. Monsieur Rousseau confirmed it: "I talked to the weather people, no wind for one week!" So what! Back to shoveling in calories. Beginning in the morning with freshly baked croissants and all the goodies that go with it, served expertly by a charming maid while we were still in bed. One of Rousseaus' friends was the owner of a large sugar plantation, and who also owned an aircraft. We were invited to view the crater of Vulcan des Furnaise, one at a time. The man flew deep into the crater and along the inner walls. Some of his fancy maneuvering increased my apprehension about the whole flying circus, which in the best of times seemed only a touch-and-go affair. Sitting far behind the windshield, my throat turned gradually to an icicle. Once back on terra firma I was a happy man. I advised Siggi not to go. She didn't!

That evening, the active local yacht club, Societé Nautique St. Pierre gave a banquet in our honor. Madame Buchett gave an amusing speech in French. She translated it into delightful English later. It was most pleasant to be with people of the same interest, and who contributed so much that made St. Pierre an unforgettable stop along our path. As a parting gift, and in the name of the membership, Madame Bouchett presented us with the club's burgee which she had designed and sewed up herself. Wind or none we left - we had to!

Our Living Quarters on La Reunion

Monsieur et Madame Rouseau

XXII

PASSAGE TO
SOUTH AFRICA

A boat towed us out to sea in almost total calm, recording
every move we were making on 16mm film. With the island
receding into only a dark mass at dusk, our memories hung
back with the fine people we had parted with. We had to admit, it was an experience never to be forgotten. (The Rousseaus retired in 1970, and the family moved back to France. In
1982 - sailing in our new ship *Thlaloca Dos* - we had a happy
reunion on the island of Corsica. After all those years we are
still the best of friends).

Only light, variable winds helped us along for three days,
until it settled from the northeast. On November 30th, we were
southeast of Madagascar, when we got the first good wind. By
the following day we had a day's run of 142 miles. Much of
that distance was due to a very favorable current.

The good wind didn't last, however, it got replaced by very
ominous looking cloud formations, the likes I had last observed
on the passage from New Zealand to Australia. We hoped it
would end with the same result as it did then, as only a passing
scare!

When the sun buried itself into the sea, the entire sky
turned into an ugly dome of black, the horizon transformed to a
brilliant crimson, where the last of the sun glimmered like an
evil eye. The color-scheme was that of freakish modern paint-

ings, it scared us into lowering all sails and to lashing every-thing securely. We observed the approaching wind as it was closing in on us; an eerie spectacle, to watch the sea being whipped up by the wind that blew the tops off the waves to horizontal sheets of water. Too soon it was upon us with hurri-cane force. The rain fell in tons, the lot screaming across in blinding sheets of liquid air, impossible to face. Poor *Thlaloca* staggered, she rolled, she pitched, a marvel she didn't shake the mast out. It was over in half an hour. The wind settled from the southeast and soon had us forging ahead again under escort of a school of dolphins, entertaining us delightfully right into the middle of the Mozambique Channel, notorious for unpleasant weather.

On December 2nd, it blew hard, but fair. Fierce squalls chased us through a very dark and very rough night. The self-steering was unable to cope with the rough seas, it forced us to do what we like the least - hand-steering! Carrying a bit too much sail perhaps, the confused seas made steering critical, I was determined to remain at the helm until morning if I had to. Despite Siggi's effort to keep me going with coffee and hot chocolate, by midnight I was *kaputt*. Siggi, for the entire time, didn't have a minute of rest either, still she bravely vol-unteered. Taking short turns, we hoped to get through the night safely.

We had made it a habit to check each other's safety line around the waist before turning in. Having done that, I went below. But below was hell. The whole vulnerability of a small boat in a rough sea and going fast, is instantly demonstrated the second one hits the bunk. The gurgling noise of rushing water along the hull is acute, and to think that only 14mm of soft cedar planking is separating you from a possible slide into eternity can indeed be frightening, especially when considering that the only lifesaving device aboard was a tractor inner-tube - and not even inflated!

Up . . . up the boat climbed like an ascending elevator, then came the push, the boat racing down the slope zigzagging as Siggi was correcting the heading. In the trough came a brief respite, then the whole process was repeated. Next I listened intently to an approaching roar, instantly aware that it was more than the usual. The boat lifted, higher and higher, fol-lowed by the drop into a seemingly endless abyss. The fin-keel quivered, suggesting a tempo far exceeding her designed hull-speed. (Later we acquired a Sum-log that registered speeds up to fifteen knots. In similar conditions the log would actually hit the end of the scale).

Acutely aware of Siggi's maneuverings in correcting the course in order to keep the boat more or less in line, I had a firm grip on the bunk's rail, waiting for what may happen eventually. When the boat finally broached, it heeling way over and had propelled Siggi clear over the cockpit dodger. I instantly sensed that it was more than just a broach. Sliding the hatch open, I faced an empty cockpit, and that made my blood curl. Ignoring the violent rattle of the sails for the moment I concentrated on rescuing Siggi, floating twenty feet away on the end of the genoa-sheet - the safety line!

She appeared to be dazed to immobility. I pulled her back aboard and made her crouch low in the cockpit, to prevent being spilled over the side again, while I busied myself on the foredeck to lower the sails. One of the halyards had parted and caused a collapsed jib and a broken spinnaker pole. The jib got under the hull, and it took me a long time to retrieve the sail that got messed-up with bottom paint in the process. For the rest of the night we lay ahull.

Siggi was still in a trance, complaining about her head, which apparently had collided with the boom when she was propelled over the side. The resulting bump on her forehead gradually turned to a dark blotch, and it became the subject of all kinds of suggestive remarks by our cruising friends later on. An honest explanation made things even worse - impossible to become a heroine in that crowd!

We finally approached coordinates where Durban should be, but a deep haze prevented all visible contact with any land. Taking bearings on a passing freighter - for Durban we hoped - we followed it's course. Eventually the haze had lifted sufficiently, and dead ahead lay The Bluff, the unmistakable landmark of the harbor. On entering the port we hoisted the quarantine flag, and we had our eyes peeled for a customs station. A passing motorboat advised us to head directly for the yacht club, and that he would notify the authorities. By then we were out of wind, and it took us ages before we finally tied up to a jetty after a voyage of sixteen days.

Moving along a row of yachts we spotted the familiar names of *Dida*, *Elsie* and *Trekka*. Bianca Lewis, a very active female reporter had seen us coming in from her strategically located apartment atop a skyscraper, was present to interview us and took some snapshots. At the club we relaxed in the thought of another passage safe behind us.

"Every reason to celebrate," Siggi exclaimed.

XXIII

SOUTH AFRICA

At the Point Yacht Club we were introduced to the club's secretary, Mr. John Pregnell, and the vice commodore, Mr. Bob Fraser, who greeted us heartily and offered us the use of their facilities. Both of the yacht clubs in Durban, the Point Y.C. and the Royal Y.C. were most caring, certainly the friendliest clubs imaginable; well tuned to assist boats and crews for the difficult passage around the Cape of Good Hope. The welcome most cruising people received in places around the world in general was heartwarming. How did we deserve it? Surely we didn't contribute much to the economy of the community. I suppose it was as one man remarked: "You guys come with a wife - not necessarily yours - with kids and a dollar in your pockets and refuse to part with any. But you bring something that stirs our imaginations, this alone is worth every dollar we spend on you!"

This benevolent attitude would change abruptly later on through the U.S. and Canada. In Canada for instance, at the Royal Canadian Y.C. in Toronto, a committee had to decide whether a 20-foot sailboat and its crew were in the appropriate class to find shelter overnight. In the meantime we were made to tie up at the end of a long pier exposed to wind and horrible motion. But this deplorable experience was still only lurking in the distance. In the meanwhile we took advantage of all the goodwill the rest the world offered without restraint.

WEST! SAIL WEST, MAN!

Actually, the first people who greeted us upon our arrival were a French couple, the Tourassons, who presented us with a loaf of bread, butter, milk and eggs. They hailed from Mauritius Island, where they had built themselves a 30-foot sailboat, with the intention of sailing around the world. It was the first boat we met that had a Ham-rig (Amateur Radio) aboard. Matter of fact, it was the only time we had heard of such an apparatus. In those days, communication equipment was still tubedriven, consequently it was of enormous size and weight. Of equally cumbersome dimensions was the paraphernalia that surrounded the transmitter. Hundreds of QSO-cards were nicely filed in metal cabinets. To concentrate all this wonderful equipment, it was installed on one side of the boat, which gave it a permanent list.

Pierre was white, Bridgit black, two of the world's most precious people. But this was South Africa, and color was not in - except white that is! The clubs refused her access. It aroused sensitivity in all of us accustomed to judging people by the simple rule of good and evil only. Someone circulated a petition, stating that the refusal of this lady was equal to rejecting all of us as human beings. If not changed, we would stay away from the club as well. Sure enough, the management caved in to our demands. A tiny victory at best, but one that made each of us in our little cruising community very happy. We all, including Bridgit, continued to receive the full respect of the membership, and there was not the slightest indication that something ugly ever happened. Perhaps it had a much more telling effect on the couple because (as we later heard) they had given up plans to sail the world, and had returned to Mauritius.

Those were circumstances the club had to sort out. To satisfy all was certainly not an easy task, especially when burdened with six overseas yachts.

We called the port office to find out whether we could be cleared in. They seemed very surprised and wanted to know how we got in, as we were not reported by the signal station on The Bluff. We could not imagine ourselves so tiny as to be overlooked entirely. However, Bob Fraser ran us over to the port office, where we completed the necessary formalities. The drive through the city, passing many department stores, convinced Siggi of territory worth exploring.

Christmas was only days away, and we wondered where and how to celebrate. This was solved quite easily after meeting Dr. Hamish Campbell. He was a fine sportsman, who spared no time, effort or expense to make the yachties' stay a most pleasant one. His spacious home became a haven to all of us yachties, and it was packed with cots everywhere, to accommodate half a dozen of us at a time. Our arrival stretched his available lodging to the limit, and we refused his generous offer. "What do you think a bloody living room is for?" He exclaimed. That we named his house, "The home of cruising orphans," we thought was most appropriate. He went as far as offering money to any of us interested traveling around South Africa. "The country is exceptionally beautiful you must see it. Do it now, and pay me back later when you can!" What a man!

That the country was just that, beautiful, we witnessed during times Bob Fraser drove us around. Every town, every village was kept immaculately clean. In stark contrast were the "colored sections". Here are quotes from our diary (1965):

"Most adobe huts in which people exist are brightly colored, showing a lot of artistic talent, and couples dancing to primitive instruments, which seem to suggest that people are happy and content. Still, there is no hiding the fact that the internal situation in South Africa is unhealthy. To blame is the country's leadership with its screwed up policies of apartheid. There must come a time when this unhealthy situation will have to change because it is morally wrong. The most identifiable weapon that upholds apartheid is the blacks themselves, who seem a lot happier and more indifferent to injustice than their counterpart in the U.S.".

By chance we met a fine German couple, Marlis and Dieter Rackelman from Johannesburg, who invited us for a few days to their home. A splendid opportunity to spend New Year with countrymen, and to see more of this exceptional and beautiful country. Leaving the fertile green coastal regions, the land rises gradually towards the interior, and the more we progressed the hotter and drier it got, and the healthy green gave way to arid conditions. Faintly visible in the distance emerged high mountain ranges; painted into a light blue sky it provided a spectacular panorama.

Johannesburg, or "Joburg" as it is called, is located 6,000 feet above sea level and is the capital of Transvaal. It is also the center of the most extensive gold mining operation in the world. A distant look from the Herzog Tower offered a very interesting view of the city and the extent of mining, with slagheaps everywhere.

We celebrated the New Year at Rackelman's cozy home - actually having a barbecue outside. Silently we wondered what the new year, 1966, would bring us. True, we had come a long way, but it left us with roughly 12,000 miles still to sail to get back home to Canada, and this included the dreaded passage around the Cape of Good Hope, which all of us sailors treated with utmost respect.

The Rackelmans drove us through the Kruger Park to observe the extraordinary African wildlife. Another trip skirted part of Bechuanaland, on the way to the capital of South Africa, Pretoria. The huge Union Building, home to the African Congress, with its terrace-shaped flower gardens was an impressive sight to behold. Next the Vortrekker Monument, a colossal stone structure, impressive in its simplicity of architecture; thoughtful justice to the simple but hardy souls in whose honor it was erected; the people who had started the evolution that made South Africa what it was.

As much we enjoyed sightseeing, after all it is an integral part of cruising, the unbearable heat at times curtailed full enjoyment. Nothing is perfect! So the saying goes.

Back in Durban, we hauled *Thlaloca* at the yacht club and gave her every attention the fear of the Cape had induced in us. We were aware it could prove her greatest test. The respect one should have of that part of the world is real, and anyone ignoring the warnings of the numerous casualties it has caused would surely be a fool.

All sorts of theories were forwarded by local sailors how best to cope with the culprit of it all, the swift Agulhas Current. The theories were as many as there were sailors! In the final analysis it was up to the deciding variable, the weather - the most unreliable partner in the business of sailing. The partner we wanted most, was a well found craft. And we made sure ours received all the care necessary.

After a week on the hard, *Thlaloca* plunged back into the water. What we had feared all along had come true, there wasn't enough water to float her out of the cradle. We had hauled her with the moon almost full - nearly maximum height of tide. The moon was waning at launch time! With the help of half a dozen men from the yacht club we tried every trick in the book to coax the cradle into deeper water. Stuck in the mud the cradle wouldn't budge an inch. Hamish, on a quick inspection on how we were doing, had left the hospital in spotless white attire, he was screaming advice on how things should be done. Siggi, looking like the rest of us with mud and bottom paint smeared over body and face - like Indians on warpath - exhausted and panting heavily, finally had enough of all that shouting. What no one had expected from this gentle woman, she hollered back: "Shut up or help. At least stop screaming!"

Next we saw, or rather heard, a man as filthy as us, screaming orders from only inches away - what a man! Doctor Hamish Campbell was the epitome of a fine comrade - a real experience in many ways.

Not until a motorboat had come to our rescue did we get the boat afloat. We tied *Thlaloca* to her old mooring. She was then ready for the last ocean she had to cross.

We followed an invitation for a trip to Zululand. Although highly interesting, but the weather was simply too hot to enjoy it fully. We were pleased to return to the air-conditioned clubhouse.

Every cruising man, or woman, met Allan Trotter, a member of the club and the owner of a well equipped service station. He never failed to offer his expertise to those in need. Some parts of our self-steering needed replacement. Allan did it free of charge. In addition, he and his charming wife invited us to a posh Italian restaurant for an exquisite dinner, within an ambiance that was equally attractive. The end of this memorable dinner was the beginning of a lasting friendship.

Dr. Hamish Campbell was a true friend to many, and we thought that he took particular interest in our well being. We followed one more of his invitations - a visit to his father. Professor Campbell was a founding member of the South African Wildlife Protection Agency, and a well-known personality in his country. A man of fame and fortune! Matter of fact, when Bobby Kennedy visited the country he stayed at his home. We were treated and entertained royally. One scene that always pops up in our minds, is the memory of the black personnel, who looked very dignified in their Cossak-like attire. They were treated as equals - with respect, rights and privileges like any white person.

XXIV

THE CAPE OF GOOD HOPE

On the morning of January 20th, 1966, Hamish came running down the jetty balancing two cakes in his hands, saying,
"You better be off, the wind is about to change." As he was in
steady contact with the weather office, he had updated reports.
I hurriedly bolted the trim-tab to the outboard motor bracket,
and hooked it up to the vane. (A trim-tab, I was experimenting
with at the time.) As we had cleared with the harbor office the
day before, it only required a call to report our leaving: "Okay,
you may proceed!"

A quick round of good-byes to the people present and we
were off. With hardly any wind to propel us we snail-paced
through the harbor. Outside it wasn't much better; when we noticed a huge tug following us very close; so close it made us
nervous. When we were about a mile offshore, which had taken
us nearly an hour, the tug suddenly spurted alongside, and a
voice through a loud hailer ordered us back into the harbor,

"Your papers are not in order!"

We were dumbfounded, because we had done everything
the law required. Because of the fact that it had taken us half a
day to get as far as we were, we found the demand unfair. We
kept our course. The tug cut in front of us, we tacked. Again
the tug blocked our way,

"Stop your silly maneuvering and do what I said," the
voice demanded. It made us furious, and we fired back with

some unpleasant comments. But, like it or not, we had no chance against the steel monster that blocked our way.

Three-quarters of an hour later, almost back at the break-water, the voice came back, "You may proceed, good luck and don't get seasick!" We showed him four shaking fists to indicate what we thought of his cruel jokes.

Back on a seaward course, and in a lumpy sea we continued gaining an offing. At dusk we were still only about five miles offshore, and The Bluff - the prominent landmark of Durban - still very much in sight. Even the renowned Agulhas Current seemed at rest. To our delight we had a school of dolphins around us performing beautifully. A knock and a splash had me look over the stern. It was hard to believe, but indeed a dolphin had collided with the trim-tab and had bent the shaft badly enough to be unusable. We had to dismount it, and that put us back to "square one," hand-steering, something we hated like the plague. Consequently, the beginning of our run to Capetown was nothing to be cheery about.

At last, we felt gentle touches of wind from the northeast. Gradually it gathered momentum, and by midnight it blew strong enough to raise a sizable sea. A boomed out jib and a reefed mains'l had us surfing down the slopes of following seas in magnificent style. In the morning we only made out a faint outline of land to starboard, we reckoned to be about ten miles offshore; apparently in the middle of a major shipping lane. It called for a constant lookout.

The wind blowing a good twenty-five knots, we lowered the mains'l and instead set another boomed out jib. All that day and the following night it was roller-coasting toward the south-west. But all good things end sometimes, and so it did on the morning of the third day. The wind had fallen light, and it left us to cope with a sea in shambles. We knew what was coming, a "Southerly Buster," as it was indicated by a black front approaching from the southwest. Back in Durban one could observe this weather pattern nearly every day. We had the sails lowered and secured in the nick of time, before the onslaught of a furious gale. It heaped the seas to pinnacles in a very short time.

Is it going to get as bad as knowledgeable people had predicted? We felt tense and were wondering. With one of us on watch to guard against possible shipping, the other was lying in the bunk, doing what was necessary to compensate the wildly gyrating motion of the boat. After sundown we expected the wind to ease, instead it got worse. Around midnight, the little man in my ear whispered a warning, "Get out there, man, and do something for your boat, or you'll be sorry!" Clad in oilskins I left the cozy cabin and stepped outside, only to be drenched at once and soaked to the skin. I untied the sea-anchor from the after deck and fastened it to ten fathoms of half-inch nylon line. I paid it out over the stern. This may read as if I knew my business - I didn't! It was a try, for lack of something else we failed to think of. There seemed to be a noticeable improvement, however. Crouched deep in the cockpit, I remained there for a long time and observed the foaming seas and listened to the howling gale. And for the x-time I pondered why apparently sane people venture into this mess repeatedly. Do we actually believe in we are sane? Are we not only dreamers? Blinded in believing we are at home in an element which in reality is out to destroy us, by forces we are unable to control nor understand. Fortunately "dreamers" are optimists who do not cease believing in their power to prevail - like the man in a cartoon: floating on a raft in the middle of the ocean, catching wind in a net!

Twenty-nine hours later we recovered the sea-anchor and made sail. Close-hauled we tacked toward the southwest. As this seemed to be a futile effort, we decided to call in on East London to await a change of wind.

There we tied *Thlaloca* to a small jetty; reflecting with disgust on the four days it took to cover 260 miles. Later we met Sid Ellis, the owner of a large furniture manufacturing company. He wanted to know what he could do for us. I mentioned the damaged trim-tab, "It will be repaired, no problem!" He instantly volunteered. He returned it the following day, expertly reinforced. In addition, he invited us to dine with him and his family at their lovely home.

Sid was involved in building a 36-foot Sparkman & Stephens designed ketch. Having available the wood, machinery and expert craftsmen, it didn't take much imagination to expect the finished product to be a piece of fine furniture. Although he was in a hurry to complete the project before the deadline of moving out of their house, as that particular section of the city was earmarked for a "Black Township ".

The following day, the Ellis' took us by car to the Transkai country. On this occasion we visited an enormous pineapple plantation, where we bought a dozen pineapples for sixty cents!

The wind kept on blowing from the southwest day after day. A situation not easy to digest, while being keyed up to conquer the cape in a hurry. However, there was no shortage of entertainment. Members of the very active local yacht club invited us one evening for a barbecue, and asked us to give a talk about our travels so far. Mr. Voss, the commodore of the club, invited us for lunch the following day, and after that drove us around to see more of the beautiful country. The car being air-conditioned had us traveling in comfort.

The weather-wise club sailors advised us to leave, predicting a northeaster imminent. On passing between the moleheads we were surprised to see what looked like the whole membership assembled, cheering us enthusiastically.

The wind was still from the south, but seemed to be backing. We beat into it. Checking on landmarks, our progress was fair. In sight of Port Elizabeth, we had the wind we hoped for. In fact, it soon increased to a severe gale, that had us thinking of heading for shelter in the nearby port. We debated at length, and decided against it. We had to get around this part of the world to free our minds.

The huge seas that were chasing *Thlaloca's* small stern concerned us immensely, as it was only a matter of time before one of the monsterous seas would swamp us. With only the minute boomed-out stormsail we scudded into an appalling night, made even more ghastly by the steamer traffic that was passing us left and right. The small anchor-light, that hung high up on the backstay, was the only sign of our presence. We hoped that the ships would exercise the same vigilance as we did. When one of the ghostly shadows approached dangerously close, we lit up the sail with the beam of the flashlight. Once the wind forced us to strike the last vestige of sail - the light reflector - things became even "hairier." One of the ships we sighted still a fair distance off pounding against the gale with spume flying high in the air like fireworks, lighting up the fearsome night, her course dead on our bow. We got the flashlight going in circles, when she finally changed her course. It was a close one! When this ghost-ship passed us only a hundred yards to port, it was a spectacle of awe; the unbelievable power a ship must possess to work against such awesome forces of nature.

In the morning we lay nearly becalmed five miles south of

The Cape of Good Hope

Plettenberg Bay. For company we had a ferociously tumbling sea. It was well known that the weather changes quickly in this part of the world, and one could almost bet that a westerly wind would follow an easterly invariably. And therein lies the inherent danger of the Cape of Good Hope. On the one hand is the strong Agulhas Current flowing up to seven knots, in a westerly direction around the cape. When a strong wind opposes this swift current - the other hand - there is hell to pay. In the extreme, even the strongest ships get in trouble. To escape an expected westerly wind, we sheltered in Plettenberg Bay.

Expecting a westerly wind, it blew fresh east in the morning, making the bay an open, uncomfortable anchorage. We left! Once clear of the bay the wind blew only light from the south. Under full sails and under an overcast sky we forged toward the southwest. Suddenly we were overwhelmed by a strong gust of wind that laid the boat on her beam-ends, nearly dumping both of us overboard - without safety lines on us! A quick reach for the sheets released the pressure and brought the boat back on her feet. The wind had increased to fifteen knots, we reduced sails and plugged on. Sailing hard on the wind, the boat pounded laboriously into a lumpy sea.

Throughout that dark and eerie night we sailed blind; always tight on the wind; always in fear we might be closing in on land; impossible to see anything. We anxiously awaited daylight for orientation. The news was good - no land!

The weather forecast predicted gale-force southeasterly winds. (Nearly every day we had reports of gale force winds, but they only rarely materialized. It seemed that the weatherpeople preferred to err on the side less open to blame.) The gale we could do without, but we accepted the southeasterly with jubilation, because it freed us of worries; of the danger of land to the north. We then were able to sail clear, if we had to! As of our position, we had no idea, since the sun preferred to remain hidden behind a solid cloud cover that prevented celestial observations.

When the powerful light on Cape Agulhas shed its blinking message on a safe bearing we were elated. Once past, we recorded a new ocean, the Atlantic, the last one we had to cross. With a reading of 35° south latitude we had reached the southernmost point of the continent. From then on we would travel constantly toward the north.

WEST! SAIL WEST, MAN!

The prediction of a severe gale in the False Bay area made us brace for another hard day sail. Fortunately, it didn't come. Instead the weather finally cleared and revealed a blazing sun that painted the ocean in dazzling blue. On passing the Cape of Good Hope, the Cape Peninsula presented itself in all its magnificent splendor; the sight of it had moved even a hardened pirate like Francis Drake to assemble the crew in devoted prayers. We were two very happy people, glad to have rounded the last treacherous part on our path around the world. Everything thereafter we considered a piece of cake!

The following night the temperature tumbled so low we hadn't experienced in years. At least not at sea. How cold it was is best described by naming the clothing Siggi wore when she came on watch: Two blouses, two sweaters, two pair of trousers (both of them mine) and foul weather skins over the lot. Her feet were wrapped in newspaper inside her boots. Unable to make it through the hatch on her own, I had to pull her through. It sure was a change from the 100°+ heat in Durban to that in the sixties in Capetown. It was there that I caught the first and only cold around the world.

Cold weather is much to our dislike in the best of times, but infinitely harder to take at sea. Dressed like Arctic explorers, the worst thing that can happen in such a situation is a loaded bladder that is screaming out for relief. A signal that has a man in desperate search for two inches of shriveled-up plumbing and (if found that is) trying to make it go through three inches of insulation. Simple arithmetic tells us it won't work - it didn't!

On rounding Duiker Point we got ourselves into a vicious tidal-race, we had to endure for hours.

Capetown, with its prominent landmark, the Table Mountain, its plateau covered with a perfect layer of clouds, revealed itself in the magic of a new day. A strong gusting wind dead on the bow, asked *Thlaloca* one more time to show her capability in overcoming great adversity, before she was relieved of all burden when tied to a mooring off the Royal Capetown Y.C., on February 3rd 1966.

Haul-out at the Point Yacht Club

Cape Peninsula

Taking on provisions at Capetown

Leaving Capetown under escort

XXV

CAPETOWN TO THE WEST INDIES

Capetown was a large modern city surrounded by an abundance of lush vegetation and mountains. This was true of the whole Cape Peninsula, where one spectacular picture is replaced by another even more stunning panorama. Climatically it was also much more appealing to us northern people than Durban for instance, where it was hot and sticky. For the first time in years we even felt chilly in our light sleeping bags, and I had caught a dainty cold. It was a grim reminder of what to expect back in Canada. It all depends what a person is used to. While we wore sweaters, some of the locals ran around barechested.

The yacht harbor, situated close to a railway shunting yard, was a bit messy, due to the locomotives that still burned coal. The prevailing wind made sure that this mess was spread evenly over all the yachts in the anchorage. And talking of wind, it was a nuisance at times. When it blew strong and gusty, up to seventy knots, it made the boats stagger under the onslaught. It required frequent checks of the mooring cables, which were kept intentionally short as the moorings were closely spaced. These moorings, of course, had to be sturdy by necessity, and it gave us peace of mind while sightseeing, or doing errands in the city, in preparation for the upcoming passage

WEST! SAIL WEST, MAN!

With us in the harbor was the 32-foot American cutter *Elsie* with her skipper Frank Casper. His sixty-years didn't deter him sailing singlehanded. We had first met in Panama, and several times since then. Frank was an unassuming, magnificent individual; impressive in his speech and very engaging when we met, yet he kept very much to himself. As he wanted to slip the boat and spruce her up for the arrival at his home port, he asked me to help, mainly in curing a persistent leak around the keel - a fault that plagued the vessel from birth to her eventual death (we found out later). I did the job because we liked the man very much, and therefore I refused any compensation.

Then there was Theo de Stadler, who was the best public relation man one could wish for. He made sure that everyone knew of our exploits - oftentimes embarrassingly exaggerated though! He had emigrated from Rhodesia many years before and had crewed on the maxi-yacht *Stormvogel* in many races and places around the world. This vessel was perhaps the most prominent yacht in the racing circuit at that time. Theo owned a steel yacht, the *Chycoron*, which he was preparing for extended cruising.

Early one morning, while we were still in our bunks, there was a knock on the hull. As Siggi looked out of the hatch she was confronted by a lady in the club's skiff. She introduced herself and handed Siggi a bundle of keys, saying that the whole family would be away on vacation and "please feel free to use our spare car, and live in the house if you like. Ask the commodore for directions!" Away she went. Next we saw her entering a loaded up car and driving off! In one single motion we had inherited a house and a car, we felt as if we had won the lottery. The whole thing smelled of public relation effort by Theo de Stadler.

It was a gesture we appreciated very much because it gave credence to the unencumbered generosity and trust of people toward us cruising folks. We used the car once for shopping, but never the house, for we thought it should remain the exclusive domain of its rightful owners.

For extensive shopping - mainly bargain hunting - there was Quinton van de Mar, who always made himself available. Before we left he gave Siggi a five pound box of fruit dainties. Bless his heart. At a later date he followed us as far as Ascension Island, where he lost his boat on a reef. A disaster of this sort is always unfortunate knowing well the time, money and effort involved to fulfill a lifelong dream.

At the Canadian Embassy we met Mr. Harold Richardson, the Canadian Trade Commissioner to South Africa. An enthusiastic yachtsman, who was building himself a trimaran. Along with Theo, he invited us to his comfortable apartment where we envied his exquisite art collection, he had collected painstakingly over many years, from many parts of the world. We concluded the visit with an elaborate dinner at a fine restaurant. Upon leaving Capetown he came aboard *Thlaloca* and handed Siggi five pounds of fruit dainties. Combined with Quinton's gift, there was enough sweets aboard to last us the rest of the voyage home - wishful thinking, as it turned out, because I had miscalculated Siggi's ravenous appetite for anything sweet. There was nothing to fear, though, because we went "overboard" in stocking up on canned fruit we bought from a warehouse that was dealing in damaged goods, priced unbelievably low. The same was true of all sorts of canned food. Once fully provisioned, we had enough aboard to last us as far as Panama, although still many months away. With all essentials completed we waited for the northwesterly wind to change to something more favorable in direction for an offing.

☆

On February 14th, we shed the mooring and moved to the small jetty off the club to take on water. By the time this was completed, the rubber tires that protected the jetty had messed up the boat. Theo de Stadler's motorsailer, the *Chycoron* was loaded with all our friends, and was standing by to give us escort out of the harbor. We were about to cast off when I spotted the extent of the ugly tire marks all along the port side of the boat, "What a mess," I remarked. It was the end of my concern, and was more interested in a cold drink once we got underway. Someone apparently had read my mind because a man came rushing from the clubhouse with a foaming bottle of beer in his hand. We already had drifted some yards away from the pier when he hollered, "Catch it!" With this remark he heaved the bottle towards me. Caught smartly, I put it to my mouth and let it run, determined that not one precious drop of the golden liquid should escape. The protest from shore I accepted as applause for a job well done.

My taste-buds finally woke up to the fact that even South African beer couldn't taste that different from the labels I was used to. What I expected to be beer was actually Teepol, a cleaning agent much used by service stations. Fortunately, enough was left to clean the boat's topside.

Siggi exclaimed, "We must take you to a hospital to get your stomach pumped out," all along feeding me canned milk. "We can't embark on an ocean passage with your belly full of Teepol," she continued. Surely she was right, but I thought the time it would take to clear the harbor would decide one way or the other, so we kept our course, while closely watching the rumblings I felt and we both heard emanating from my gut; no doubt the Teepol was doing its assigned job thoroughly. The Admiral, now very angry, rose to her full stature of authority, enquiring the opinion of our escorts, who by then were loaded with the real stuff, the answer came in a rousing song:

" . . .you're forever blowing bubbles . . . "

The lesson I had learned: Always read the label. But, heck, the label read "beer!"

We expected an easy passage to St. Helena, 1.700 miles to the northwest. When we had cleared the harbor, the wind was back to northwest, forcing us to sail tight on the wind. After several tacks we had cleared the land sufficiently to feel safe for the night. The radiating city lights remained with us all night, compensating somewhat our disgust about the contrary wind. The confused sea had raised customary uproar in our stomachs, and in my case expelled most of the cleaning agent. I thought that the "hose" between my mouth and stomach was the cleanest piece of tract inside my body, as it got scrubbed twice - down and up!

So as not to get bored we witnessed a great show, a magnificent performance by virtually hundreds of seals darting about in a frenzy. These funny creatures compensated much for the discomfort we felt otherwise. Our logline and rotor was of special attraction to them. As mentioned earlier, we once had lost the back end of the register to what we think was a large fish. To prevent a repeat, we hauled the rotator inboard.

The unsettled conditions eventually improved drastically and gave us an excellent run of 856 miles the first week, with surprisingly little favorable current present. With a strong southeasterly wind in control, *Thlaloca* was really flying, with warm and sunny days throughout.

Bang! A crash! Listening from below, we thought the mast had collapsed. Rushing topside we missed the sight of the two boomed-out foresails. The shackle that held the double halyard block at the top of the mast had chafed through. As a consequence, the sails were dragged under the hull of the boat, and obviously were under much stress while the boat was forging ahead. Once the sails were recovered, with still more bottom paint added to what was already there from similar accidents in the past, I faced the unpleasant climb of the swaying mast to reattach the block. What I thought would be a speedy job lasted for more than two hours, and sapped me of every ounce of my strength. Four times I went up and down the mast to rest or collect another tool. Aloft I clutched the mast tightly, as it was swaying from side to side, and with the boat pitching maddeningly, made it almost impossible to free a hand to do the job. My fear that the mast would break, as it did back in Colnet Bay, had us both worried. There was nothing Siggi could do to steady the motion of the boat despite careful steering. Finally, the shackle and block were back in place. After resetting the boomed-out "twins" I retired below unable to make another move.

Early morning of the nineteenth day after leaving Capetown we sighted the jagged outline of St. Helena. One must wonder how this small island survived the onslaught of the seas throughout millennia. More surprising how anyone ever found it. Without a doubt, Napoleon must have been bitter when he was forced to exchange an empire for something so minute.

Our general chart of the South Atlantic indicated the location of Jamestown, the settlement, on the northwest side. Accordingly we thought it smart to sail west about the island. We paid for this screwed-up logic with five hours battling cat's-paws in what had become the lee of the island. Mighty relieved we were when the hook went down off the town, though still a long way off the landing place, on account of shallow water.

☆

A longboat with the officials aboard bumped alongside shortly after, who informed us how lucky we were we had not arrived a week earlier. The swells had been so bad it made landing impossible. It had washed out the seawall fronting the town and had smashed the doors on all storage sheds. We went ashore with the officials. There we made arrangements with a boatman to ferry us back and forth, as it wasn't advisable to take our own dinghy, as the surge was such it took considerable skill to make a dry landing.

WEST! SAIL WEST, MAN!

Upon landing, we made the first important discovery, a water tap on the side of a building, that immediately established priority. With the tap only about three feet above the concrete floor, we did some fancy exercises to rinse the salt off our bodies. Refreshed, we were eager to "hit" the town, located on the bottom of a great gulch, and it appeared very clean and neat. With no industry to speak of, the adult population was largely made up of retired people from Britain and some from South Africa who much appreciated the island's healthy climate. As we were in need of fresh produce, we looked for the nearest general store, and there met Mrs. Benjamin, the proprietor's wife, who revealed her exceptional interest in seafaring people. She invited us to their neat home, where we met her husband later that night. They offered us their home as a land-base for the duration of our stay. We took regular advantage of this generous offer, as it enabled us to remain ashore all day and enjoy the house for the occasional rest and cool-off. A touching demonstration of their hospitality was when the Benjamins mobilized their car, that had been blocked up in permanent storage for a year, to drive us around the island.

When we approached the island from seaward, we appraised it as a barren rock, but were pleasantly surprised when we witnessed the abundance of greenery of the interior. On top of a plateau the BBC. (British Broadcasting Corporation) was constructing a huge communication link, a direct "hotline" between Britain and Africa. The roads were small and winding, but in excellent shape and we could well imagine the complexity in building them. The drive was concluded with a visit to the Governor's House. On the lawn fronting the building crawled Jonathan, a giant tortoise, said to be 140 years old.

An elderly South African couple drove us to visit Longwood Mansion, where Napoleon had lived during his exile that began in 1815. He died there six years later. The building served then as a museum. All there was to see has little historical value, as most was substitutes and believe-to-be's. Longwood property and the grave site, where Napoleon was buried originally (before he was exhumed and transported to France) was decreed by Queen Victoria to be regarded as French territory, and a French consul was there to look after it.

We spent a day in the well stocked library and read excerpts from a dozen books on Napoleon. It amazes me how a man who was responsible for so much destruction, murder and misery could ever be revered. Especially by those who condemn violence most vehemently. I suppose, that the deciding factor in judging good and evil, fame and infamy, depends on whom one does harm to!

One day, when we returned from shore, we noticed a familiar yacht in the anchorage. It was the *Salaamat*, with her skipper John Woodstock and three other men. We had first met in Durban, then in Capetown. Their trip which had originated in Malaya was to end in England. Later, this heavy displacement yacht of 48 feet was lost on a reef off Antigua, the West Indies.

With the arrival of *H.M.S. Puma*, a British frigate, and two freighters, began a marvelous time for the town, and for us in particular. The town turned instantly from a sleepy enclave into a beehive. Local opinion predicted a sharp population increase in about nine months time!

For the upcoming cocktail party on the *Puma* we were invited by two officers, Bob Trevethon and Ken Dillon. Bob as head of the navigation department went out of his way in supplying us with every chart we would possibly need. Ken was in charge of the demolition and emergency control center. He invited us to be part of a demolition exercise on a wreck near the island. With half a dozen frogmen we boarded the *Salaamat* and headed for the spot, where we anchored. It was diving in heavy gear, helmet and the whole paraphernalia, something new to us. We were treated as greenhorns - which indeed we were - and no mercy was given in exposing us to most rigorous exercise. Fairly stated, we enjoyed the feast that followed decidedly more. The pantry of the *Puma* had wisely provided a large pork roast. The delicious emanating aroma gave cause to place myself conveniently near it; on top of the cabin and leaning against the wheelhouse with a long sharp knife handy. Also a case of good Limey beer just to the right of me, what more could a man ask for after a day of grueling work?

On the eve of *Puma*'s departure, we were invited to a farewell party along with a dozen VIP's from the island, they included the Governor, Sir Dermod Murphy, who was to leave on the man-O-war for the island of Tristan de Cunha. We felt sad to part with our acquaintances with whom we had spent many enjoyable hours, but in a few days we also had to leave. We gave them a last salute with the foghorn as they slowly steamed away.

261

WEST! SAIL WEST, MAN!

As I always did before departing on a passage, I inspected the boat's bottom and steering gear. After careful inspection of the water I inched myself over the stern and dove around the boat, knocking the odd barnacles off the hull. Suddenly I caught a glimpse of a dark shadow, it scared me enough to be back on deck in half the normal time. Another good look, and there it was, a giant ray! Immediately I warned the *Salaamat* of the potential danger to life and limb, but failed to impress them. One of the local men who was aboard answered with a grin on his face, "We play with them!" Well, they can, but not I!

Over the past days we had cast fleeting glances at the five hundred and ninety-nine steps of the Jacobs Ladder which leads up one side of the ravine to old fortifications. So far we had the luxury of saying *mañana*, but tomorrow we would be at sea - so, no more *mañanas!* Our self-respect demanded the ultimate sacrifice of a stiff climb!

We both sweated and puffed our way up the well worn steps, to be rewarded with a splendid view of the town and the anchorage, where *Thlaloca* was only a dot on a blue ocean - the ocean her keen bow would be slicing tomorrow.

We walked around a bit and inspected a couple of old rusty cannons. The land was very barren and outside of a few cactus plants, there was hardly any other vegetation. This concluded ten wonderful days. Decidedly better days than Napoleon ever had!

☆

Before noon on March 15th. we set sail for Ascension Island 700 hundred miles away. We had ten pounds of frozen meat and a large tin canister of lifeboat biscuits aboard, given to us by *H.M.S. Puma*. The biscuits were hard, but super-tasty. The following days were happy ones, for me at least, as Siggi was forever frying meat, while I sat in the cockpit continuously eating!

Again, the weather remained without equal. Our *Thlaloca* was surfing along under the press of two restless wings. This sail across the South Atlantic will stick in our memory for ever. It was sailing as it should be but too often isn't.

On the morning of the seventh day we sighted Ascension Island, slowly rising out of the sea to the impressive height of 2,817 feet. The island is a massive nesting ground for many species of birds, especially Sooty Terns, and they were aloft in huge numbers, hunting for food. We passed the tall rock of Boatswain Island close to port while sailing along a very rugged shoreline, to an anchorage off Georgetown.

A small boat, powered by an outboard motor, came alongside with the magistrate of the island, who asked for our passports. When we asked about drinking water, he assured us that we could fill our bottles, although it was pretty scarce. One worry less! The wind was gusting 35 knots, and with the helping hands of the two boatmen we secured the boat to an enormous mooring, suitable for large ships. This was no place for a boat to get adrift while ashore, with no suitable craft available to retrieve it.

During normal weather, the anchorage is well protected. Rough weather makes it untenable and it was said that the swell breaks in five fathoms. All small craft were then lifted by crane ashore.

The water in the bay was unusually clear, and anything flipped over the side attracted a school of small black fish. We fed them with a whole box of "bloody" corn flakes, still from Mauritius. It was fair to say, we were as sick of it as was the crew of the *Sycamore Hill*.

Ascension Island could well be an island of the Galápagos Archipelago. It is of volcanic nature, therefore it looks quite gloomy. With no harbor and scarce on potable water, it had no real value to anyone except to birds for nesting. Modern times, however, changed this considerably. During World War II, the Americans established an air base to combat German submarines. After the war, with the advent of space exploration, it gathered continuous importance as a tracking station; a multi-million dollar investment. As on St. Helena, the BBC. was constructing a huge communication link.

After a good night's rest I pumped the dinghy and had a stiff row against the prevailing winds, towing seven plastic water containers behind. Siggi followed later in one of the local boats. Once ashore we noticed an air of great activity, due to numerous construction projects. The roads were dry and dusty, and every passing vehicle raised a cloud of red dust. When we asked a man for water, he directed us to another man who had the key to the supply tank. There we filled our bottles, and for the time being left them with our dinghy close to the landing.

From a man on St. Helena we had an introduction to a Mr. Hartley Booth, a very keen yachtsman. We found him in the

new building of the cable station. As he was in wire-contact with his friend, he already knew of our coming. The building was nicely air-conditioned, and it was a treat to be inside instead of the intense heat outside. After all, we were only 8° south of the e
quator. It was arranged that we should have dinner with them, and after, Mrs. Booth would drive us around the island.

When we arrived there at noon, the Booths awaited us with a sumptuous dinner. Being employed by such a worldwide communication company must be very rewarding. Transferred to many stations around the globe, they had collected an intimate knowledge of people, customs and places, plus many rare souvenirs. Over excellent roads we had an extended drive, but outside of lava flows, cactus plants and the occasional land crab, there was nothing of interest, and we could hardly fathom the people's expression, "We like it here!"

As the car climbed a steep winding road, we noticed an increase in vegetation. Atop the island we observed the most remarkable contrast to the arid landscape of below, because quite suddenly we were surrounded by lush greenery, which covered a wide area. Evidently, the occasional cumulus cloud deposits enough moisture conducive to the development of productive farmland.

Peter Critchley, his wife and several paid hands were working a farm that supplied most of the vegetables for the inhabitants. They also raised pigs for fresh meat. After some delicious home-baked cake and coffee on the verandah, Siggi admired the extensive patches of beautiful orchids Mrs. Critchley was raising. After the visit, we drove back to the settlement. There we collected our passports, and a boatman motored us back to our *Thlaloca*. Two days after our arrival on Ascension Island, we were off again. Under the boomed-out twin staysails we made the fastest offing ever. A fresh southeasterly wind again the provider of excellent daily runs. Looking back two hours later, haze had blanketed the island from vision, ahead of us lay 3,100 miles of ocean to Barbados Island, in the West Indies.

☆

We hoped to cover the distance in a month. A look at the Pilot Chart suggested that it was advisable to cross the equator near the island of Fernando de Noronha, about 200 miles northeast of Cabo São Roque, Brazil, it being the narrowest part of the doldrums - an area of calms and unsettled weather.

As if our little ship sensed this to be her last major run, she performed magnificently, escorted by a school of six dorados, their colorful bodies darting about speedily in an effort to catch flying fish. Gradually they left one after another, until only one remained. It stayed with us for two thousand miles. It's hunting skill was extraordinary, it would make the flying fish leave the water and then follow their flight close under the surface of the water, and at times catch one of them still airborne. Usually, it knew exactly when they had exhausted their flight, and snatched one of them the second it reentered the water. The show was highly entertaining, and we grew very fond of it's presence. First thing every morning, we scanned the ocean for it's glittering shadow. Then, one day, the "glitter" wasn't around; we searched and hoped for it's reappearing. But it was the permanent end of the great show, we felt sad at losing a faithful companion.

As on previous passages, only the very small flying fish crash-landed on deck. They were too small to supplement our food supply. On one day we flipped forty-three of them back into the sea. The larger ones had enough energy to wiggle themselves back into the water. Whenever a large one had landed in the cockpit, the commotion generally brought the whole crew on deck. In the darkness we hunted it down by feel alone and a great deal of excitement on our part. By daylight they were destined, via the frying pan, into our stomachs.

The first week we sailed 836 miles, but then the wind became fluky, with dark rain clouds filling the graying sky. When the wind had dropped to zero, the rain fell in buckets. We soaped our bodies and let the rain rinse us clean. We refilled the empty water bottles, and this removed any concern of running short on water.

By looking over the stern, with my head below water, I was shocked by the sight of all the goose barnacles which covered the entire hull. I fetched one of the aluminum paddles to use it as a scraper. Hanging over the side, I cleaned as far as my arms could reach. There were plenty left, but since the wind had come up we raised sails. Further cleaning of the hull had to wait until the next calm.

Along our route was an abundance of bird life, mostly wide-awake birds that have their nesting ground partly on Ascension Island. Sailing before the wind we did not use the mainsail, the boom became therefore a favorite resting place for ocean birds. They were a jealous lot. The first bird that had landed would squabble in a most profound manner to scare off the following birds from landing. When this happened in the middle of the night, it irritated us to a point that we chased them off. But minutes later they were back, with even louder palaver.

One morning we noticed an old bird sitting on the boom. When we saw the mess it had made all over the sail, cabin and deck, we realized he had an intestinal disorder. We scolded him for what he had done. He moved his little head from side to side, the round black eyes sad, as if begging, "Please don't drive me off." No doubt, this bird had only a short time to live, as indicated by the wing feathers which resembled only sparsely dressed spikes. Eventually his hunting instinct got the better of him, and he flew off, barely getting airborne.

One of the little fellows landed on my head. Testing his trust, I lowered myself into the cabin, he made no move to fly away. I placed him on the chart table, where he seemed happy and content. When I realized the consequences I might have to deal with in case of similar obnoxious toilet habits as with the last chap, I quickly placed him on the boom instead.

On April 5th. we crossed the equator at longitude 36°30' west, after having sailed twenty-six months in the Southern Hemisphere. Besides that, we toasted *Thlaloca*'s average speed of 125 miles per day over the past 1,500 miles. This included a favorable current from 7 to 16 miles a day.

From then on we expected the excellent sailing before the wind we've had so far to become decidedly more unfavorably, as we ventured deeper into the northeast trades. During the next calm-spell I pumped the dinghy and scraped the rest of *Thlaloca*'s "goosy" bottom. It should help her sliding more smoothly over the remaining 1,600 miles to Barbados.

Ever so slowly we inched our way through variable winds, calms and squalls. Every once in a while the northeast trades made a feeble effort to gain an upper hand, just to be overpowered by winds from other directions. For lack of anything else to do we sailed towards a couple of objects popping about in the distance. They turned out to be glass floats, the type the Japanese were using to buoy their longlines (used for fishing). We had sighted and ignored these floats on every ocean. We decided to take the two with us home for souvenirs. They were encrusted with barnacles and all kinds of minute ocean life. We cleaned the lot and tied them to the backstays. Shortly after we sighted one of the typical Japanese trawler passing us a mile astern.

April 11th began with moisture laden front, packed with a hefty wind, bearing down on us from the northwest. Once it had passed over us, we expressed a sigh of relief. We could hardly believe when the whole mess returned with the same ferocity. We were elated when the sky finally cleared and sparkled in a friendlier hue. Eventually, the wind blew from the northeast and remained there.

Wind and sea on the beam was never comfortable sailing, because every wave that bounced on the hull would sent a geyser of water into the cockpit. To protect ourselves from the salty exposure we had to wear oilskins, even though the days were sunny and glorious. A salty body meant that we would drag the salt into our bedding, as our limited water supply would not permit washing it off. Another detriment to getting salty, were our sensitive "bottoms." Sitting for days on a hard plywood deck, liberally sprinkled with non-skid, the constant chafe would in a short time peel the skin and allow the salt to creep into the open skin. It resulted in agonizing discomfort. Unable to sit, we would be more on our knees until the skin there had gone as well.

Back on Rodriguez Island we had made the acquaintance of two doctors to whom we mentioned our problem. They had mixed together a concoction only a highly trained chemist would have been able to identify. Whatever it was, it helped. When an application became necessary we called for an *Arschparade,* (a sort of roll-call to expose ones hind end). We then pasted each other's bottoms with a thick layer of this smear. In time this stuff stagnated to a hard shell. After a dozen application, this shell had the resistance equal to the armor plating of a Tiger tank! Unable to wash it off, we had to wear it off. When the people ashore observed our peculiar walk in wonderment, we could only accept their sympathy with a smile. The true cause they would never have understood.

At times the wind blew strong and we became concerned about our aging mainsail. We thought of replacing it with the stormsail. We shackled the tack of the sail to the main halyard, and to a rope-loop, I had spliced around the mast. The clew was attached to an adjustable downhaul, fastened to the goose-

267

neck. The head was tied to the end of the boom. While hoisting, the halyard carried the tack with the rope-loop aloft, to a height best suited to give the sail satisfactory shape. It worked! We couldn't win races with the rig, but could have kicked ourselves for not having thought of it before.

Our daily runs were nothing spectacular those days. On some of them we even bucked an up to fifteen-mile a day counter current. However, the broadcasting stations of the West Indies came in stronger and clearer every day, and we began to realize that our adventure, namely, closing the ring around the world, was drawing rapidly to its conclusion. We had our minds set on a special celebration once we broke the last 500 miles to Barbados - beginning with pancakes for breakfast.

Siggi checked the larder thoroughly, which by that time was pretty well depleted of necessary ingredients. Of the three eggs still left, two were bad. The surviving one made a good batter anyway. To avoid a mishap, Siggi had the bowl parked in my bunk, nicely secured with pillows. It so happen that a fierce jolt of the boat upset the bowl. We scraped most of it back. Once served with jam we still detected a definite taste of bunk flavor!

For dinner it was sauerkraut, bully-beef, canned potatoes and a special dessert, consisting of a big bowl of vanilla custard with raisins. To make absolutely sure nothing was going to happen this time, I held the custard-bowl between my feet in the cockpit, while heartily eating my dinner. As the devil would wish, I had to use my feet to balance one of *Thlaloca's* fancy moves, which resulted in splattering the precious custard all over the cockpit floor. Nothing ever was wasted aboard our ship - not fish-flavored custard, nor anything else! All further celebrations were canceled as we realized it just wasn't our day.

On April 22nd. we sighted Barbados, and soon were engulfed in prolific downpours, which lasted well into the following day. Sailing along the shore we inhaled the land air deeply, the first in thirty days. It was already past eight p.m., and as dark as a dungeon, when we arrived at what we thought to be the quarantine anchorage in Carlisle Bay. We could hear the surf breaking ashore, therefore reluctant to approach the shore any closer in the pitch-black night. We dropped the anchor in ten fathoms. Between the rain squalls we took our time getting the boat in shipshape for the officials in the morning.

As always we tied the anchor light to the backstay, as this was handy for immediate inspection from inside the cabin. Elated and happy that the trip was over, we went below for a well earned sleep.

Three hours later we were awakened rather abruptly by a terrific bang, and both of us jumped for the hatch. But it was jammed by the broken boom. I finally had to use force to free us and to get into the cockpit. All we could see was the fading outline of a trading schooner sailing into the darkness, the crew chanting calypso in a drunken stupor. We were left with a hole in the hull, both backstays and the steering vane had been carried away, a broken boom, a bent traveler, a smashed riding light, and a torn out chainplate. Our first action was to catch the swaying lamp, which was moving back and forth with the torn loose backstay. Siggi caught it and said, "It is still warm!"

We concluded, that the people on the schooner were too drunk, therefore unaware of what had happened. Again calamity had struck and we were devastated. At that moment we had a real desire to thank God for having saved us from possible injury, even death; because we realized only too well that had the vessel hit us amidship it would have been the end of the boat, and with the broken boom blocking the hatch, no escape possible in time before we had sunk. Lucky for us, the collision had occurred in the cockpit area. The boat, light as she was, had simply been pushed aside without much resistance, what indeed had saved her and us!

In the morning, when the officials came by to clear us. We reported the collision but failed making any impact on them. We moved over to the Royal Barbados Y.C., where we anchored in two fathoms. Shortly after, a police craft came alongside and took us to headquarters, where the accident was taken to protocol painstakingly the West Indian way, "a word a minute." In the meantime the police had found the rascal, who freely admitted the hit and run. No further action was taken. We followed the advice of some yacht club members who told us, "Forget it! Nothing will ever come of it."

At the club we were given honorary membership. We met many helpful people who provided us with the necessary contacts and tools. Mr. Hood, the vice commodore, gave us permission to use the club's workshop, and also gave us a used boom, which I had to whittle to shape and size. With all that help from the club members, we soon had the damage under control. One morning, when we looked out, we found the dinghy's painter chafed through and the dinghy had drifted out to sea, to be gone forever. We wondered what would be next.

The *Trekka* came in after a 29-day passage. Cliff and Marian Cain, a wonderful couple we had met in many places around the world, were en route home to Monterey, California.

With all our time spent in repairing the damage, there wasn't much left for sightseeing. Moreover, time was at a premium, because we had to be clear of the Caribbean before the onset of the hurricane season. Until then we still had many miles to sail.

XXVI

CLOSING THE RING

We raised the anchor and left Carlisle Bay for Panama on May 11th. The day was wonderfully sunny, and the trades were blowing full bore. On the end of that 1,300 miles passage would be the thrill of a circumnavigation of the world. A glance at the Pilot Chart suggested that we could expect help from a strong current. But it worked out rather disappointingly. On one day only did we plot a boost of 26 miles; on two days we actually recorded 8 miles per day less than the log reading. It shows that ocean-currents hold promises inconsistently, a fact we had grown used to over the past years.

Our course should have cleared the island of Aruba by 40 miles. We sobered from a sleep instantly when I got up to have a glance around and saw a long line of lights close by. I took the tiller and steered northwest. Surely, if this was land we should be on a reef any minute. Slowly we convinced ourselves that it must have been a large fishing fleet. Once the lights had dipped beyond the horizon, we felt relieved, and gladly handed the steering back to the vane. We went below and resumed where we had left off. But with our nerves all adrift, sleep eluded us for the rest of the night.

With shipping getting heavier towards the Panama Canal, it called for a steady lookout. Since we had lost our good anchor light in Barbados to the hit and run incident, we hoped that the *el cheapo* light we had bought at a Barbodo's "ironmonger"

WEST! SAIL WEST, MAN!

store would be as effective.

Off the tip of Colombia, the sea became very angry once more. It was downright scary. We never thought that we would ever again find ourselves in seas that resembled those we had off the southern tip of Africa. We dragged the sea-anchor behind and scudded before the monstrous breaking seas at three knots, until the weather moderated a day later. After that the wind fell light, a welcome break after a storm, although we grew sick of it pretty soon. No worry, though, the northern end of the Panama Canal was only a day's sail away. Had we not said this once before, when we were approaching the canal from the other end?

The sea had calmed to a glassy appearance, and there was nothing else to do but to sweat it out. I was sitting on the cockpit floor with my legs resting on the dodger that surrounded the cockpit when I noticed, a couple of times already, a jerky motion of the tiller. When it happened again I got up, when at the very same moment a sword-like dorsal fin was moving slowly along the starboard side. When I burst out, "killer-whale," to Siggi below, she emerged out of the cabin like a shot.

Awestruck we stared at the dorsal and hoped that the beast would be a good-natured fellow, if not, *Thlaloca's* ½-inch cedar planking could be pierced as easily as newspaper. He moved back and forth astern, suddenly disappearing below the boat, and our souls cried out for mercy. Again it was the rudder that became the object of abuse. Up he came straight as a rod, flashing his entire body except the tail. Back he plunged onto the flat sea with the sound of a cannon shot. We'll never know whether his fantastic leap was to show off his wonderful white belly or an expression of joy at meeting us; or was it some other motive we were unaware of? The show was over, and we were elated. This was one of many rare moments a less startled person as we were would have thought of a camera.

It seemed that the gods of wind and weather were in unison, determined not to let us off the hook lightly, as indicated by a dark wall approaching from the east. As the front moved slowly overhead, it dumped a lot of rain, blown horizontally by a fierce wind, blotting out visibility. Lightning bolts punched the sea around us, and the thunder exploded with ear shattering bangs. Quickly I secured the sails and boom. I had a hand on the traveler to hold myself, when I saw fire shooting half way up my arm. Strangely, though, I didn't feel a thing. Siggi, inside the boat, had felt a charge going clear through her body. We both shivered from fear and being chilled by the cool air; I so much, that I hadn't noticed the loss of my partial dentures. Siggi remarked, "Gosh, you do speak funny, what happened to your teeth?" I jumped back out into the cockpit, and among the jumble of sheets and sloshing water found them. The only bright spot within a surrounding gone mad. Once the storm had passed, it left us with only very light winds.

Unknowing to us, another yacht, the ketch *Seawind* with Malcom and Muff Graham, was in the same storm and got hit by lightning, doing considerable damage. We met them on our arrival in Cristóbal.

The following morning we sighted land, and by late afternoon we were within two miles off Punta Manzanillo. At that point we were thirty miles from the Panama Canal. Bearings on landmarks confirmed that we were making only very little headway in the light wind against, what appeared to be, an opposing current.

The same conditions prevailed the next day. The lighthouse on Isla Grande remained on the same bearing, even though the bubbles astern indicated movement through the water.

The days were beautiful but unbearably hot. We could not rig any kind of awning as we had to take advantage of every dollop of wind. During the night it fell dead calm, and a bearing on the lighthouse confirmed our fear that we were drifting back. To prevent it, we anchored in 26 fathoms (according to the chart). This we could only do with the 60 fathoms of ½" logline Gock Campbell, the skipper of the *Sycamore Hill*, back in Mauritius, had given us.

The anchor held. We checked the current with our log, and it was running at ¾ of a knot. Around midnight we felt a light breeze. It was a long haul to recover sixty fathoms of line, being careful not to have the lot all tangled up.

Later, the wind ceased again. Down went the hook! What first appeared like a dragging anchor, turned out to be a parted line. Obviously the line wasn't much good, being only of hemp. But the loss of one of our anchors and a couple fathoms of chain was something we could ill afford.

We used the outboard motor sparingly. With less than a gallon of fuel left, we wanted to save some for maneuvering inside the harbor. The traffic was heavy, and at one stage a ship had to take drastic action to avoid a collision. The source of our survival was our vigilance (and that of the ships, as the case just stated). The trouble was, that the ships were generally lit up like Christmas trees, making it difficult for us to clearly ascertain their course.

The following day we only made five miles, and the heat nearly drove us nuts. Trying to make Puerto Cabello to wait for wind, was as impossible as reaching for the moon!

The night brought a shove of wind that enabled us to advance within sight of the Cristóbal breakwaters. There we got becalmed again. With the fuel down to a pint, our spirits were low and drained to even less when we noticed our drift away from the "finish line." Eventually "someone upstairs" sent a message to the appropriate channel to deliver to us the zephyr of wind that propelled us over the magic line, a few minutes before 12:00 G.M.T. on May 25th, 1966. Thus we completed the circle around the globe, having sailed 27,000 nautical miles in 2 years, 3 months and 20 days, from Panama to Panama.

XXVII

BACK WHERE IT ALL
BEGAN

When a pilot boat came alongside, I jumped aboard with all the necessary papers, while Siggi kept on sailing. As our boat had been measured previously, in January of 1964, it was only a matter of a few formalities. We were directed to anchor on the "Flats" to be cleared by customs and immigration. While this was going on, the pilot boat kept pace with *Thlaloca*. This was the first time for me to see our little ship from another perspective, while she was moving along under sail. She looked so very lovely, and I was immeasurably proud of her and my beautiful wife and comrade, guiding her to the exact spot where we made our momentous decision in January of 1964, to sail westwards.

From the anchorage I caught a ride ashore, where I made arrangements with the Cristóbal Y.C. for a berth.

It was a splendid feeling to be back, and to visit with old friends. We boarded the train for the short run to the Pacific side, to see Peggy and Bill Arbaugh, the man who twenty-seven months previous had advised, "West, sail west, man!" Now he said, "I think you got yourself into a jam!" He was right again. Now we had to sail the course we were unwilling to take that many months back. We stayed three days with them, without a care in the world.

Peggy, an excellent hostess, outdid herself to make us feel

at home. During a conversation, I mentioned to Bill our need of charts. "Don't worry, you'll have all you will ever need," he said. We drove miles, to a shed, where Bill had stored a couple of hundredweight of brand new charts, Sailing Directions, Pilot Charts and Light Lists. We were given a free hand to whatever we wanted. By the time we had the lot stored aboard the boat, she was down another inch on the waterline.

Back at the club we had plenty of company; people who wanted to know if we really had sailed around the world in "this thing." Siggi, always annoyed when people referred to our *Thlaloca* as "this thing," answered: "No, we did not!"

"Well, someone told me (us)!"

"Oh, you are probably talking about this boat, in that case, yes, we did," she would answer.

One day, a very charming lady came over to our table and introduced herself and said, "My husband does not think it is polite to just walk in on people, but I'm so curious about your trip. Would you please join us at our table for a drink?" Thus we had the pleasure in meeting David and Julie Jenkins. Mr. Jenkins was the judge at the District Court. They resided in a very beautiful home within the Canal Zone. It became our favorite hangout over the following days.

Every time we set a departure date, it was postponed because of numerous invitations. With us was the British yacht *Spurwing* with Sir Percy Harris (Pewin, he wanted to be called) and a young New Zealander, Mac White. Pewin was the last governor of North Cameroon. It was most interesting to listen to his many tales, articulated in precise Oxford English. He was sailing a small but very comfortable yacht, en route to New Zealand to join his married children there.

Mac and Muff on *Seawind* were repairing the damage to the mast, engine and electronic instruments, caused by lightning during the same storm we were in. They had been on the go for the past five years, and were on the last leg home to California to complete their circumnavigation. They were fun people to be with, and we wished we had met earlier. Over the following years we corresponded, until one day there was no more mail. We were shocked to learn that this wonderful and generous couple had been murdered by a doped-up couple on Hawaii's Palmyra Island in the Pacific. This tragic story is the subject of a book: *And the sea will tell.*

The political controversy - Panama versus the Canal Zone

- was still very much the same as it was during our last visit, two years before, a very delicate touch-and-go affair. One day we were warned not to cross the border, then, the next day it was all right to do so.

A very big man sat across from our table, looking at us searchingly, as we did at him. Both parties had a welcome surprise when we finally recognized each other. It was Captain Haff, who had piloted *Thlaloca* through the Panama Canal in January of 1964. So, twice more we crossed the peninsula to be his guests at his home.

We set our final sailing date for June 5th - the next day.

XXVIII

HOMEWARD BOUND

It is true we had circled the globe, but home was still 2,500 miles to the north. We then had to face up to a voyage that seemed impossible more than two years before. There was one fundamental difference, though, the height of the tradewind season (the winter months) was past. Therefore, we could expect less forceful winds. The new danger, an early hurricane, was a real threat we hoped to escape with our renowned luck.

Our itinerary called for making Baranquilla, Colombia or even farther northeast, then sail north through the Windward Passage (between Cuba and Haiti). Whether this was feasible depended on the strength of the wind and current.

We sailed off early in the morning. A fair southeasterly wind and a good current had us well on the way. The twenty-three miles to Los Farallones Light were sailed in six hours. Inbound had taken us three days!

Next day we plotted a run of 107 miles. After that it was back to familiar rain squalls and light winds. Overall, the weather remained pleasant enough. On the third day we sighted the Colombian coast and sailed northeast along the barely discernible land mass. According to the Sailing Directions we could expect a weak north-setting current, and also a chance of favorable land breezes. Instead, the weather had changed dramatically. With the stormsail and closely reefed mainsail *Thlaloca* pounded to windward. A short time later we were

279

down to bare poles. We kicked the sea-anchor over the stern (with the windage of the boat forward, she always behaved better with the drogue aft).

With many South American radio stations filling the frequency bands, we were unable to find an English speaking station that could inform us of inclement weather on the way. Perhaps it was just as well. This way we were unaware of the fact that a depression had formed east of the Serrana Bank, north of our position. A hurricane (Alma) was in the making. Of another development we were unaware of, that a most unpleasant passage had just began.

Between fast moving clouds I managed to catch a glimpse of the dying sun for a line of position. Not very accurate but better than nothing. Following behind me through the hatch was a volume of water that had bounced over the stern and charged through the whole length of the boat. We mopped up a lot of water. Still, the bedding remained soaked, and the inside of the boat a bloody mess!

Before noon the next day, the boat lay broadside to the sea, which wasn't normal. We recovered the sea anchor. It came in easy because only the ring with tattered pieces of canvas attached was left. It had finally succumbed to old age. Instead we dragged behind us two tires from a mini-van, we had picked up in South Africa. The tire's designated purpose was to use them as fenders in the locks of the Erie Canal, once we get there. We were pleased to find out that they worked as well as the sea-anchor.

In the afternoon we had enough of it. We recovered the tires, set a staysail and rigged the stormsail in place of the mainsail (as we did on the passage to Barbados) and let *Thlaloca* hammer her way to windward.

In a book written by Mulhauser he says: "Rough weather reduces things to a state of intolerable discomfort in small ships, and makes life a misery". Truer words were never spoken, as we found out during the following days; an ordeal that lasted seven long days and covered 360 miles. Our brave little ship smashed and pounded her way to windward, and it was close to a miracle that she did not fall to pieces, or the mast be driven right through the bottom of the boat; particularly then when she fell off a wave into the trough with a crashing jerk. This played havoc with our nerves. It was real awful.

We can't remember that we ever slept on that passage because of the constant pounding and the high-pitched wind-noise in the rigging.

The current was a problem as well. Within the axis of the current we were set 32 miles to leeward in one day, and an average of 17 miles per day on the whole. No loom of any light looked more inviting than that on Morant Point, Jamaica. We decided then to break the trip, instead of continuing through the Windward Passage.

Throughout the advancing day, the beauty of Jamaica revealed itself more and more, from the 7,000 foot Blue Mountains to the lovely green of the slopes. The long channel into Kingston Harbor may be marked well for large ships, but with the wind blowing gale force from the east and the sun in our eyes, we had concerned moments in identifying the markers. Once around Harbor Shoal Light we entered the smooth water in the lee of Port Royal, and tied up to a pier to be cleared.

The first question by the customs and immigration people was, "How did you make out during the hurricane?"

"What hurricane?" Was our question.

We were given a full account. We treated the news somewhat dumfounded since it didn't jibe - especially wind directions - with what we knew of the law pertaining to a hurricane. Whatever, we had survived a very tough trip, and we had reason to pat *Thlaloca's* fat belly, in appreciation for a job well done.

Siggi phoned Mike Campbell, whom we had met in Cristóbal, and who made us promise to visit him and his parents should we stop at Jamaica. He told us to wait as he would meet us with a launch to tow us up the channel to the Royal Jamaican Y.C.. This was a welcome offer, as it saved us a five-mile beat against a strong easterly wind.

At the club, *Thlaloca* was offered a stout mooring, a necessary requisite to have mental peace while exploring the island. Both in beauty and history it has much to offer.

Mike's parents had a villa up in the mountains from where we had a splendid view of Kingston, and the bay beyond. They also owned the Rip Tide Motel, which was beautifully located on Discovery Bay. We spent two days there, doing exactly the things tourists do.

Columbus had landed on the island in 1494 during his second voyage. In later years it was settled and heavily fortified. In 1670, the island was ceded to Britain, and down through its history had two well known personalities in responsible positions. One was Sir Henry Morgan, a former buccaneer, who was made Lieutenant Governor in 1674. Today he returns to memory through a certain brand name of rum. In his time, however, he was a remarkable man, and his many exploits make interesting reading. The other man was Horatio Nelson as naval commander, before his rise to fame and immortality.

It was estimated that Jamaica held the largest bauxite deposit in the world. Alcan (Aluminum Company of Canada) was busily engaged in its exploitation. The ore was transported from the pit by miles of conveyors, and over cantilevers loaded onto ships. Bauxite and fruits were the two main resources of the island's economy. Tourism came next. The extent of this business was easily estimated by the number of aircraft that were coming and going in an apparently endless stream.

The old Spanish architecture was a reminder of the island's past glory. The city of Kingston presented modern buildings, and appeared very clean. As we did not consider ourselves exactly tourists, we found the prices of food very high - unaware of the drastic changes on mainland US. and Canada during the past three and a half years of our absence. This shock was still to come.

We watched the development of a depression moving in over the Windward Islands. As a precaution, we had a talk with an official of the Canadian Embassy, on whether we could expect protection in case we were forced to seek shelter in a Cuban port. The answer we received was ambiguous to say the least, true to his profession of a diplomat. On the whole, I personally would not hesitate to sail into any port regardless of reports. I look upon it as a challenge, and believe strongly that the world is full of good people, and that Siggi with her magnificent smile would keep us out of harms way! The depression became no threat to us, and we were off on June 21st.

We set small sails to a fresh easterly wind. Almost immediately the mainsail split along the leach a good three feet. We quickly reefed the sail some more and continued. On the way we saw several derelict hulks of banana boats. We were just discussing how similar they looked to *Cristal*, the vessel that helped us out of the awkward situation in the Gulf of Panama 2½ years before, when we saw through the binoculars that one of the wrecks was indeed the *Cristal*. We were sad having witnessed her rather disgraceful end.

Homeward Bound

Our mainsail needed mending. We tied up to a jetty for a couple of hours and did just that. Sailing upwind along the Jamaican coast, we were in for a hard beat. We arrived in Morant Harbor before noon the next day, where we decided to linger until the wind had calmed a bit.

It was a very lovely bay, surrounded by high hills. The healthy green of extensive banana plantations speckled with red roofed houses against the background of the Blue Mountain range presented a spectacular picture. The water a transparent light green invited us for a refreshing dip. Truly a gorgeous place to hang around for a while, but when the forecast predicted less forceful winds, we were off after only six hours.

The powerful light on Morant Point guided us a long way into the Windward Passage. A wonderful moonlit night provided excellent visibility. In the distance we spotted a blinking light, which we took as a signal for help. We steered for it. When we got there, we found a small boat with a couple of fishing poles rigged over the side, and a man slumped over, obviously asleep. We roused him with a toot from the foghorn, and asked him if he needed assistance - he was at least two miles offshore - "I'm all right!" he said.

Throughout that night and well into the new day, we had a good run. From then on the wind had fallen close to zero. Off to our starboard loomed Navassa Island, soon to be gobbled up by low lying clouds. A lot of shipping during the nights forced on us a careful lookout.

For two days the sea was like a mirror, on which the sun beat with mind-deadening intensity. We were deeply elated every evening when this glowing ball of fire dipped below the horizon and painted the sky to the west in a color of gold, eventually red, and then twilight to night bringing out twinkling stars as messengers of hope for a new day - perhaps even some wind! Very often over the past years had we watch this intimate life of nature from the middle of nowhere. Very soon we would only have time to remember the splendor of these fleeting moments as some of the most pleasant in our lives.

Four days out of Jamaica, with the Windward Passage and the high mountains of Haiti and Cuba behind us, we approached Great Inagua, the southernmost island of the Bahamas, where we anchored in the lee of it.

Present were several inter-island schooners, each with a large crew of natives. These boats were locally built, and neither of the island's craftsmen used power tools in fashioning these crude but apparently seaworthy vessels. Out at sea it was a delight to see them sailing along under bulging canvas. Also at anchor in the bay lay a large motor launch, normally engaged in treasure hunting, we were told by one of the divers. It was surprising to learn how profitable it could be. But apparently also dangerous to men and costly in equipment.

As Matthew Town on Great Inagua was a Port of Entry, we cleared into the Bahamas with the officials. We took a walk in the neat village and came across a well stocked general store, where we bought some bread and bananas. In the afternoon we departed.

A blustering southeast wind had us sailing fast, past Acklins Island to starboard and Long Island to port into the Exuma Sound. Approaching the Great Ship Channel, the seas really piled up, breaking noisily behind us. Such dramatic effect could only be the result of the tide running against the strong wind. Once through the pass, however, the sea calmed, and we were sailing in the transparent water of the Great Bahama Bank. The transformation from deep to very shallow water was so abrupt, that it needed some getting used to it. We didn't take lightly the warnings of shallow coral heads, and we thought of anchoring for the night, but declined because of the short chop that would have made lying to an anchor very uncomfortable. So we stormed on, through a night ablaze with a full moon.

Taking bearings on the powerful light on New Providence Island kept us informed of our position. On the western edge of the bank we took several soundings, making sure we were truly in the Tongue of the Ocean, where we set a course for the Berry Islands.

By morning the wind was still blowing strong. We thought it better to shelter in the lee of Bird Key until the wind moderated for the crossing of the Bahama Bank. By a hair we missed hitting a floating 50 gallon drum. We shuddered at the thought of the consequences in case of a collision!

We found good anchorage on the windward side of Frazer Hog Cay, perfectly protected by an extensive sandbank to windward. Next day the wind had calmed. Before leaving, we tied up to a jetty to take on water. Immediately we were engulfed by a cloud of viciously biting mosquitoes. They were so bad we neglected to moor the boat properly, as we were too busy fighting off this terrible nuisance.

Our hurry to escape the hungry beasts quickly was curtailed by a couple who invited us for a drink to a nearby bar. Arlene and Frank Snedaker, with their crew of four healthy looking teenage children, were cruising the Bahamas in a trimaran. We all agreed to meet in Fort Lauderdale, their hometown, should we decide to visit there.

There wasn't much wind when we left, and the insects pestered us for a long way. It was a problem we had forgotten about since the Marquesas Islands in the Pacific.

Once past the Northwest Channel Beacon, we lay still on a glassy sea. The weather forecast spoke of only calm conditions that made us regret our decision of the day before, when there was plenty of wind. Unable to run the motor for any length of time for lack of fuel, we had to make the best of the lightest breath of wind. There was traffic both ways, between the Bahamas and Florida - Bahamian vessels and the occasional yacht. During the night we anchored for a while to ascertain the current. It was running south.

Next day we found the appearance of the water very "sandy", and a sounding gave us only five feet - six inches less and we are aground! Checking with the chart, it indicated shallow water north of our course. A noon sight confirmed we were too far north. We had neglected to consider the current being tidal - setting south and north. Before nightfall we raised Sylvia Beacon, and anchored two miles to the east of it.

Siggi prepared one of her classic meals, *a la Thlaloca* (vegetables, bully-beef and rice). This had been our standard meal for years now, yet each time we had it, it tasted even better! After the meal we lay on deck for awhile under a sparkling sky and pondered over our future life back in civilization, without our *Thlaloca* and the sea for our daily companions.

At noon the following day, we tied up to a jetty at Cat Cay. It was once a bustling resort for the affluent sailing society, with gambling and the lot. Now with extensive developments on other islands - Bimini Island to the north in particular - had reduced Cat Cay to only a refueling stop for boats traveling between Florida and Nassau. A hurricane many years ago had devastated the island. To restore it to her former standard, should take many more years.

With our kitty quite low, scratching bottom, we could afford only two gallons of gasoline. It got us into a fruitless argument with the gas attendant, because he gave us only one and a half gallon, the rest he left in the hose. The evidence was so overwhelming in our favor, it made the argument ridiculous. Still, he wouldn't budge!

Later we anchored near the lighthouse on Gun Cay, awaiting wind for the passage across the Florida Strait. We passed the time with swimming and diving until sundown, when we had another meal *a la Thlaloca*.

At 9:30 p.m. we noticed a southeast wind, to which we quickly hoisted anchor and sails. To compensate for the expected northerly set of the Gulf Current, we laid a course for Fowey Rocks, which we thought should be about right for Miami. Around midnight, the wind became fluky, it forced us to use the motor sparingly.

A noon-sight next day put us already five miles north of Miami. Obviously, Miami was only a memory, and Fort Lauderdale in question, as land was still ten miles to the west, indicated by only a cloud bank. An American destroyer steamed slowly by us, with half a dozen binoculars peering down on us from the bridge.

Finally, at three o'clock in the afternoon, we spotted the first solid structures on land. Still the current was strong, creating huge fields of eddies that slowed our pace to a crawl despite a fair wind and motor power. The gulfweed was thick and got into the prop of the motor repeatedly, to a point it made using the motor a waste of effort.

It was a relief when we sailed through the breakwaters of Port Everglades. We were back on mainland U.S. after an absence of almost 3½ years. We sailed around the harbor for along time in search of a customs station, but without success. We finally tied up to a pier. A very unfriendly security guard wanted us to leave at once, but we talked him into giving us a chance to make a phone call. The unfriendliness of the official left little doubt that we were back in North America!

But one should never judge a country by a single screwball. The officials we dealt with a few minutes later were extremely polite and courteous. After that we secured a berth at the world's largest marina, Bahia Mar. There was telephone connection directly to the boat and newspapers every morning. It was all fine living, but two dollars per day was a fee our depleted kitty could not afford. The marina had its own public relations department which asked us for interviews and a television appearance. We agreed, in the hope that it would reduce the berthing fee. Well, it didn't!

We called our Bahama acquaintances, the Snedakers, to help us find a more reasonable berth. Frank had a talk with Mr. Olson, the dockmaster of the City Moorings in the New River. The place was a delight in that we were in constant contact with people. Mr. Olson (Oli) was an old hand in sailing and did everything to make our stay very pleasant. The city's public relation people came out to welcome us to the city.

Evidently, we were well known, largely due to the publicity we had received at the Bahia Mar Marina. Across from us, on the other side of the river, lay the large and beautiful motor yacht *Longhorn*. A man standing on the after deck hailed over, "Hello Canada, come over for a drink, anytime!" There we had the pleasure of meeting Mr. F. Galway, a retired Canadian Admiral, who then was the head of the Longhorn Finance Corporation, and chairman of several Canadian corporations. He was certainly a very wealthy person, as also indicated by the Rolls Royce he was driving. What occured next is one of the extraordinary happenstance that can be expected only once in a lifetime - and we blew it!

"You kids must be broke?" Was the first question we were confronted with. The truth was we had just received a hundred dollars from my mother per wire. And with one hundred bucks hidden away "deep in the bowels of our ship," we weren't about to admit that we were broke.

"Well, what if you had more than you have right now?" I speak for myself, and I admit I was getting hot around my collar, and my heart started to pump excessively. "No, Sir, we really have plenty to get home, and there we have jobs," (wishful thinking). By that time he became annoyed by our constant refusal, he finally burst out in frustration, "Why don't you take the stuff, it is only laying around!" All we could stammer was, "Thank you, Sir, we have enough money!"

"Would you accept an open check, you can write in whatever amount you please?"

Admittedly, our "innards" were so confused and in uproar, we could hardly speak.

"We don't accept money," were the only words we could think of.

Mr. Galway then called Bob, his captain, and introduced us as a "world famous Canadian sailing couple," (Only very few people had heard of us at that point; and only a few more were added in the future).

The conversation just quoted is only a short excerpt of what had taken place that exciting evening. To tell it all would fill pages, and would border even more on fiction.

There is no doubt, that had we taken his offerings in money and the introductions to most influential people as a gift from heaven, we would have come out "smelling like roses".

Fifteen minutes after ten o'clock the following morning, Bob, the captain, handed us an envelope, "A gift from the Admiral," he said. Inside we found 500 dollars!

We called a meeting with Mr. and Mrs. Olson and the Snedakers and presented the case. We asked for their advice on what was the right thing to do - accept it or reject it. The verdict: "Keep it!"

Perhaps it sounds as if we were overly fastidious, but it was our policy throughout our voyage - and in general - not to accept unusual gifts unless we could somehow repay generosity in kind - at least make a sincere effort in that direction. Elsewhere I have already stated that we received a lot more than we could possibly give in exchange. But when someone, a complete stranger at that, handed us 500 bucks it knocked the scantlings from under our feet. Conversely, for the first time in years we were on solid footings. All at once we felt very rich! Rich not only in money, but that someone actually saw in our adventure an accomplishment worthy to be rewarded.

Later that day we went to Mr. Galway and thanked him. Additionally, we made it clear, that we considered the money as a loan, we would repay it as soon we were able to do so.

A year or so later, we wrote to his then known address to let him know that we were prepared to fulfill our promise, paying back the loan. There was no reply. By way of the "coconut-drum" we eventually received the news that he had passed away due to cancer. May his generous soul rest in peace forever!

☆

"The American Venice," as the city of Fort Lauderdale is called, is truly a magnificent place to linger. We fell in love with it, and like in so many places around the world we were reluctant to leave, but we had to! Several suspicious lows were reported, but so far nothing to be dreaded. We had planned to sail the ocean as far as Beaufort, North Carolina.

Homeward Bound

We departed from Fort Lauderdale on July 15th. A nasty
swell greeted us on the ocean, that was doing its best to roll us
over the side. With only light winds to steady the motion, our
progress was bouncy and slow. Our ears open to weather reports, we took a deepening depression over the Leeward Islands
as a good reason to head for Port Canaveral. We had no desire
to test our luck at this late stage of our voyage. In the middle
of the night we closed in on Cape Kennedy. We didn't have a
detailed chart of the place, instead we followed the descriptions
in the Coast Pilot. The many lights had us confused, but with
patience and soundings we worked our way towards the bell
buoy, where we finally spotted the range lights into the harbor.
For the rest of the night we anchored off the main channel. Although it was quite bumpy, we managed a good sleep.

We awakened to the noise of passing motorboats as they
were heading out for fishing early in the morning. We raised
the anchor and sails and progressed into the Intracoastal Waterway for an altogether new experience. We gained latitude with
patience and mosquito repellent. Our "eggbeater" was much too
weak to budge some vicious tidal currents, which always
seemed to run contrary to what we had figured out. Every day
we tacked dozens of times, and the result at the end of some
days were so meager we were thoroughly disappointed. Too
many times we had to anchor and waited for the tide to change.
The supposedly prevailing southwesterly wind was just as
screwed up. Only twice did we get a good sail out of it.

At Charleston, South Carolina, we slipped into a marina
for a thorough rest. Our steering vane proclaimed the words,
"Completed 32,000 miles around the world". It always attracted a number of people who were anxious to speak to us.
Invariably, someone would call the local paper or the television
station for an interview. In Charleston we were asked to sail
about the harbor while a T.V. crew filmed our maneuvering.

When we reached Norfolk, Virginia, the rivers and canals
were behind us, and the ocean beckoned us again. Norfolk's
huge naval base was full of warships of every description. The
Yacht and Country Club harbored us overnight.

The following day we motored in a dead calm, and we had
to wait until late afternoon before a feeble wind came up from
the southeast. There was still enough light for a couple of good
photos of the Chesapeake Bay Bridge-Tunnel, a 17-mile combination of bridges and tunnels crossing the mouth of Chesapeake

Bay. The wind strengthened on the beam and held through the night for a fair sail up the coast.

That fair sail was only a memory when daylight broke, and a dense fog engulfed us. Then near the Delaware Bay, shipping converged for vessels bound up and down the bay, as indicated by blaring fog signals all around us. We hoisted our aluminum bucket as substitute for a radar reflector, and hoped the thing would protect us.

In the early morning hours of August 10th, we heard the engine of an approaching ship, and the sound grew louder every second. It missed us by not more than a hundred feet, steaming on a northerly course. Realizing how close we had come to being run down rattled our nerves. We had to get out of this trap. Lack of wind forced us to chance the last reserve of fuel, and in addition swung the paddles lively when we stopped the motor to listen to traffic and a whistle buoy, for which we were headed. We finally found it and identified it on the chart. From there we plotted a course for Cape May Harbor.

In the afternoon we entered the harbor, from where we continued into the New Jersey Waterway. This "ditch" was far more intricate than the ICW leading south from Norfolk, and the bridge attendants by far not as friendly and cooperative. At one stage we anchored in front of a bridge, as the bridge tender obviously refused to acknowledge our signals. A passing motorboat came to our rescue. The good man moored his boat to the bumper guard and climbed the bridge, making the attendant miss some of the soap opera on television while he operated the span for us.

Once we had passed through the Manasquan Inlet, we enjoyed a marvelous sail as far as Sandy Hook, where we anchored in the lee for the night. At midnight, however, a fresh wind blew up from the northwest, making the anchorage untenable. We proceeded, and for the rest of the night dodged the heavy in and outgoing traffic of New York Harbor. We were elated when daylight came and we found rest from the arduous night in the lee of Coney Island, where we anchored. It was a Saturday and we watched an impressive number of all kinds of craft heading for their favored fishing spot; their wakes rocking us to sleep.

It was already midday when we awoke. We hurried and made sail. The sun was shining and it was hot. We sailed beneath the largest bridge in the world, the Verrazano, which

Homeward Bound

spans the Narrows - between Brooklyn and Staten Island. Beyond emerged the unmistakable skyline of Manhattan, and the most famous monument in the world, the Statue of Liberty which, since its existence, has greeted millions of people in pursuit of a better life.

We were lost! Where could we possibly find a suitable anchorage for the night in this bustling place? The skipper of a passing motorboat directed us to the Liberty Yacht Club, in the back of the "Old Woman" (as the statue is called in the local jargon). As it turned out, the so-called yacht club was nothing better than a stranded barge, to which were tied half a dozen boats in various stages of decay. The only pleasant part of the club were the people, everyone was super-nice.

Of particular interest was Charlie Jensen, a member of the club, who spared us every minute of his time to drive us around New York, a city that failed to impress us. Charlie was a most remarkable fellow. For several years he had been a U.S. Army boxing champion, and had won the Golden Glove. Despite his advanced age he still acted as if he could beat the world, and never realized that he was a bit punch-drunk. We remained the best of friends until he passed away a few years later.

In the foggy morning of August 16th, we quickly motored across the Hudson River to clear the heavy traffic midstream. The long line of finger-piers on the east side of the river didn't look much better than the yacht club we had just left. To one of the piers lay the 82,000 ton liner *Queen Elizabeth*. Although *Thlaloca* was 81,999 tons smaller in tonnage, she could claim having sailed every ocean "Her Majesty" ever did - albeit at a slower pace!

Once past the George Washington Bridge, we were clear of the harbor proper. Up the Hudson River to Troy, we enjoyed days of delightful sailing, gliding past magnificent mansions of a bygone era, surrounded by artfully manicured gardens and groomed lawns. But we also felt the colder climate creeping up on us, that had Siggi digging out the woollies, we had last worn in Capetown, South Africa. In Troy we were faced with the problem of removing the mast for the 162 mile passage to Oswego. Near a bridge we spotted a high wall and tied the boat to it. But passing motorboats kicking up a nasty wake made the job of lowering the mast impossible. Help came from the bridge tender. Having observed our predicament, he suggested

291

tying *Thlaloca* under the bridge. The good man and I pulled the mast out of the boat easily. While Siggi was guiding the heel of the mast, we lowered it to rest horizontally on the prepared supports on deck, a framework of light timbers, Charlie Jensen had provided.

Shortly after we entered the first of the 31 locks of the New York Barge Canal, which we traveled over the following days. All was peace and quiet and we enjoyed it thoroughly, until we were a couple of miles out on Lake Oneida. A fresh wind from the west had come up, dead on the nose. The Seagull hammered away trying its best to overcome the adversity, but the eastern shore we had left an hour ago was getting noticeably more distinct, meaning that the wind was the more powerful factor in the equation. We turned 180 degrees, and tied up to the town terminal of Verona Beach to await more favorable conditions. Storm warnings were up for the next two days. A welcome break to spruce up the boat for the homecoming in Toronto.

We wanted to rig a short mast, to enable us to carry some sail across the choppy Lake Oneida. A nearby trailer park had a restaurant, where I asked permission to chop down a tree in the forest that surrounded the park. Also I wanted to borrow a saw. A big man sitting at the counter overheard the conversation I had with the owner, "Come with me to my place, I'll fix you up," he said. He was Vic Farina, the owner of the Dwarf Line Motel nearby. Not only had we collected a tree but also an invitation to be his guests for the length of our stay. As any good Italian-American, he believed in good food, and his specialty were "belly-busters" (pancakes) and steaks, both in enormous sizes. We got to know many people, including newspaper reporters, who wanted highlights of our voyage around the world.

☆

Once in Oswego, the boat got her mast back. A day and a half later we sailed into the harbor of the Royal Canadian Yacht Club in Toronto, Ontario - only a few miles short from where our dreams had evolved and *Thlaloca* was conceived. No one was there to greet us. This we found rather strange. Later we were told that our claim of having sailed around the world in a 20½-foot boat was considered a hoax. We don't blame them. They made up for it when the truth was established.

As New-Canadians we were proud having sailed the new Canadian flag around the world - as the first sailboat! For us it

was the culmination of an unforgettable adventure. I had a glimpse of the world I yearned to see since childhood, and I'm so fortunate to have shared the wonders with a person I love dearly, my beautiful and brave wife - who suggested:
"Let's celebrate!"
Among the people, who eventually crowded around us, one asked, "Would you do it again in this 'thing'?"
"This 'thing' happens to be a 'thing' with a soul, called a boat," Siggi shot back in anger. "However, my answer to your question is, 'NO!'"

Jury-rigged mast across Lake Oneida

Arrival in Toronto, Ontario, Canada

APPENDICES:

1

People and their boats

we met on the way

2

Boat and Equipment --------------------
--------------------Accidents and Sickness'

APPENDIX 1

THE JOHNSONS AND THEIR YANKEE

It is our firm belief that no other sailing couple in the world has lived a fuller life than Irving and Exy Johnson. It is hardly necessary to elaborate on their adventurous exploits, as a score of books, articles in the *National Geographic Magazine* and even a documentary movie do it so much better. What we like to do, however, is to tell of our experiences with a couple that inspired us enormously: the quiet spoken natural story-teller, efficient, powerful Irving, and petite Exy - every inch a true lady and so lovely in and out. Our eventual meeting happened after we had sailed our *Thlaloca* across the cold and foggy North Atlantic, from New York to Münster, Germany in 1968. We had departed from Sheepshead Bay YC., N.Y. and sailed on the Great-Circle-Route to Falmouth, England. It was a slow passage - 41 days! That it took that long we could only blame the light easterly wind combined with a bumpy sea that curtailed our progress the last 500 miles. In Münster, the boat was hauled and laid up behind Siggi's parents house. Being already late in the season precluded any continuation of the voyage. Instead we flew back to Canada to rejoin our jobs and earn the funds necessary to bring her back to America. In 1971 we were back. Propped up in the yard for 2½ years, the little ship had weathered a lot and it required a full six weeks of hard work before she was ready to face the ocean.

We hired a trailer and transported her twenty-five kilometers to Münster, where we placed her under the crane of the

WEST! SAIL WEST, MAN!

Wasserschutzpolizei (one word, no kidding!) - Water Safety Police - who showed exceptional willingness to put her in the water. Yes,"water", I said! Like hell they did, instead they put her smack on top a pile of rocks. It was enough to make us weep. Siggi did, I cursed.

"How can you do a stupid thing like this? I asked the operator. "I told you there is only one meter of water," he countered. This was news to us. Whatever, we had to find another half a meter of water somewhere.

Help came in the shape of a powerful motor yacht, whose owner suggested to hook into the slings and drag the boat laterally, while still in the air, away from the shoreline where there was plenty of water. It worked perfectly, and only minutes later we were tied up to one of the piers of the Monasteria Y.C. with the bad incident only a memory - except perhaps a nagging thought about possible damage to the keel - oh well!

Loaded down heavily with all kinds of goodies from Siggi's parents store we cast off the moorings on September 12, 1971. With the Seagull outboard motor on full throttle we were charging towards the Rhine River at 4½ knots - on course for the English Channel and the Bay of Biscay. One thought was paramount, we had to move fast to get south before the onset of normally bad fall weather; with snow falling already in some parts of the Eifel Mountains - and the Bay of Biscay lurking as a formidable obstacle, we could not reasonably expect to cross before October, even November.

At the huge Ruhrort Lock, we were squeezed into insignificance by half a dozen barges, all of them had their screws turning in order to hold position - for us an absolute nightmare! The skipper of the barge nearest us, who had previously asked us about our destination, apparently concerned by what we had in mind, suggested that the quickest way south was by way of rivers and canals. This suggestion Siggi immediately hailed as words of a true genius, while I had the gravest doubts about our "eggbeater" astern, plowing against a five-knot current in the Rhine River. What decided the issue was the skipper's offer of a tow as far as Köln (Cologne). Furthermore, it should be easy to find a tow as far as the Mosel River. We then would be out of the Rhine River. With this much assurance I stood no chance to argue against it.

By a hair this proposed passage ended almost right there. We had already handed our longest line to the barge. While he was carefully taking up the slack, another barge opened up full throttle. The wash got hold of *Thlaloca's* fin-keel and got her sailing smack towards the other side of the lock where she crashed against the steel lining. To save us and the boat we had no other choice but to let the line go. The barge, of course, had to continue. Very much shaken up, I tried to start the motor - it wouldn't! The lock operator flooded the chamber to flush us out, while we worked the paddles like galley-slaves to get out of a 500-foot long "madhouse," with barges already moving in from ahead. Exhausted and out of breath I was desperate, I turned the paddle flat and gave the Seagull a hefty whack - it started, and out we were!

This abominable maneuver had cost us not only a lot of good line, but our tow as well. Back to square one, on course for the Bay of Biscay. "Too bad," said Siggi. "It was not meant to be," said I! But our renowned luck was with us again. Looking around we saw in the distance a barge, and a man waving vigorously, sure enough, the skipper had waited for us. Fifteen minutes later we were following in the wake of a very foolish adventure, as poor *Thlaloca* was torn through the turbulent water at eight knots, and it looked as if she was ready to founder at any moment. Her bow-wave stood way above deck level, her stern so much depressed that the water stood four feet behind us like a wall. The genius had turned into a rascal and our enthusiasm into despair. We lived through agonizing hours, tormented by fear and guilt about exposing our gallant vessel to such abuse.

Once we arrived in Cologne we said, "Thank you, goodbye" to our helpful skipper, and "never again" to ourselves. This attitude changed almost at once, when we sat under one of Cologne's giant bridges for one solid hour with the Seagull hammering away full throttle, and the blooming "bridge hadn't moved one inch!" We allowed the current to take us back into the harbor.

At a shipchandler we bought 200 feet of three-quarter-inch polypropylene line, of a beautiful orange color; it floated and the color was distinctive. After refilling the empty fuel bottles we faced "father Rhine" (a German expression) again. Needless to say, with the same result. This madness had to stop. We either hook a tow or face the Bay of Biscay after all. The trouble was, that none of the slower moving barges showed the slightest interest in a sparkling new orange-colored line, one end of

299

which Siggi was swinging expertly in cowboy fashion over her head, standing on the bow. It was a *Swiss Express* that finally bit. Express means fast, and fast was the least we wanted. But beggars are no choosers, we had to!

Our Sumlog registered up to ten knots through the water. Even faster than the last tow, but it seemed *Thlaloca* was taking it more graciously or, perhaps, we had gotten used to it. Despite oilskins we got soaked to the skin. We were sick with worry. We were cold and hungry. Again we felt guilty of abusing our vessel. At the confluence of Rhine and Mosel the pounding stopped, and so did cold, hunger and guilt. After heaving over to the *Swiss Express* a quart bottle of *Dornkaat* (Schnaps) with a thank-you-note attached, we recovered the tow line, started the Seagull and headed into the smooth water of the idyllic Mosel River.

Following the Mosel Valley, the waterway snakes through the hilly ranges solidly covered by vineyards. Here and there the rich foliage was broken revealing fortifications the Romans had erected more than a thousand years ago; or neat villages in delightful colors. The beauty of it all made our hearts leap with pleasure. The wine-festival was in full swing, and we freely indulged in the golden liquid that even the Romans found beneficial. The atmosphere we found overwhelmingly conducive in judging this kind of travel a lot more appealing than ocean sailing. The friendly town of Konz and its small intimate yacht club detained us for a week while we waited for the arrival of a *Trip Tique* and a *Permit du Circulation*, directly from Paris. It was a busy week we spent with different club members, everyone determined to make our stay a most pleasant one.

At the town of Apach we passed into Luxembourg where, as a mark of saying "hello" we suppose, the rats had a dance on *Thlaloca's* freshly scrubbed foredeck during the night. This had us scared enough that we cast off and anchored midstream, where we took our chances with possible traffic as the lesser evil.

Our further course traversed the huge industrial complex around Metz with all its ugly and soot covered buildings, and the water of the canal contaminated with all kinds of trash; especially plastic sheeting that floated just below the surface. It got into the prop and choked our motor countless times.

It changed abruptly when we entered the *Canal d'Este, Branch Sud*. The only unpleasantness of this canal was the ninety-nine locks that had to be negotiated. Otherwise it was gorgeous. Autumn had changed the color of nature dramatically, and often we thought of our far away adopted homeland, Canada, where we last saw a similar display.

In one of the locks we placed *Thlaloca* dead behind the American sailing yacht *Yankee*, in a position where we couldn't be overlooked. To be sure, it was in the nature of these fine people that no one was ever ignored! We introduced ourselves. And when the lock gates had opened, Irving handed us the end of a long line (which we later exchanged with our orange one) and said: "Here, hang on!" And hang on we did for the next three weeks!

Not only had we gained reliable propulsion, we had reduced our navigation to follow a broad stern with the name, *Yankee, Mystic*. We were determined to follow this name until prudence told us to part, as not to become a burden and jeopardize our precious friendship.

Truly, if someone's desire is to experience tranquillity and find in nature the stimulus for poetic thoughts, a trip through that seemingly unspoiled part of the world is highly recommended (Exactly the reason why we visited the same places again years later with *Thlaloca Dos*). Also, being with the Johnsons, who knew that area intimately, we had valuable guides who enhanced our view immensely.

Once through the *Canal d'Este* one enters the beautiful Saône River which at times in the spring and autumn, depending on the amount of rainfall, can be treacherous. We had no excessive rain, consequently smooth sailing all the way. Along the Saône is one little river, the Seille, which so far the Johnsons had not explored, but were eager to do so. Since we had nothing to lose, quite the contrary, we were game.

The delta-like entrance to the river was cause for confusion. That something wasn't kosher came to mind when a sandbank barred further progress. It is well known that sandbanks come and go, and in Irving's point of view an obstacle that had to be erased by battering it with fifty tons of steel, propelled by a 6.21 GM Diesel. Nipping away ever so slowly, the churned up sand colored the water over a large area. Right then came to mind an article I had read years ago of a similar incident the Johnsons had written about in a book or magazine. Also faced with a sandbank they had employed block and tackle in addition to motor power to get the fifty-ton *Yankee* across -

301

to explore the countryside beyond! Had it not been for an old Frenchman in an equally old leaking pram, who informed us that the real entrance was farther south, no doubt, the call for block and tackle would have been next.

Thus we came to a primitive lock dating back to a time when Napoleon was scorching Europe. Hand operated, of course, it was leaking like a sieve, but held water long enough for us to slip through. This little river was a delight. We saw no sign of life other than numerous cattle grazing in rich green pasture and gazing at us dumfounded; not sure what to make of us, of what was certainly a rare occurrence.

The river was never properly charted, consequently its depth erratic. It was interesting, that tiny *Thlaloca* drew several inches more than *Yankee* (as designed). Not surprising then, whenever *Yankee* hopped over an obstruction, we braced ourselves for the inevitable much more severe jolt only seconds later. It gave us goose pimples every time, and if the intervals were short, they raised pimples on top of the ones we already had. We soon came to a small town, which in any case was the end of the navigable part, so we returned - bouncing over the same obstructions again. Still, we found the excursion a thrilling experience. Later in the day we made fast to the pier of Port du Plaisance in the city of Lyon, where by degrees *Thlaloca*'s pale-blue topsides acquired a rich oily look as she got doused constantly by the wash of heavy traffic. Not even her deck was safe from this filth.

From Lyon, the passage south was on the Rhône River with all its unpredictable currents and dangers. Irving and Exy were so kind and let us have their log of that passage. We are grateful that we are allowed to quote from it freely. Therefore, any part of the following within quotation marks is from their log:

"October 9th, Tournus (a town) I phoned to find out the depth of the Rhône. Sounds very low. I phoned Pariset, (a river pilot) water is very low; only 2.27m at Chasse. Possibly some water to be let out on the 18th."

To raise the water level in the Rhône, the Swiss occasionally opened their sluices and send a slug of water into the river that would temporarily raise the water level to enable the commercial traffic to move. This of course entailed international negotiations that were prone to delays. It all looked like an extended waiting period of which the Johnsons took advantage by

taking their guests, Ruth and Hope Atkinson for a riverboat excursion on the *Canal de Nivernais*. We were invited to make
Yankee our home for the length of their absence; a suggestion
we accepted without delay. So it happened that for the next
five days I walked the deck of *Yankee* in a manner that left no
doubt in the minds of the many envious Frenchmen who
strolled by that it was my ship.

The year was 1971, a time when the Vietnam War was a
hotly debated issue. Excessively perhaps in France, where the
Communist Party was very strong. Under contention was their
belief, that it was only an "American War," forgetting completely their own deplorable involvement in Indochina and Al-
geria. It gave us great satisfaction in making certain that the
American flag was flying unobstructed, and we only hoped that
some of the characters who thought themselves brave by dumping garbage on other American flagged yachts would demonstrate "guts" to confront us eye to eye.

"October 19th, Irving decided to take *Yankee* down river
by himself. Apparently, Pariset, the pilot, was a heavy drinker
and had caused damage to several yachts (a pilot takes several
yachts in convoy). Irving's decision unfortunately causes a lot
of bad blood. But who needs a drunken pilot highly paid to run
my ship aground when I can do it as well sober? At least I
know whom to blame!

" . . . there is a real war of nerves around here. Everyone
is talking about, how much water there will be, what the different yachts draw, taking a pilot or not, etc.. I hate the atmosphere . . . dread the Rhône . . . always a bum feeling in Lyon.
Hein and Siggi came for dessert, to eat a cake Siggi had made
us."

The only unburdened people amongst the lot were the two
characters on *Thlaloca* whose only job was to follow the letters
Yankee - Mystic .

"October 20th. This was the day I had dreaded - starting
down the Rhône, and now the emotion over Pariset's ire was
added to the dread. Of the eleven yachts at Lyon all but the
Chinese Junk got going. We had to wait for the lock quite a
while, but got out at 9:20. Then into the current!

Ruth and Hope did a lot of keeping track of the kilometer
markers for Irving, as he has to know its location on the chart
every inch of the way. Hope's comment: 'It's like going
through Woods Hole all day."

WEST! SAIL WEST, MAN!

We thought it would be an easy operation - just follow in the wake of *Yankee* - but we had greatly misjudged the workings of the strong current, the swirling eddies, on *Thlaloca's* under-body. When we observed Irving, wheeling constantly port and starboard, and add to this our tiller-action in keeping a course anywhere near that big stern, one could easily imagine that trouble was only a matter of time. Siggi, who did her best to ease the tension, was describing in detail all the things she had in mind baking for Christmas, to which I retorted, "The way it looks at the moment it will be more like smoked barnacles, we will scrape off *Thlaloca's* bottom when she is high and dry on a sandbank!" This remark did not make a hit at all, for thereafter she was as quiet as I was. We both wondered how it would eventually end.

After seventy kilometers, reputedly the worst, the current lost its turbulence and gave us a chance to look left and right where we recognized the sheer beauty of the countryside; the ever so green grass of the pastures, the glorious forests and freshly plowed fields that emanated an earthy fragrance; an enticing urge to just stop and meander the trails along the river's edge. And there were graceful swans that drifted majestically in the lazy currents outside the deeper channel. Birds caroled their individual songs that combined to a harmonious chorus. We could afford to listen and look at nature unencumbered by motor-noise and navigational attention - the people on the *Yankee* could not!

"The Mistral was blowing harder all the time . . . "
A Mistral is the name of a wind that develops over the Alps and blows with fury down the Rhône Valley. Since we were moving south and a Mistral always blows from the north, we therefore had a following wind. Entering a lock with all the maneuvering involved, it was prudent to proceed on our own.

The fury of the wind drove *Thlaloca* with excessive speed towards the lock chamber with no way to slow down - Seagull outboard motors had no reverse. What are we going to do? I had already the end of the orange line in my hands, about to jump into the cold water to swim for a ladder to tie up before the big crash. Then I heard Siggi's voice from the foredeck screaming against the wind, SEA-ANCHOR!

Our sea-anchor was much too large to be stored below deck. It was lashed to the after deck. This magic word propelled my 200 pounds of blubber - read muscles - into immedi-

304

ate action, and within seconds I had the drogue floating astern. Thus we came to a reasonably soft landing alongside the *Yankee*. We are certain it was the first time a sea-anchor was used in a river. The one and only record we care to brag about! One regret however - I can't claim credit for such a smashing idea.

Peace of mind was only brief, though, when a dozen voices hollered at once, "Watch it!" Here came the steel-monster *Mark Twain*, driven by the wind and totally out of control. In an instant, Irving had the "Jimmy" (engine) going. His efficient crew recovered the mooring lines, and off we were deeper into the lock chamber. A moment later, the barge bounced from one side to the other before it came to a halt. A real close call!

Yankee's log describes the next incident:

"October 21, started as a fairly easy day, but finished in near tragedy. *Thlaloca*, as always, towed astern on the floating orange line. A made-over barge, the *Mark Twain*, with only three-foot draft, usually followed. We planned to use the remaining 1½ hours of daylight to get to Ardoise where there was a barge-loading place. When we approached, the current, which had been whirling for several miles, was terribly strong. We tried to tie up to the verticals, but the current kept pushing us out, so we decided to back up and tie to the barge lying there. *Thlaloca*, with Siggi in the bow, was managing the towline. The *Orion* (another boat that was following Irving's piloting) was standing by, with the *Mark Twain* very near. Hope and I were working on the lines at the bow when at the same moment we realized something was wrong, and we heard the woman on *Orion* scream. Apparently, the *Mark Twain* had run down *Thlaloca*. Utter terror. I thought that Siggi was in the water - that awful Rhône and getting dark. Ruth at the stern line saw it all and thought *Thlaloca* had sunk. Hein and the *Orion* lady had been yelling at *Mark Twain* to stop coming closer, but the man at the bow, her owner, Mr. Schubert, ignored the warning. We couldn't understand how she could run that boat down. Hein and Siggi were so shaken, they were practically in shock. It was terrible.

"*Thlaloca* wasn't taking any water, and we hoped no ribs or frames are broken. Siggi had a hot shower here and we had them both to dinner, and all of us felt gradually better. The young man who steers *Mark Twain* came over to see if anyone got hurt and he got harsher words from Irving than from Hein.

WEST! SAIL WEST, MAN!

The owner, Iver Schubert, who looks like Hemingway and dresses like a riverboat captain, was in the bow and made no move or gesture to stop the running down. We feel that he was more to blame than the young man. We can't see what is the matter with him. Siggi slept in the girl's cabin, and even Hein brought his sleeping bag into the cockpit of *Yankee*, as the Rhône charged by noisily. We asked Siggi this afternoon what she first did when she came to Canada, 'Scrubbed floors,' she answered brightly. That's Siggi. We have continually marveled at her and Hein: Their unfailing good manners, their wonderful attitude towards each other, their intelligence, their spirit, their accomplishments. If only more of the human race were like them."

By writing down this account I feel a tremor going through my body, to think what could have happened had Siggi lost her grip on the line . . . swept underneath the barge . . . into the prop . . . down river? The real irony of this unhappy episode came when Mr. Schubert sent word that he liked to see me on *Mark Twain*. Expecting some apology, perhaps his willingness to compensate us for the lost items and the repair of *Thlaloca*'s damaged port side; first he let me wait for fifteen minutes, and when he finally made his grand entry with brass buttons and tunic all gleaming, he merely stated: "You make your claim to your insurance company, I to mine. Let them fight it out!" He walked away. This man had reason to thank his physical malady (he was an invalid) otherwise he would have been hurt - not for his refusal to accept responsibility, rather his repugnant arrogance.

"In the morning we started down the Rhône again - *Mark Twain* did not follow! Irving's successfully piloting at twelve knots continued until we reached the water backed up from a new lock, always plenty deep. We were now passing the city of Avignon where the imposing Palace of the Popes looks down over the river and the marvelous old bridge.

"At the lock we were lucky that a barge was just starting in, so we did not have to wait for all the yachts that we figured were 1½ hours behind us - with two not speaking to us now! From here it was only a few kilometers to where *Thlaloca* would turn off into the canal to Beaucaire. Irving was still piloting carefully, but his much corrected chart did not make clear the channel for the turn off. The new lock had changed the picture. There were some beacons around, but you never know what they mean - mostly nothing helpful.

"We took a turn around one of the beacons and went aground. Well, this wasn't as bad as most places as the current had lessened a lot. A river workboat was near and offered to give us a pull. But they did not understand the situation and mostly got us aground harder. Then they looked at their watches - nearly 12 - and departed for the hallowed 12-2 period.

"By now, *Thlaloca* had also gone aground. *Orion*, a large motor yacht, actually quite old (also a parasite in *Yankee's* wake) was standing by. So we started our drill. Irving got out the 125 lbs. anchor, got it into the dinghy and started to row it out - not easy. We were not hopeful about its working, as anchors simply don't hold in the Rhône, and there wasn't a bollard or tree anywhere. All this took time, and we were sure the yachts would soon be showing up. 'Pariset will have the last laugh,' Irving said. The *Orion* offered to have a pull. So Irving untied the line from the anchor and gave it to them. Wendy on *Orion* made fast, but as it turned out not through a chock. It parted and shot at us, and instantly into *Yankee's* propeller. We were back twelve years with a huge towline around the prop in the Rhône. So, get out the wet-suit-top, long-johns and face mask and into the cold Rhône for Irving. By this time, *Thlaloca* had been pulled off easily, and Hein and Siggi beside themselves at the realization that the only reason we got into trouble was because of our concern to put them safely into the canal to Beaucaire. They were close and Hein jumped into the water to come and help. I got a line to him as swimming in even lesser Rhône current is no good. We couldn't find a second face mask, but he and Irving went to work. I did get Hein a longie-top.

"It wasn't easy, but there were some things better than twelve years ago - though I didn't think being twelve years older was better for Irving. But the current wasn't as strong and there was Hein to help. They could stand on the bottom, the heads under, and they could see. Of course, *Yankee* looked exactly what she was, and all the other yachts had to do was come around the bend and they do get the picture. We all tried to tell ourselves that didn't really matter, at the same time couldn't keep our eyes off a particular bend in the river.

"Well, they finally got the line off and we put it aboard the *Orion* again - through the chock this time! She was a better vessel than I judged, as she had good power, twin screws and fair depth. So, heave, and we were afloat again. We got the line back aboard, Hein back on *Thlaloca* - which *Orion* took now in tow as she was bound for Beaucaire too. We all were waving good-by with feelings when Pariset came around the bend! No one had seen us. I did a dance!

"We all missed *Thlaloca* at the end of her orange line, with the Canadian flag fluttering above her self-steering mechanism. We had an emotional farewell, and they presented us with a nice picture of themselves on the boat, a fat chocolate-bar for Irving and an envelope. When we later opened it, it contained 50 francs (10 dollars). They live in real austerity - or rather do-withoutness, but they are no deadbeats, and the ten dollars was a typical gesture. We will never forget them, and I just wish you could meet them some day.

"Altogether, our last three weeks were the most eventful, exciting and fun of the summer. How marvelous that Irving can still do something like the underwater stuff in the Rhône without ill effects. This Rhône calls for the real Johnson, so please stand up!"

☆

Yes, indeed, may the real Irving Johnson stand up. Unfortunately, he can't, because he has rounded his last cape. As with all great men they never die, they just pass away. Siggi and I consider ourselves fortunate for what providence gave us, the chance to be with Irving and Exy for three wonderful weeks, an experience we will cherish forever.

Up the Rhine River

Irving and Exy Johnson

The *Yankee* and *Thlaloca*

A lock dating back to Napoleon's time

FRANK CASPER AND
HIS ELSIE

"Did it ever rain in Tahiti?" Confronted with this question we would hesitate for a few seconds, but then we would think of Frank Casper and the answer would be a definite "yes".

It never rained much, but when it did we wore a shirt, and this was that much more than the normal, except shorts, of course. Among the milling crowd always present along the row of a dozen yachts moored off the main street, moved a six-foot-two man: Black southwester, black fisherman-type raincoat to his knees, a pair of gray woolen socks halfway up his slender, hairy legs and his feet stuck in brown rawhide leather boots with high cuffs laced tightly. On the end of one arm dangled a large netted bag slightly bulged with two potatoes and a sliver of cabbage and one small onion. He had just come from the market. Meeting him he gave us his broad smile and instantly praised the superior qualities of the sales lady who served his daily needs. This was Frank Casper. That he was an unusual person we knew from our first meeting in Panama; that he was special we found in our subsequent meetings around the world.

Twenty years of world cruising and living aboard brought us the pleasure of meeting many outstanding people all quali-fied to be mentioned, but none we knew better than Frank. Why he is so vividly in our memory is perhaps because he was difficult to get to know. Not that he was arrogant or shy, just a private person who minded his own business.

Over the following two decades we met many times and

corresponded regularly. When we finally coaxed him aboard (*Thlaloca Dos* in later years) we considered it an achievement. There he would grant us a glimpse in his inner self that was foremost an example of extreme modesty. Not once did he use adjectives to color an experience that otherwise would have been a hair-raising story. He spoke a precise English, like an engineer for Underwriters had to. Praise always fell on other people - of much we were the recipients. With Frank around, we were never short of invitations.

At one time we were approached, along with Frank and two other long distance cruisers, by two reporters from a radio station for an interview. One of the question was:

"Are you making any money out of your travels?"
It was amazing to hear of the huge amount of money the other two were making. Siggi and I feebly admitted the fifty-seven dollars we had made that far. We felt like inferior beings until Frank saved us by saying, "I made that much less!"

His good ship *Elsie*, a cutter thirty-two feet long, was built in Germany shortly after the war for a fellow by the name of Hannes Lindemann, who had made headlines by sailing a Klepper canoe across the Atlantic. Lindemann with his wife made one Atlantic crossing in *Liberia* (*Elsie's* original name) from Africa to Miami. There his wife bailed out, and the boat was sold to Frank. He renamed her *Elsie*, commemorating his late wife.

One unpleasant deficiency of *Elsie* was that she was iron fastened - as nonferrous metal was unobtainable those days. We still see her enter Papeete, the hull oozing rust all over the otherwise handsome vessel. She also was plagued by an annoying leak around the keel. Perhaps every shipyard in the major ports around the world had a go at it to stop it - and so did I - but to no avail. He would write us, for instance:

"Sailed to England. One gale. Had boat out in Plymouth, repaired leaks. Down to twenty pumps now . . . " This was written on an ancient typewriter with characters that jumped up and down like the ocean waves he was riding on almost constantly. Frank completed his circumnavigation in 1966 - the same year we did in *Thlaloca*. The Slocum Society gave him honorary life membership for an outstanding single-handed voyage. Frank notified the Society that he was unable to accept the recognition because he had a crew member aboard from Florida to Panama! Later he was awarded the Blue Water Medal of the

Cruising Club of America.

We expected to meet again in Europe in 1981, but fate intervened when a spiky reef off the Bermuda Islands ended his life. It was the way he wanted to make his departure from earth we are sure of. We only hope he died without suffering. All of us who knew him will testify that Frank was a wonderful and sincere man; a fine seaman - we miss him a lot.

Frank Casper on *Elsie*

311

BILL NANCE AND HIS CARDINAL VERTUE

Perhaps the most remarkable man we had the pleasure of meeting was Bill Nance, an Australian, on *Cardinal Vertue*. That was in November 1964 in New Zealand. Strangely, though, his was the shortest meeting of any person we elected to write about, but one that made on us a most profound impact on account of his extreme modesty.

To many people, the Griffiths were like a giant magnet. One of the regular visitors was Bill on board the old *America* (Griffiths home while building the new *Awahnee*). On the whole, however, Bill and his brother, Bob, were working diligently on *Cardinal Vertue*, to ready her for the voyage around Cape Horn. The year was 1965, and as far we know there was no record of a tiny boat, 25 feet in length, that had rounded this notorious cape.

One can be almost certain that anybody else with the same intent would make sure that the news media would blare it out with great fanfare, and the departure would be attended by a huge crowd of people.

We had an inkling that his departure was imminent. When we missed his boat at the usual spot one morning there was no doubt he had left before dawn. Bob Griffith immediately chartered a seaplane and half a dozen of us piled in and searched for the boat. We failed to find any trace of it. Two months later we received a postcard: "Have arrived in Buenos Aires."

WEST! SAIL WEST, MAN!

It was eleven years later when one day, to our welcome surprise, Bill sailed into the Chesapeake Bay, Virginia. He was on his way to Europe when a hurricane forced him to run for shelter. We were pleased to discover that he was still the same unassuming, modest and pleasant chap we so much admired back in New Zealand.

Bill Nance (left). A joyful meeting on board *Thlaloca Dos*

Jean Gau and his Atom

Jean Gau with his Tahiti Ketch *Atom* circumnavigated the world twice and with these credentials was among men like Gerbault, Pidgeon, Muhlhauser, etc., prime examples of courage and daring we "greenhorns" sort of looked up to and liked to emulate. In order to understand this clearly, it helps to recall the time, 1963, when only a handful of yachts - perhaps only six from Panama - ventured out to conquer the world's oceans. It is only natural that we looked forward with excitement to meet one of the brave who, we hoped, would tell us something of what to expect.

Jean we first met in Balboa, Panama. A man with not an ounce of excess body weight, he appeared to us very French; very flamboyant. Despite his many years in the United States (a naturalized citizen) his speech was heavily accented and at times hard to follow. His enthusiasm for sailing matched his passion to paint. He would tell the story many times, meeting Winston Churchill in the Azores when both men propped up their easels at the same spot.

Over the following years we met in different ports as our courses were much the same. We always had reason to marvel at the excessive length of time he spent on passages - seventy-two days from Panama to Tahiti, via Pitcairn Island, where bad weather prevented his landing.

In those days there were no self-steering devices on the market (at least we had not seen any) and a Tahiti Ketch, we imagine, was not an easy vessel to make self-steering with the help of sails only and still maintain speed. In conditions not

315

right (he told us) he simply hove-to, brought out the easel and painted. Sometimes for days on end. This behavior is understandable in calm weather, but with any wind blowing regardless of direction and not moving, this philosophy is difficult to grasp.

Surprisingly, it was Frank Casper, who would never criticize another man's action, remarked, that he suspected the *Atom* to be unsound - thus Jean's reluctance in sailing to windward. This may be partly confirmed by Jean's refusal to invite knowledgeable people aboard *Atom*; people who could possibly detect weakness' in the vessel and point them out - and destroy dreams! .

Visiting each others' vessel is an age-old ritual, Siggi thought to press for. The occasion was our meeting (the last as it turned out) in Sheepshead Bay, N.Y.. To celebrate the special moment she had bought a cake and suggested eating it on board the *Atom*, the much larger vessel. We didn't. Instead we crammed into *Thlaloca*'s tiny cabin with hardly room to wiggle, and the hatch closed to keep out the rain. Among the three of us there was only one happy person - Jean!

☆

In Durban, South Africa, one senses immediately that the passage around the Cape of Good Hope may well test boat and equipment to the limit. Perhaps men and women as well. As in any endeavor, to be successful requires a portion of luck. That we had. Not so Jean! In a storm the *Atom* rolled, shedding her masts and much equipment. He eventually made harbor and repaired the damage and replaced lost equipment. A year later as originally planned he completed another circumnavigation.

His exceptional rebound from the many disasters surrounded him with an aura of invincibility. However, one incident in Panama convinced us that Jean was after all only a person like you and me with all our human failings: He was about to leave for the open Pacific. Having started the engine he went forward and raised the anchor. On the way aft, to take control of the boat, the engine quit and refused to start again. Exposed to a strong tidal current, the boat was carried with it. In total panic Jean gesticulated and babbled excitedly in French and English a call for help. Ron from *Gannet* and the two of us were sitting in *Thlaloca*'s cockpit having a beer, we all screamed, "Drop the anchor!" He did, and it effectively ended the commotion.

☆

316

People and their boats we met on the way

Eventually, the *Atom* was lost off the African coast. Declining health forced Jean to remain shore-bound in Southern France, where he later died. Though with us will always remain one memory we much cherish: We were approaching a pier at the Sheepshead Bay Yacht Club in New York to tie up, and Jean was there to greet us; we hadn't seen each other for years. He acted in his normal posture, swinging his arms wildly and very excitedly shouted in his heavily accented English to any passerby, "These are my friends, my friends . . . !"

Sheepshead Bay. Our last meeting with Jean

317

BOB, NANCY, RIEDI
GRIFFITH
AND THEIR AWAHNEES

Together we lived and worked to build the ferrocement yacht *Awahnee*. This, Siggi and I very much appreciated because it was the source of income we needed to continue our travels. Whatever one may think of ferrocement, we leave to the judgment of the individual. It suffices to say, that many New Zealanders at that time (64/65) were building truly wonderful boats in this rather unfamiliar material applied to boatbuilding. The new *Awahnee* we created was far from a masterpiece. That this vessel sailed the oceans so successfully over the following years was a tribute to the strength of ferrocement; coupled with the superb physical and mental strength, as well as the enormous experience in ocean sailing, the Griffiths had collected over decades in this mode of travel.

In this regard it is appropriate to recall some of their exploits. And one that really demonstrated their resourcefulness was when their first *Awahnee* ran onto a reef in the Red Sea. The boat was holed so badly, it came to rest on the coral bottom. Only by diving was it possible to waterproof the large hole somewhat. This done, the boat was pumped dry - or nearly so. Anchors were readied next and placed aft - from where the boat had plowed in - and winched to tension. It was followed by dynamite (yes, dynamite, that was bought in New Zealand to ward off possible pirates) placed and detonated along the escape route. It caused a mini tidal wave that lifted the boat momentarily, and the tension on the anchors propelled the boat aft. Several applications of this sort eventually freed the *Awahnee* to sail the oceans again. Later, in Port Said, Egypt, the boat was repaired properly. One interesting little story Nancy told us: when she handed the yard-workers new brushes to paint the topsides. Later, when she checked on the progress, she noticed the bristles on the brushes only about an inch long. Questioning the workers about it they seemed much surprised because they had never seen bristles longer than that, and thought it unusual, therefore had cut them off!

About the subsequent loss of the first *Awahnee* in the Pacific, I already touched on earlier.

☆

Another exceptional mastery of a troublesome situation occured on their passage from Rarotonga to New Zealand, in the old and somewhat decrepit yacht *America* (when we wisely chose to sail to the Tonga Islands instead). On the way they encountered most horrible weather. Bob, a veterinarian surgeon by profession, developed an excruciating toothache under a metal crown. He repaired the malady with the help of a ¼-inch electric drill run off a Honda generator. During the same passage, Nancy, his wife, became extremely ill, when she was passing kidney stones. Surely it was Bob's expertise as a doctor that helped Nancy to pull through - no doubt, with the mysterious medicines and gadgets Bob carried along in a large banged-up suitcase. Later, in New Zealand, I called upon Bob for a remedy to cure one of my illnesses. Whatever medicine it was the "stuff" nearly killed me. I'm immensely happy that Nancy was obviously of a hardier physique than I because of the fact that she survived the much more potent dosages administered to her!

Real tragedy struck when Riedi, their handsome and strong son, who had sailed all the hundreds of thousands of miles with them fell to his death off a cliff in the Marquesas Islands.

Bob is also gone now. Death may be understood when it happens to the sick and feeble, even though still in the prime of life. But when it happens to a man like Bob who radiated so much physical strength and health, it touches deeply. But such is life! Of the "trio" we knew so well only Nancy is still afloat somewhere. Where she is, we don't know, too many years have passed between then and now. We are sure, though, that she is still that indomitable person; always caring; always fun; always handy with a delightful story. Aboard their vessels she was the real heroine, as Siggi was and still is aboard ours.

With the passing of Bob and Riedi Griffith, Frank Casper, Jean Gau, the Hiscocks, the Smeetons, Bernhard Moitessier and Peter Tangveld, we mourn people we knew so well, along with an era that has vanished for good, because times have changed dramatically. I'm aware that today's "cruisers" resent being reminded that only twenty or thirty years ago seafaring life was vastly different, because boats were simpler; equipment was simpler. And no one should argue the fact that "simpler" could well be synonymous with enhanced enjoyment. Today's sophisticated approach to cruising should not serve as a guideline to a lifestyle that after all should be relaxing and unencumbered; it should not curtail the adventurous spirit of the individual in quest to explore the oceans of our world for even one day, because most of the advertised "exotic" equipment has little value in the real world.

Studio 57

Left, Bob Griffith setting the stern post in place in the frame-work for his new concrete boat. Right, Jean Griffith, foreground, and Sigrid Zenker wiring the netting reinforcement on to the metal frame-work.

APPENDIX 2

Boat and Equipment
☆
Accidents and Sickness'

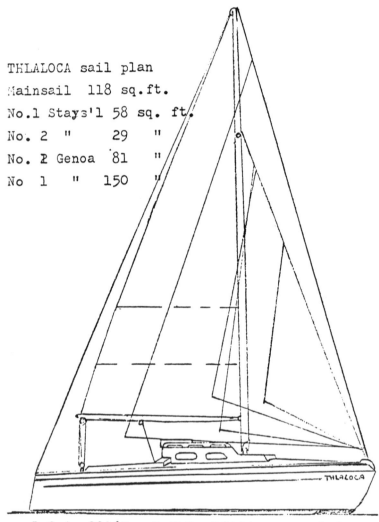

THLALOCA sail plan
Mainsail 118 sq.ft.
No.1 Stays'l 58 sq. ft.
No. 2 "   29   "
No. 2 Genoa 81   "
No 1   "   150   "

L.O.A. 20'6" , L.W.L. 18'6", Beam; 6'6"
Draught; 4'6"

Sail plan of *Thlaloca*

THE BOAT AND
EQUIPMENT

Thlaloca measured 20½ feet overall, a beam of 6½ feet and a draft of 4½ feet. Her hull was of ½-inch strip-planked Western Red Cedar over steam-bent white oak ribs on 4½-inch center. Keelson, clamps, stem, all were of laminated hardwoods. The beams - deck, cabin, cockpit, as well as carlings were of Sitka spruce, again laminated. Laminating is a process that gives relatively small timbers superior strength. The boat (hull and topsides) was completely sheeted in fiberglass and bonded with epoxy resin.

The fin keel was a 3/8-inch steel plate, to which was bolted the iron ballast casting. Her hollow spar was of laminated Sitka spruce. It supported the following sails: 1 mainsail, 1 masthead genoa, 1 #2 genoa, 2 jibs, 1 stormsail, 1 spinnaker.

Equipment: Built-in compass, hand-bearing compass, radio, sextant, inexpensive bulkhead mounted clock (for chronometer), barometer, divider, 2 navigational protractors, Nautical Almanac, HO 249 Tables, charts, stopwatch, one pair of binoculars, hand held windspeed indicator, flashlight, cabin light (kerosene), gimbaled one-burner stove (kerosene), sea-anchor, 2 anchors, 2 fire extinguishers, 2 spinnaker poles, 2 life vests, flares, inflatable dinghy, Walker spinning log, 2hp Seagull outboard motor, 2 wooden paddles, anchor light, foul weather gear. Water - usually 30 gallons - was carried in plastic containers; and so was kerosene for stove and lights, and fuel for the outboard motor.

WEST! SAIL WEST, MAN!

Thlaloca was a very capable and sturdy vessel, but too little to provide any comfort for two people over the long haul. Nevertheless, she was our baby and we cared for her accordingly - as she did for us!

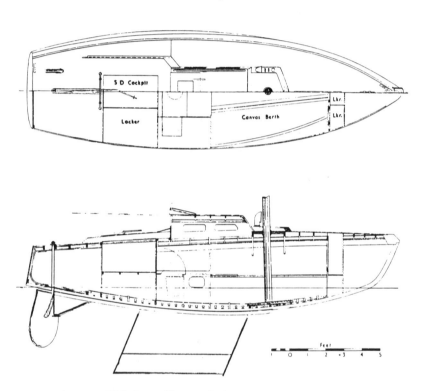

Thlaloca General Arrangement

ACCIDENTS AND
SICKNESS'

Today, with excellent medical advice readily available in books, it should be possible to deal effectively with the normal, and in many cases foreseeable sickness' that may be met in cruising off the beaten track. It's the unexpected accident that may pose a real problem, and a lot more so for the person who has to find treatment and solution to a specific problem. What I address here is the shorthanded vessel - a couple out there alone and without communication with the outside world. Specifically, I like to go a step further on the ramification of the accident I described in *Fiji to New Zealand* - had the calamity happened to me instead of Siggi!

I recall our first long passage from the Galápagos to the Marquesas Islands, when I was stricken with what I thought to be appendicitis. All the symptoms that were described in the medical book were present. Ignoring them did not help. When I wakened during the night and I felt very lousy with cold sweat and feverish, I thought back twelve years when I was working as a lumberjack. Our boss was a Swede of enormous size and he had the physical strength of an ox. In temperatures of 30° below zero he used to walk about with the tops of his underclothing and jacket unbuttoned, exposing a hairy chest. The very statue of invincibility. One day he did not feel well, and he refused to be flown out. The following day a plane came. I still see him walking towards it with his customary smile. Half an hour later he was dead - still on the plane - with a burst appendix.

It got me thinking: What if something like that was going

to happen to me? Siggi would be unable to manhandle me in the cramped space of *Thlaloca*. I made up some excuse, that I was sleepless and preferred to be in the cockpit for a while, tied up, of course! By removing the access cover to the lazaret and sticking the legs in there and with a cockpit cushion for a pillow, one could make himself quite comfy. By dawn I had recovered to my former self. Whatever ailed me, I don't know.

In the extreme scenario - someone becomes incapacitated or worse - a partner would have to face a situation that for sheer horror I leave to the imagination of the individual. Still, it should be addressed, to give a physically less endowed partner, who initially must be in a state of panic, workable mechanics to hoist a lifeless body on deck, or a helpless person out of a cramped space. Paramount is to assure that the partner is able to continue the voyage with minimum delay.

Every time I broached this subject with Siggi she refused to listen. Then your partner should be able to read about it. Place the instructions in the log book or any other place you prefer. Make it known, and he or she can take advantage of it should it become necessary.

My experience on the passage from Fiji to New Zealand should underline the seriousness of this problem because had I been the person hurt in that cramped space instead of Siggi, I can't imagine her getting me out of it despite her formidable strength and inventiveness under pressure. Think of it, speed is critical to ease a person's agony, and it may well save a life.